FORGIVENESS, RECONCILIATION, *and* RESTORATION

Pentecostals, Peacemaking, and Social Justice Series

PAUL ALEXANDER AND JAY BEAMAN, SERIES EDITORS

Volumes in the Series:

Pentecostal Pacifism: The Origin, Development, and Rejection of Pacific Belief among the Pentecostals
by Jay Beaman

A Liberating Spirit: Pentecostals and Social Action in North America
edited by Michael Wilkinson and Steven M. Studebaker

Forgiveness, Reconciliation, and Restoration: Mulitdisciplinary Studies from a Pentacostal Perspective
edited by Martin W. Mittelstadt and Geoffrey W. Sutton

Forgiveness, Reconciliation, and Restoration

Multidisciplinary Studies from a Pentecostal Perspective

EDITED BY

MARTIN WILLIAM MITTELSTADT

AND

GEOFFREY W. SUTTON

PICKWICK *Publications* · Eugene, Oregon

FORGIVENESS, RECONCILIATION, AND RESTORATION
Multidisciplinary Studies from a Pentecostal Perspective

Pentecostals, Peacemaking, and Social Justice 3

Pickwick Publications
An Imprint of Wipf and Stock Publishers
199 W. 8th Ave., Suite 3
Eugene, OR 97401

www.wipfandstock.com

ISBN 13: 978-1-4982-5517-2

Cataloging-in-Publication data:

Forgiveness, reconciliation, and restoration : multidisciplinary studies from a Pentecostal perspective / edited by Martin William Mittelstadt and Geoffrey W. Sutton.

xxii + 244 p. ; 23 cm. — Includes bibliographical references.

Pentecostals, Peacemaking, and Social Justice 3

ISBN 13: 978-1-60899-194-5

1. Forgiveness. 2. Reconciliation. 3. Pentecostalism. I. Mittelstadt, Martin William. II. Sutton, Geoffrey W. III. Title. IV. Series.

BJ1201 .F70 2010

To Sandra Sutton and Evelyn Mittelstadt

For their love and support

Contents

Historical Perspectives

Psychological Perspectives

A Sociological Perspective

An Educational Perspective

Series Preface

Pentecostal and Charismatic Christians comprise approximately twenty-five percent of global Christianity (around 600 million of 2.4 billion). This remarkable development has occurred within just the last century and has been called the "pentecostalization" of Christianity. Pentecostals and Charismatics experience Christianity and the world in distinctive ways, and this series invites discovery and development of Pentecostal-Charismatic approaches to peacemaking and social justice.

The majority of early twentieth-century Pentecostal denominations were peace churches that encouraged conscientious objection. Denominations such as the Church of God in Christ and the Assemblies of God said "no" to Christian combatant participation in war, and some Pentecostals and Charismatics are exploring this history and working for a recovery and expansion of this witness. The peacemaking aspect of the series focuses on pacifism, war, just war tradition, just peacemaking, peacebuilding, conflict transformation, nonviolence, forgiveness, and other peacemaking-related themes and issues within Pentecostal-Charismatic traditions and from Pentecostal-Charismatic perspectives. We launched the series with a twentieth-anniversary reprint of Jay Beaman's *Pentecostal Pacifism*—an appropriate look back to the generative years of the Pentecostal movement when many denominations believed that nonviolence was a hallmark of the gospel of Jesus Christ.

Some early Pentecostals also confronted the injustices of racism, sexism, and economic disparity. Others perpetuated the problems. Yet the Holy Spirit leads us now, as then, to confront injustice prophetically and work to redeem and restore. Pentecostal-Charismatic Christians around the world are working for justice in a myriad of ways. This aspect of the series focuses on gender, race, ethnicity, sexuality, economics, class, globalization, trade, poverty, health, consumerism, development, and other social justice related themes and issues within the Pentecostal-Charismatic tradition and from Pentecostal-Charismatic perspectives. We understand that peace and justice are not separate concerns but different ways of talking about and seeking *shalom*—God's salvation, justice, and peace.

Forthcoming volumes include both original work and publication of important historical resources, and we welcome contributions from theologians, biblical scholars, philosophers, ethicists, historians, social scientists, pastors, activists, and practitioners of peacemaking and social justice. We especially welcome both scholarly and praxis-oriented contributions from majority world Pentecostals and Charismatics, for this series seeks to explore the ways that Pentecostal-Charismatic Christians can develop, strengthen, and sustain a peace-with-justice witness in the twenty-first century around the world. Royalties from sales of these volumes are often donated to Pentecostals & Charismatics for Peace & Justice (www.pcpj.org), a 501(c)3 network advocating for Jesus-shaped and Spirit-empowered peace with justice.

Paul Alexander

Contributors

DIANE AWBREY (PhD, University of Missouri-Columbia) is associate professor of English at Evangel University. Although her area of concentration is Renaissance English literature, she has also published in religious and business venues. She has served on faculty at Central Bible College, Springfield, MO; Friends University, Wichita, KS; and St. Michael's College, Colchester, VT. She has also been a writer, editor, and curriculum developer for the Kauffman Foundation of Kansas City and Global University. Currently, she is leading the Evangel University faculty in a comprehensive redesign of its general education program.

ROBERT BERG (PhD, Drew University) is Professor of New Testament and the Director of LifeWorks: The Center for Leadership & Life Calling at Evangel University. As an ordained minister with the Assemblies of God, he has served on pastoral staffs in New York and Arkansas. His writings include works on the Gospel of John.

RENEA BRATHWAITE (PhD candidate, Regent University) is recipient of the Robertson Scholar, and adjunct professor at Regent University. A summa cum laude graduate of the Assemblies of God Theological Seminary, he is the managing editor of the forthcoming *Dictionary of Pan-African Pentecostalism*, a volume produced under the auspices of The Seymour Project headed by Estrelda Alexander, PhD. His research interests include Pentecostal history and theology, black liberation theology, feminist theology, and biblical hermeneutics.

Jeff Hittenberger (PhD, University of Southern California) serves as Provost/Vice President for Academic Affairs at Vanguard University of Southern California. He previously served as Director of Graduate Studies at Evangel University and as Dean of the School of Education at Vanguard University. He served as a Rotary Ambassadorial Scholar at Mohamed V University in Rabat, Morocco, has served as a consultant and researcher in Cameroon, Mali, South Africa, Israel, and Haiti, and has authored numerous publications.

Martin W. Mittelstadt (PhD, Marquette University) is associate professor of New Testament at Evangel University. Originally from Winnipeg, Manitoba, Canada, he now lives and works in Springfield, MO. His publications include numerous works on Luke-Acts including *Spirit and Suffering in Luke-Acts* and *Reading Luke-Acts in the Pentecostal Tradition*. Recent research projects that stimulated interest in this monograph stem from his studies on the convergence of Pentecostal and Anabaptist theology and praxis.

Johan Mostert (PhD, University of Pretoria) is Professor of Community Psychology at the Assemblies of God Theological Seminary. Originally from South Africa, he now lives in Springfield, MO. Before his appointment to AGTS he was National Director of the Welfare Department of the Apostolic Faith Mission of South Africa (the largest Pentecostal denomination in SA) for 11 years, and spent five years as a consultant to various churches and international development agencies in the fields of HIV/AIDS and Community Development. He earned five degrees in theology, psychology, and social work, and was certified as a Counseling Psychologist and Social Worker in South Africa.

Patrick Mureithi (BS, Missouri State University), a Kenyan, is an Artist in Residence with the Communication Department at Drury University, Springfield, MO. His recently completed documentary, *ICYIZERE: hope*, documents the progress of survivors and perpetrators of the Rwandan genocide of 1994. He is currently working on a documentary about Eye Movement Desensitization and Reprocessing (EMDR) entitled "The Eye is the Window" (www.josiahfilms.com).

Lois E. Olena (DMin, Assemblies of God Theological Seminary) is Visiting Professor of Practical Theology and Jewish Studies at the Assemblies of God Theological Seminary where she also serves as DMin

Project Coordinator and editor of *Encounter: Journal for Pentecostal Ministry*. She has published on the Holocaust, race relations, and wrote the official biography of Dr. Stanley M. Horton, *Stanley M. Horton: Shaper of Pentecostal Theology*.

MARILYN QUIGLEY (MA, Missouri State University) is associate professor of English at Evangel University where she directs the composition program and teaches literature as well as creative writing. Her publications include a children's musical, *From Pit to Palace,* based on the life of Joseph; several short stories for religious presses; and *Hell Frozen Over*, which follows the experiences of her uncle and many of his comrades who endured the Battle of the Bulge. She serves as secretary on the board of the Missouri Literary Festival.

TONY RICHIE (DMin, Asbury Theological Seminary; and DTh, London School of Theology) is Senior Pastor at New Harvest Church of God (Knoxville, TN) and adjunct lecturer/professor at the Church of God Theological Seminary (Cleveland, TN) and Regent Divinity School (Virginia Beach, VA). He represents the Society for Pentecostal Studies to the Interfaith Relations Commission, National Council of Churches (USA), and on the Interreligious Dialogue and Cooperation Task Group of the Commission of Churches on International Affairs, World Council of Churches (Geneva, Switzerland).

GEOFFREY W. SUTTON (PhD, University of Missouri-Columbia) is professor of Psychology at Evangel University. He also serves as a consulting psychologist, lecturer, and author. He continues to contribute articles on faith and psychology for various journals. Born in London, England, he immigrated to the United States and now lives in Springfield, MO. He is a director on the International Board of the Christian Association for Psychological Studies.

MERVIN VAN DER SPUY (ThD, University of South Africa) is a professor of counseling psychology at Providence Theological Seminary, MB, Canada. A native of South Africa (SA), he immigrated to Canada in 2001. After earning degrees in pharmacy and theology, he became a pastor with the Apostolic Faith Mission (Pentecostal church in SA) and served as liaison chaplain in the Defense Force. He was the founder-president of the Association of Christian Counselors in South Africa and was an executive board member of the International Association of Christian

Counselors and vice-president of the International Network of Christian Counselors. He was nominated by the minister of health to serve as a member of the SGB for Psychology of the South African Qualifications Authority. He has developed a *Paraklesis Counselling Model*. His research interests include the work of the Holy Spirit in counseling and pharmacologically informed psychotherapy in Christian counseling.

MICHAEL WILKINSON (PhD, University of Ottawa) is Associate Professor of Sociology and director of the Religion in Canada Institute, Trinity Western University. He has published on Pentecostalism, globalization, and religion, including the books, *The Spirit Said Go*; *Pentecostal Immigrants in Canada and Canadian Pentecostalism*; and *Transition and Transformation*.

EVERETT L. WORTHINGTON JR. (PhD, University of Missouri-Columbia) is a Professor of Psychology at Virginia Commonwealth University. He is a member of the Counseling Psychology (APA-accredited) program and is affiliated with Social Psychology and Developmental Psychology programs. His research interests include forgiveness, relational spirituality, the hope-focused marriage approach to enrichment and counseling, and religion and spirituality (especially Christianity).

Acknowledgments

We wish to thank all of the contributors to this volume without whom this book would not be possible. Without exception they gracefully accepted our feedback.

We are indebted to Evangel University student Martin Campbell for his tireless work in editing and re-editing numerous revisions of these chapters. Given the multidisciplinary approach, Martin was instrumental in formatting the essays to Pickwick style. We wish to thank Travis Cooper for his careful work in producing indices.

We are thankful to Paul Alexander for his initial approval of our book proposal and for his support in the project. We appreciate the publishers for recognizing the merit of this book and providing editorial guidance to us throughout the process.

We thank LifeWorks: The Center for Leadership & Life Calling at Evangel University for a financial grant to bring this project to fruition.

Finally, we wish to express our appreciation to our wives, Sandra Sutton and Evelyn Mittelstadt, for their kindness in affording us the time away from other tasks as we sought to meet our deadlines.

Introduction

Pentecostal Perspectives on Forgiveness,
Reconciliation and Restoration

One fall morning a group of children walked across the fields in their small community to begin a typical school day. Their teacher began by reading about grace from Acts 4:32–33. They sang and prayed before dividing into groups for their lessons. Nearby a gunman followed his malevolent plan of revenge against God. At approximately 11:05 a.m. on Monday, October 2, 2006, five Amish girls were fatally wounded and five others critically wounded in the picturesque village of West Nickel Mines, Pennsylvania. What captivated the world's attention was the Amish response of forgiveness and reconciliation as they reached out to the family of the homicidal-suicidal destroyer of their children. Members of the Amish community including families of the victims forgave the killer and embraced the wife of the murderer during her time of loss. They attended the funeral and showered this young widow with numerous acts of kindness. In the midst of these acts of grace, a common refrain from the media suggested that the Amish were backward and repressive, therefore unable to grieve as "normal" human beings.

Fortunately, a number of Anabaptist scholars wrote timely narratives in an attempt to help the public understand this expression of *Amish*

Grace.[1] These scholars did a masterful job of demonstrating the centrality of forgiveness in everyday Amish living. According to the authors, daily repetition of the Lord's Prayer, reflection upon a bloody history of persecution, and the teaching of Jesus on forgiveness and reconciliation postured these people for forgiveness. In other words, the Amish response flowed out of regular practices that emphasize the critical role of forgiveness in Christian life and thus should not be surprising.

As we reflected on this and other stories of forgiveness and reconciliation, we began to muse over our Pentecostal heritage. How might a Pentecostal community respond to such an atrocity? What role does forgiveness and reconciliation play in Pentecostal life and mission? We wanted to investigate how Pentecostals have reacted to offenses they have perpetrated and experienced. We wish to understand what it means for people of the Spirit to face evil, to deal with anger and conflict, and respond with love and charity. Such questions led to this book. We were unable to locate any work written specifically on forgiveness and reconciliation through Pentecostal lenses. This work serves not to fill the gap or provide definitive answers, but to encourage serious theological discussion, deliberate reflection, and consideration of concrete practices for Pentecostals living in a world marred by anger, hatred, violence, and revenge.

To accomplish our goals we sought input from a diverse group of scholars who could examine select experiences of Pentecostals from the perspective of different ethnic backgrounds and varied scholarly disciplines. Compared to other Christian traditions, the contemporary Pentecostal movement is still very young; yet we are among the fastest growing groups of Christians on the planet. Although there are different fellowships, we have in common a belief that the Spirit of Christ, manifest so powerfully in the lives of the apostles, continues to work in the lives of contemporary followers of Jesus. In this volume, we have focused specifically on forgiveness and reconciliation. Some authors focus more on forgiveness, while others seek to understand reconciliation. All seek to understand how God's Spirit is at work to maintain and restore relationships within faith communities as well as between groups of people from different faith and religious traditions.

---

1. Donald B. Kraybill, Steven M. Nolt, and David L. Weaver-Zercher, *Amish Grace: How Forgiveness Transcended Tragedy* (San Francisco: Jossey Bass, 2007). See also John Ruth, *Forgiveness: A Legacy of the West Nickel Mines Amish School* (Scottdale, PA: Herald, 2007).

In concert with our interdisciplinary approach, we arranged the essays according to disciplines. Martin Mittelstadt takes readers to Luke-Acts, a favorite text of Pentecostals. He challenges Pentecostals to read the Lukan story not only as a template for evangelism or its emphasis on Spirit baptism, but also as a rich resource for a theology of reconciliation. Mittelstadt suggests Pentecostals read Luke-Acts not primarily as a gospel story focusing upon individual conversions, but as the gospel of peace, a story of reconciliation between individuals and peoples with a history of conflict and division.

Next, we include two literary perspectives. Robert Berg offers a poignant analysis of William Young's controversial best seller, *The Shack*. Berg provides a short synopsis of the story and then addresses several of the theological and practical concerns of critics. In the end, Berg finds in *The Shack* a consummate *testimony* to forgiveness. Berg locates Pentecostal resonance with *The Shack* upon the practice of testimony. Pentecostals unashamedly find in this story a basis for common celebration and experience of a loving God who walks people through periods of bitterness and anger to God and others. Marilyn Quigley and Diane Awbrey analyze the problem of unforgiveness illustrated by Katherine Anne Porter in a short story, *The Jilting of Granny Weatherall*. In a touching self-disclosure, Quigley juxtaposes her path to forgiveness with that of Granny Weatherall. Quigley's story is an eloquent example of that quintessential mainstay of Pentecostal services, a personal testimony of God's Spirit at work. The authors also provide a Pentecostal lens on forgiveness when they analyze Quigley's spiritual battle to forgive in the context of comforting her dying mother-in-law. Whereas Berg offers critical theological commentary on the nature and value of testimony via a bestseller, Quigley and Awbrey *get personal*—they share a living testimony of the struggle toward forgiveness.

The next section consists of three essays on forgiveness through the lens of history. Renea Brathwaite takes readers back to the early years of North American Pentecostalism. Brathwaite rehearses the success and failure of the racially integrated Azusa Street Revival and its aftermath. Though Pentecostals made early inroads toward racial reconciliation, they fell prey to a world not yet ready for integration. Brathwaite calls upon contemporary Pentecostals to enlarge their theological vision and demonstrate a gospel with characteristics of forgiveness and embrace. Lois Olena follows with the gripping story of African-American Pentecostal preacher Robert Harrison. Harrison displays tremendous grace as he embarks on a long journey toward credentialing in the Assemblies of God. Both Brathwaite and Olena chart Assemblies of God struggles with societal norms and interpretation of Scripture and call upon Pentecostals to learn from their past and lead the way in embodiment of integrated communities of faith. Tony Richie takes a slightly different approach and addresses the responsibilities before Pentecostals in the context of inter-religious dialogue. He suggests such dialogue must begin with serious conversations on past failures and conflict, lead to forgiveness, and end with reconciliation in order to focus upon common objectives for the betterment of humankind.

In the "Psychology of Forgiveness," Geoffrey Sutton begins the section on scientific perspectives. He discusses forgiveness in the context of reconciliation and restoration, by providing an overview of psychological research, which includes not only opinions about these ideas but also experimental findings on effective strategies for helping people forgive. Fitting with our overarching goal, Sutton examines these motifs from a Pentecostal perspective, while looking at the sad tale of a pastor who confesses sexual sin to a shocked congregation. Johan Mostert and Mervin van der Spuy, both formerly of South Africa, recount the gripping drama of terror at the dawn of the post-apartheid era. In "Truth and Reconciliation in South Africa," they recount their attempt to grapple with powerful forces of change as leaders in their respective Pentecostal communities. Their personal struggles and honesty prove riveting as they tell of their amazing journey through the South African story. Canadian sociologist Michael Wilkinson concludes the section with analysis of the burgeoning public apologies and requests for forgiveness of the last few decades. Wilkinson offers a sociological view of forgiveness and reconciliation in his review of requests for forgiveness expressed by Canadian government and religious leaders toward descendents of those victimized by harmful policies and procedures from centuries past. In addition to exploring a theoretical perspective, Wilkinson illustrates Christian and Pentecostal responses to the particular offense toward First Nations people who suffered within the Canadian residential school system.

Finally, we look to the field of education. Nearly one million people were massacred during the 1994 Rwandan intertribal melee. Jeffrey Hittenberger and Patrick Mureithi examine the results of an education program to teach forgiveness and reconciliation to Tutsis and Hutus, two peoples with a long and dark history of conflict on the Rwandan landscape. Hittenberger and Mureithi examined the components of an educational model in view of psychological research and consider how Pentecostals might contribute to education for forgiveness and reconciliation.

We believe a primary strength of this volume is its diversity. We sought Pentecostal scholars from different traditions, different academic and professional disciplines, and different ethnic backgrounds. Our contributors include scholars from various Pentecostal traditions including Apostolic Faith Mission, Assemblies of God, Church of God (Cleveland. TN), and the Pentecostal Assemblies of Canada. These scholars have graduate degrees in various disciplines including Education, English, Nuclear Engineering, Psychology, Sociology, Social Work, and Theology. Finally, contributors hail from Barbados, Canada, England, Kenya, United States, and the Union of South Africa. As editors, we were mindful of the need to retain the sense of diversity for the reader, while editing for style and format consistent with other volumes in this series. Some chapters will have a different *feel* as the authors express themselves in a scholarly manner unique to their discipline. Finally, we hope this volume will prove fruitful for a variety of audiences. We hope it will find a home in university and seminary classrooms, pastoral libraries, and weekly book studies led by followers of Jesus from many faith traditions. While we hope to stimulate thinking about a Pentecostal perspective on forgiveness and reconciliation, we also hope to engage readers from a wider audience who share our enthusiasm for transformative themes.

Geoffrey W. Sutton *and* Martin W. Mittelstadt
Springfield, Missouri, USA
January, 2010

A Theological Perspective

1

Pentecostals and the Gospel of Peace

Spirit and Reconciliation in Luke-Acts

Martin William Mittelstadt

A child raised in a Pentecostal church hears early and often of the importance of Scripture memorization. I remember receiving repeated challenges to memorize the words of Jesus in Acts 1:8, namely, "you will receive power when the Holy Spirit has come upon you; and you will be my witnesses in Jerusalem and in all Judea and Samaria and to the ends of the earth." These words, possibly more than any other words, provided me and many other young Pentecostals an early synopsis of Pentecostal teaching. Pentecostals treasure intimate experience with the Holy Spirit and ensuing power for witness. While this teaching remains central to catechesis, Pentecostal identity surely extends beyond Spirit reception and empowerment. Indeed, many Pentecostals search with insatiable passion to enlarge their Pentecostal vision through fresh reading of the Scriptures. One such experience constitutes the background for this essay.

During recent readings of Luke-Acts, I began to focus upon Luke's emphasis on peace and reconciliation. Today, as Pentecostals strive to

3

articulate their pneumatological heritage for the current generation, I believe a fresh look at Luke's investment in peace and reconciliation may invigorate and enlarge their missiological vision. While Pentecostals typically limit salvific language to individual reconciliation between humans and God, Luke goes further. For Luke, peace does not function as an inner state of being, but as a means of identifying humans often with a history of unforgiveness and conflict now reconciled not only to God but also to each other.

In this favorite text for Pentecostal identity, I believe Luke envisions Spirit-led proclamation of the gospel as reconciliation. I propose the following course. First, I lay a foundation for this study based upon methodological guidelines well suited for thematic discovery. By employing a literary approach, I continue with a brief introduction to Luke's interest in the Spirit as well as peace and reconciliation. Second, in tracing the convergence of Spirit and reconciliation in Luke-Acts, I argue that Spirit-inspired witnesses solicit intentional embrace of the counter-cultural gospel of peace. On numerous occasions Luke correlates Spirit-reception and the breaking of boundaries marked by long histories that include marginalization, division, and conflict; these boundaries are replaced by the formation of an alternative community. At the same time, Luke does not avoid the implications of the rejection of reconciliation as paramount to rejection of the gospel. Finally, given the centrality of a Spirit-inspired gospel of peace, I suggest that the convergence of Spirit and peace in Luke-Acts provides fresh possibilities for contemporary Pentecostal mission.

METHODOLOGY: A LITERARY ANALYSIS

The following methodological parameters serve as a guide for analysis. First, while it is possible to read Luke's gospel and Acts as separate texts, an approach encouraged by their division in the canon, I examine them as a two-volume work. Luke's introduction of Acts as a continuation of "all that Jesus did and taught" (Acts 1:1) establishes his desire to furnish a comprehensive and coherent narrative unity with inner integrity, overarching themes and repeated patterns.[1] Second, I envision Luke as

1. Henry Cadbury coined the term Luke-Acts in his *The Making of Luke-Acts*. Further, I use the name "Luke," either to refer to the Gospel of Luke or to the author of the Third Gospel and the Acts of the Apostles. While I hold to the traditional identification of Luke as a physician and co-worker of Paul, I also believe this should not benefit or challenge the conclusions of a literary analysis.

a literary artist; a gifted storyteller adept at connecting short vignettes into one long coherent narrative. His readers must take the whole story into account via narrative developments, plot lines, character roles, irony, repetition, anticipation, and fulfillment. Finally, these literary features, commonly associated with modern novels, short stories and films, provide the key to his theological intentions.[2] As an artist with considerable literary skill and a rich imagination, Luke develops and sustains various motifs in order to convey his vision of Jesus Christ and of the mission that follows.

In order to prepare for the convergence of Spirit and reconciliation, I must introduce a specific literary convention employed by Luke. Luke regularly utilizes programmatic and literary prophecy, that is, a strategic literary device at critical junctures within the narrative to direct interpretation of the subsequent narrative.[3] When effective, programmatic and/ or literary prophecy helps the reader to anticipate the course of the story. Luke typically develops themes in the following manner: 1) previews often found in songs, oracles, and speeches anticipate the purposes of God to be realized through Jesus and his witnesses in the subsequent story; 2) repeated words or phrases often found early but also throughout the narrative receive special attention for understanding the story; 3) commission statements disclose divine purposes and tasks for particular characters and ensuing keys to the plot; 4) readers are assured that anticipatory statements come from the lips of reliable characters who often speak under the direct inspiration of the Holy Spirit.

The following well-known examples demonstrate Luke's reliance upon this literary convention. First, Luke programmatically directs the geographical course of the Third Gospel and Acts. At Luke 9:51, Jesus begins his journey toward death in Jerusalem and in Acts 1:8, the resurrected Jesus commissions his disciples upon reception of the Spirit to take the gospel from Jerusalem to the ends of the earth. The Third Gospel marches toward Jerusalem while Acts advances away from Jerusalem. In another literary prophecy, the Lord speaks to Paul through Ananias. Ironically, Paul will not only serve as a primary apostle to the Gentiles,

---

2. The following authors offer helpful instruction on literary/narrative analysis: Johnson, *Literary Function of Possessions*; Kurz, "Narrative Approaches to Luke-Acts"; "Narrative Models for Imitation"; *Reading Luke-Acts*; and Tannehill, *Narrative Unity*.

3. See Johnson, *Literary Function of Possessions*, 88; and Tannehill, *Narrative Unity*, 1:21–23.

but as a former persecutor must suffer as he proclaims the gospel to the Gentiles (Acts 9:15–16). The subsequent narrative delivers repeated fulfillment not only of Paul's powerful proclamation but also his severe suffering on account of the message. In a similar manner, I suggest that Luke introduces his theology of peace and reconciliation via literary and programmatic prophecies and then provides substantial fulfillment in the subsequent narrative. I turn now to a brief overview of the importance of the two motifs under consideration.

SPIRIT AND PEACE—THEMATIC PROMINENCE IN LUKE-ACTS

The preeminent role of the Holy Spirit in Luke's writings is well documented. Given Luke's frequent references to the Spirit in the Third Gospel and his incessant use of "Spirit" in Acts 1–12, scholarly interest in Lukan pneumatology particularly among Pentecostals comes as no surprise. Roger Stronstad, one of the foremost Pentecostal scholars to capitalize on emergent literary analyses, describes Lukan pneumatology not as initiatory, but charismatic, vocational, and prophetic.[4] The Spirit inspires prophecy, worship, witness, and guidance for the inauguration, development and expansion of a new charismatic community. In the Third Gospel, Luke anticipates a new community based upon numerous Spirit-filled announcements that point to Jesus. As the Lukan narrative unfolds, Jesus serves as the consummate man of the Spirit. The paradigmatic Jesus embodies the gospel message and fills his followers with the same Holy Spirit in order to assure extension of the gospel. Luke's emphasis upon these crucial stages resonates well with his weighty referencing of the Spirit in the programmatic birth narrative (Luke 1:15, 17, 35, 41, 47, 67, 80; 2:25, 26, 27), the inauguration of Jesus' ministry (Luke 3:16, 22; 4:1 [2], 14, 18)

---

4. *The Charismatic Theology of St. Luke* continues to be the enduring assessment of Lukan pneumatology by a Pentecostal to be taken seriously within the larger scholarly community. Stronstad challenges the dominant view of the scholarly community by interrogating attempts to harmonize the pneumatologies of Luke and Paul. While scholars correctly emphasize Paul's understanding of the Spirit primarily as soteriological, Stronstad concludes that this kind of identity transfer silences Luke's pneumatology. Stronstad questions the theological dominance of Paul's singular use of the phrases "baptism in the Spirit" (1 Cor 12:13) and "filled with the Spirit" (Eph 5:18) compared with the twelve uses of the same two phrases by Luke ("filled with the Holy Spirit": Luke 1:15, 41, 67; Acts 2:4; 4:8, 31; 9:17; 13:9; 13:52; and "baptism in the Holy Spirit": Luke 3:16; Acts 1:5; 11:16).

and travel narrative (10:21; 11:13; 12:10, 12), and the expansion of the new community in early Acts (more than 25 references in Acts 1–12).

While the scholarly debate concerning Lukan pneumatology continues at a feverous pitch, the same cannot be said concerning Luke's interest in reconciliation. Recent bibliographical overviews on the history of interpretation in Luke-Acts provide no category for peace, forgiveness, reconciliation, or conflict resolution.[5] Due to length restrictions, I concentrate on Luke's extensive use of the term "peace."

The underlying political context for Luke's narrative (and historical) world is marked by Roman occupation, war, brutality, and persecution. The political power of the Roman emperor and his empire stands as a critical backdrop for Luke's theological integration of gospel and peace. Luke uses the word "peace" fourteen times in the Third Gospel and seven times in Acts, compared to minimal usage in Matthew (four), Mark (one), and John (six).[6] Based upon a simple word count, Luke appears to be more interested in associating the word and concept of peace with Jesus' story than other Gospel writers. Whereas a broken world remains inclined toward power, self-interest and conflict, Luke presents the challenging way of peace, a message of radical love based on God's desire for communities built upon human inclusivity. Spirit-led characters announce the coming of Jesus who incarnates the gospel of peace. As Jesus models this gospel of peace, his followers continue to embody and proclaim his life and a message of reconciliation. I believe this lacuna deserves extensive attention throughout broader academic and ecclesial communities. Given Luke's strategic use of peace and the Spirit, I turn now to the intersection of these two motifs.[7]

---

5. For example, Bovon, *Luke the Theologian;* and Swartley, *Covenant of Peace.* Swartley assesses twenty-five major studies of New Testament theology or ethics and observes that no single study considers the peace motif in Luke and Acts (x).

6. Luke 1:79; 2:14; 2:29; 7:50; 8:48; 10:5; 10:6 (2); 11:21; 12:51; 14:32; 19:38; 19:42; 24:36. Acts 7:26; 9:31; 10:36; 12:20; 15:33; 16:36; 24:2. Luke's use of peace produces only one parallel use in Mark (5:34 par. Luke 8:48) and another parallel use in Matthew (10:34 par. Luke 12:51).

7. While commentators provide specific exegesis on the ensuing texts, few attempt to make literary and theological connections. I found the following works most helpful in the exegesis below: Borgman, *The Way According to Luke*; Kilgallen, "'Peace' in the Gospel of Luke and Acts of the Apostles," and Swartley, *Covenant of Peace.*

THE WAY OF PEACE: PROPHETIC ANTICIPATION (LUKE 1:79; 2:14; 2:29)

Luke begins the gospel story with a rather lengthy narrative of Jesus' birth (Luke 1:5—2:40). Only a short vignette of the twelve-year-old Jesus in the Temple separates the birth narrative from the adult ministry of Jesus. The birth narrative creates lively expectation for Luke's readers. The angel Gabriel announces to Mary that her child will be great, the Son of the Most High, and sit on the throne of David without end (Luke 1:29–33). Similarly, Luke records songs and oracles of exhilaration by Mary, Elizabeth, and Simeon to accentuate the enthusiasm created by the birth of Jesus. In the midst of this poetic narrative, Luke introduces his readers to the exciting possibilities for peace by way of three anticipatory declarations.

First, Luke begins with the exuberant carol of a new father. Zechariah celebrates the birth of his son by singing of John's mission; John the baptizer will be a prophet of the Most High and prepare a path for the long awaited redeemer, savior, and deliverer of Israel. At the conclusion of his oracle, Zechariah switches emphasis to the mission of Messiah: "to give light to those who sit in darkness and in the shadow of death, to guide our feet into the way of peace" (Luke 1:79). Luke's employment of this literary prophecy anticipates the sphere of the messianic mission. Zechariah is filled with the Spirit (Luke 1:67) certainly not in a salvific manner, but to prophesy and to proclaim the impact of this child. From Luke's point of view, the Spirit-led Zechariah sings as a reliable character announcing divine purposes for the Messiah. Using peace as the conceptual and literary climax to Zechariah's hymn, Luke creates a mood not only for Messiah's ensuing birth but also for the subsequent mission. Zechariah's song, fresh with hope for redemption and deliverance from enemies, captures the prevalent longing for the restoration of Israel from the dominant oppression of the Roman Empire. Such hope becomes magnified with Luke's introduction of the birth account during the reign of Caesar Augustus (Luke 2:1). On the heels of Zechariah's expectation, Luke intimates that Jesus' message of peace may conflict with that of the emperor and *pax Romana*. With hopes of peace in conjunction with the messianic mission, Luke moves immediately from Zechariah's oracle to the birth of Jesus.

Following a brief narration of Jesus' birth, Luke provides readers with a second anticipatory announcement. Just as Zechariah heralds peace as a human announcement of Jesus' coming, so also a heavenly host offers praise in response to Jesus' birth: "Glory to God in the highest, and on earth peace among those with whom he favors" (Luke 2:14).[8] Although the exact meaning of this announcement continues to be disputed, praise for messianic news of peace moves from humans to the heavens. "Among those with whom he favors" may refer to people who convert to God or those favored with God's good will. Whatever the extent of human cooperation, divine intervention demonstrates that God is acting on behalf of humanity to provide a foundation for this peace.[9] Further, if earlier references to the sphere of Jesus' influence begin with caution, this heavenly song certainly signals an expansive vision for peace among people everywhere.

For the purposes of this essay, I propose several implications. First, though this second announcement includes no reference to the inspiration of the Spirit, the weight of the angelic declaration is surely equivalent to Zechariah's Spirit-inspired song. Second, Luke chooses to declare the primacy of peace. Although myriad possibilities exist for the significance of the baby Jesus, Luke's choice demonstrates an important connection between gospel and peace. Finally, the nature of this peace remains unclear at this point in Luke's narrative. While interpretative analyses include personal and/or corporate peace as well as emotional or spiritual peace, readers must remain attentive to the socio-political context. Early declarations concerning the Messiah encompass a broad range of emotions such as the restoration of Israel and deliverance from enemies. However, Luke's readers know all too well that the reign of the Lukan Jesus fails to provide a political revolution following the pattern of the Greeks under Alexander the Great, the Maccabeans or Imperial Rome. Since the Lukan Jesus rejects objectives gained through violent revolution, readers must remain patient as Luke unveils an alternative model for peace with possibilities for all people (Luke 2:10, 14).

Luke employs a third anticipatory declaration by way of Simeon. During purification rites on behalf of Mary (in the presence of Joseph), Simeon announces the long awaited consolation of Israel. Under the inspiration of the Spirit, Simeon sings of God's salvation: "now you are dismissing your servant in peace, according to your word" (Luke 2:29). Simeon's oracles (Luke 2:29–32 and 34–35) offer both clarifying and confusing elements for the reader. In the first oracle, Simeon continues

8. Note the irony of a literal translation; the heavenly army announces peace on earth.

9. See Kilgallen, "Peace," 68.

to enlarge the scope of Jesus' message along the lines of the angelic announcement; the much anticipated glory of Israel includes a twofold reference to salvation prepared in the sight of all nations and as a light to the Gentiles (Luke 2:30–31). Simeon's words clarify Luke's salvific theology of reconciliation. With the inclusion of those outside of Israel, Luke renounces any notion of Jewish exclusion and nationalism. In the second oracle, Simeon directs his attention toward Mary. By way of Simeon, Luke introduces a pattern that sets the tone for a divided response to Jesus. Earlier anticipation of peace receives qualification; Israel will not be immune from the decision-making process and must choose to follow or reject Jesus. In fact, everyone including Mary must come to grips with the divine purpose of Jesus.

Again, I offer further implications. First, Luke emphasizes the reliability of Simeon and his oracles through a triple reference to the Holy Spirit (Luke 2:25, 26, 27). Simeon's inspired words solidify the expansive scope of Jesus' ministry but also introduce the possibility of rejection, in fact, its divine necessity. Second, while some may diminish Simeon's announcement of personal peace as formulaic, this reference deserves literary and theological consideration. Since the aged Simeon does not reappear in the narrative during the adult life and ministry of Jesus, this expression of peace appears all the more remarkable. Simeon senses not only peace without immediate fulfillment, but his prophecy of salvation beyond Israel anticipates an inclusivity that dismisses divine favoritism based upon ethnicity or nationalism. Finally, while Simeon points not only to the universal availability of salvation, response to Jesus will be mixed. Like Zechariah's earlier song, Luke employs Simeon's oracles as programmatic prophecies to guide interpretation of the subsequent narrative. Luke tempers over enthusiasm by cautioning his readers. Luke utilizes Simeon to initiate the divine necessity of division served by the call of Jesus. Jesus anointed as the guide into the way of peace and heralded by angels for his message of peace brings people to a point of decision. The ensuing narrative demonstrates that the Lukan gospel anticipated by Spirit-inspired speech and marked by reconciliation between people(s) requires alignment with Jesus. Simeon's oracle prepares Luke's readers for such a divided response.

JESUS AND THE WAY OF PEACE—PARADIGMATIC AND PREPARATORY

Luke now equipped with anticipatory declarations of a messianic mission transitions to the adult ministry of Jesus. The Lukan Jesus serves as the exemplar for the gospel of peace; Jesus filled with the Spirit embodies this message of reconciliation. But Luke goes further. Jesus not only proclaims the message of peace but also instructs his followers concerning future fulfillment and rejection of this message. The Lukan Jesus fulfills earlier declarations while commissioning his disciples to proclaim reconciliation and follow the path of peace in a broken world.

Luke's narration of Jesus' paradigmatic ministry produces two vignettes with the announcement of fulfilled peace. In Luke 7, a sinful woman sits before Jesus wiping his feet with her tears, kissing his feet, and pouring perfume on them. Simon the host Pharisee rebukes Jesus for his association with such a woman only to receive a challenging retort from Jesus. But Jesus receives the woman, forgives her sins, and proclaims: "Your faith has saved you; go in peace" (Luke 7:50). In Luke 8, Jesus feels a human touch and the ensuing release of his miraculous power. An unclean woman suffering from twelve years of uninterrupted bleeding comes forward, falls at the feet of Jesus, and announces her healing. Jesus responds: "Daughter, your faith has made you well; go in peace" (Luke 8:48). While some scholars view these statements as formulaic, such a dismissal may prove hasty. From Luke's perspective, these women serve as fulfillment to an earlier literary prophecy by the Lukan Jesus given at the synagogue in Nazareth. At the inauguration of his ministry (Luke 4:16–30), the Lukan Jesus announces the nature of his mission based upon a reading from Isaiah 61. Jesus filled with the Holy Spirit at his baptism and led by the Spirit against the devil in the wilderness now announces the anointing of the Spirit upon his life and ministry. The Lukan Jesus declares his mission to the poor, the outcast, and the marginalized. As Luke embarks upon narration of this Spirit-inspired ministry, the women in Luke 7 and 8 are only two of several examples of such literary fulfillment. By producing peace for these women, the Lukan Jesus also fulfills earlier anticipations of peace. These stories do not only associate Jesus' words of peace with physical health, and wholeness but with hope for societal restoration. Jesus' words reverse exclusion and division by supplying both women the possibility of full reentry to their respective families and community groups.

As the Lukan narrative moves along, the nature of peace enlarges. The narrative takes a dramatic turn, when the Lukan Jesus begins to provide instructional qualifications of the peace motif. The majority of references to peace in the Third Gospel occur in the central section of the gospel narrative (Luke 10:5, 6 [2]; 11:21; 12:51; 14:32; 19:38, 42 [2]). Luke introduces this section at 9:51, the first of numerous references concerning Jesus' journey to Jerusalem (Luke 9:53; 13:22, 33; 17:11; 18:31; 19:11, 28). Scholars often refer to this entire section as a travel narrative (Luke 9:51–19:44). While Jesus marches toward impending death in Jerusalem, the travel narrative serves as the context for Jesus' extended farewell discourse. In this regard, Luke's arrangement is not only geographic but dramatic. The Lukan Jesus prepares his apprenticing disciples for his departure and their future. Jesus challenges his disciples with the demands of the kingdom of God. He calls would be followers to wrestle with questions of status, possessions, family, persecution, and peace. He invites followers to a journey of radical discipleship that requires total reorientation of their lives.

According to Paul Borgman, Luke's travel narrative functions as an extended chiasm with the theme of peace as the outer extension of the spiral. Borgman designates Luke 9:51–10:24 as "peace to this house" and Luke 18:35–19:44 as "the things that make for peace."[10] This initial spiral functions as an *inclusio*, bookends for the entire central section. In Luke's introduction to the travel narrative, peace occurs three times (Luke 10:5, 6 [2]) followed by two references in the concluding scene (Luke 19:38, 42). By introducing the peace motif prominently at the beginning and conclusion of the travel narrative, Luke emphasizes the centrality of peace to Jesus' entire mission.

In the introductory scene, with his attention squarely upon Jerusalem, the Lukan Jesus sends seventy disciples ahead to villages he intends to visit. As they come upon a home, the disciples are to greet dwellers with this address: "Peace to this house" (Luke 10:5). Jesus instructs his disciples that if their message comes upon a child of peace, peace shall rest upon the household master. While the salutation "peace to this house" may indicate an ordinary and formulaic greeting, the context suggests otherwise. Luke deliberately associates the offer of peace with the mission of the disciples. The household master must deliver the appropriate response. Jesus instructs the disciples that peace is a gift and may in fact be rejected. Given

---

10. Borgman, *The Way*, 8–9.

the larger context, Jesus sends the seventy as envoys of peace declaring the rule of Christ to all open recipients. Once again, Luke strategically locates emphasis upon peace not only as a foundation for Jesus' mission but also as the standard for the future mission of the disciples.

The tension created by the offer of peace comes full circle at the conclusion of Jesus' journey to Jerusalem. Jesus enters Jerusalem amidst joyful shouts of praise: "Blessed is the King who comes in the name of the Lord! Peace in heaven and glory in the highest heaven!" (Luke 19:38). With monarchical praise, a large company of followers envisions Jesus as the genuine king of Jerusalem. More importantly, through the joyful song of "peace in heaven and glory in the highest," readers recall earlier declarations of Jesus' royalty by the angelic choir. But as the angelic song at the nativity tempers hope of unequivocal peace with the qualifying phrase "among those with whom [God] favors" (Luke 2:14), so also the Lukan Jesus quickly recognizes potential misunderstanding by qualifying the current setting. A sobbing Jesus follows a pharisaic rebuke with a startling qualification: Jerusalem fails "to grasp the things that make for peace" (Luke 19:42).

In contrast to the song of peace in heaven, Jerusalem will not possess peace. Instead, Jesus forecasts war and the destruction of Jerusalem. Following King Jesus should lead to the welfare of Jerusalem, yet Luke indicates that rejection by Jerusalem ultimately leads to its downfall. Furthermore, Luke provides a certain kind of literary fulfillment not only to the earlier anticipatory announcement of the angelic choir but also to Zechariah and Simeon. The physical journey of Jesus to Jerusalem functions as paradoxical fulfillment of Zechariah's messianic hope for a guide to "the way of peace" (Luke 1:79). Jesus' qualification of peace also reflects Simeon's forecasting of a division within the people of God (Luke 2:34–35). Luke's literary skill is so effective that readers are not shocked to see Jesus' lament over a city that does not recognize the time of God's visitation (19:41–44).[11] In doing so, these Spirit-inspired oracles find literary fulfillment. It is also important to emphasize that Luke continues to direct readers away from political aspirations commonly associated with messianic rule. Jesus' announcement of Jerusalem's impending destruction requires

---

11. Note numerous examples of Jesus' rejection. There is continuity between what Jesus encounters here and earlier. His teaching is rejected (Luke 6:11; 16:14; 19:47; 23:5); John is rejected (Luke 7:30; 20:5); and opponents watch Jesus closely to catch him (Luke 6:7; 11:54; 14:1; 20:20, 26).

further qualification of Jesus as the king of peace. This qualification surely startles a crowd hoping that Jesus' triumphal entry into Jerusalem would restore the glory days of Israel.[12] Readers must continue to wrestle with an alternative for peace. When Luke begins narration of the universal expansion of the gospel in Acts, readers will recognize that the peace of Christ supersedes all ethnic and national boundaries.

FULFILLMENT OF THE GOSPEL OF PEACE

In the closing section of the Third Gospel, Luke narrates several appearances of the resurrected Jesus. Though readers recall Jesus' earlier instruction concerning impending death, eleven disciples find themselves afraid and confused. Following Jesus' death they ponder the consequences of their association with the crucified Jesus. But all of this changes when joyous disciples from Emmaus come with good news of Jesus' resurrection. While the Emmaus disciples share their encounter, Jesus appears suddenly and greets the eleven, "Peace be with you" (Luke 24:36). Once again, these first words of Jesus carry more weight than a customary greeting. Readers recollect similar declarations to marginalized women (Luke 7:50; 8:48) and Jesus' earlier charge to the disciples: "whatever house you enter, first say, 'Peace to this house!'" (Luke 10:5). Just as the disciples' offer of peace needed to be received at the homes they visited, Jesus now enters the "home" of his disciples to gather children of peace (Luke 10:6).[13] And just as Jesus instructed his disciples concerning the familial implications of peace, so now the resurrected Jesus assures the disciples that their commitment to him and to one another provides the foundation for a new community and the expansion of Jesus' life and teaching. Jesus grants

---

12. At his arrest, the Lukan Jesus plays on this pervasive political desire by telling his disciples to purchase swords. Ironically, the disciples reveal that they already have two swords (hardly enough to ward off enemies), to which Jesus retorts that two is enough (Luke 22:36–38). When one of Jesus' own disciples slices off the ear of a servant of the high priest, Jesus rebukes the disciple and heals the ear (Luke 22:49–51). Clearly even the disciples remain confused concerning the nature of the Jesus' messianic mission.

13. Scholars remain divided on the textual authenticity of the greeting in Luke 24:36. Proponents in favor of its originality cite its attestation in all the best Greek manuscripts. Furthermore, I and others would also argue that the literary connections cited above make it seem doubtful that the text was altered for alignment with John 20:19. Luke repeatedly employs this greeting to provide fulfillment of the peace motif. For a summary of the textual evidence, see Fitzmyer, *The Gospel according to Luke X-XXIV*, 1575.

the disciples a fresh vision of peace and commissions them to proclaim his gospel of reconciliation to all nations beginning in Jerusalem (Luke 24:47–48). By the conclusion of the Third Gospel, Jesus' investment in the peace motif is secure. As Luke embarks upon his second volume, this investment begins to reap further dividends; the disciples not only demonstrate their grasp of the gospel of peace but begin to proclaim its message. Of course, Luke expects his readers to continue observation of this message and its implications.

Acts includes fewer references to peace but they are no less strategic. I turn to two specific references, namely, Acts 9:31 and 10:36. These verses serve respectively as a summary and synopsis of Luke's gospel of peace.[14] Luke's description of the church at peace (Acts 9:31) and his introduction to Peter's homily at the household of Cornelius as the "good news of peace" (NIV, Acts 10:36) fulfills anticipatory goals introduced in the Third Gospel. These statements, like crescendos within a song, provide climactic descriptions of the gospel envisioned by Luke.

Through narration of the formative years of the emerging community, Luke associates the increasing momentum of the gospel with the realization of peace. Acts begins with the end of Jesus' earthly ministry. The Lukan Jesus leaves the disciples with a promise; as he ministered in the power of the Holy Spirit, Jesus assures his disciples that they too would be anointed by the Holy Spirit (Luke 24:49; Acts 1:8). Upon reception of the Holy Spirit as promised on the Day of Pentecost (Acts 2:4), the disciples engage in immediate proclamation of Jesus as Lord resulting in thousands of favorable responses by Jewish audiences (Acts 2:41; 4:4; 5:14). Note Luke's strategic establishment of a political context; Peter announces, before "devout Jews from every nation under heaven" (Acts 2:5), that Jesus is both Lord and Messiah (Acts 2:36). The speech begins in response to the collective bewilderment of a Jewish crowd that hears Galilean disciples speaking in a host of languages from across the Roman Empire. By creating a calculated map of the imperial terrain, Luke reverses the claim that all the nations of the earth rest under the dominion of Caesar. Instead, Pentecost points to an alternative vision of universal authority created by the Spirit, ruled by Jesus, and devoid of borders. Again, readers recall the Lukan birth narrative and realize fulfillment of earlier prophetic oracles

---

14. While length restraints do not allow for analysis of every reference to peace in Acts, Luke's vision for the gospel of peace finds thorough fruition in the two references under examination.

concerning the universal significance of Jesus. Shepherds anticipated "joy for all people" (Luke 2:10) and Simeon envisioned Jesus' impact extending "in the presence of all peoples, a light for revelation to the Gentiles" (Luke 2:30–31). John the Baptist announced that "all flesh shall see the salvation of God" (Luke 3:6) before Luke traces Jesus' lineage to Adam, the paternal progenitor of all humanity (Luke 3:23–38). By way of the Pentecost narrative, Luke envisions a new community, not directed by the convoluted propaganda of *pax Romana*, but under a new banner that might be deemed *pax Christi*; Luke offers initial programmatic fulfillment of Jesus' command for the disciples to proclaim the gospel "to all nations" (Luke 24:47), to take the message from Jerusalem to Judea, Samaria and to the end of the earth (Acts 1:8).[15]

Further, it comes as no surprise that this same gospel message also receives a divided response. Through their proclamation of the gospel, Peter, John and other disciples declare their allegiance. Peter proclaims Jesus "both Lord and Christ" (Acts 2:36). Peter and the other disciples declare that they must obey God rather than any human authority, whether Jewish or Roman (Acts 4:19–20; 5:29). As the Lukan story continues, witnesses persist in spite of verbal threats, imprisonment, and physical punishment. Tension only increases as Stephen becomes the first martyr (Acts 7:54) and persecuted followers are forced to flee Jerusalem (Acts 8:1).

But it is in the midst of this remarkable growth during intense opposition that Luke's concept of peace begins to unfold. In Acts 9:31, Luke summarizes the state of the mission: "So the church throughout all Judea and Galilee and Samaria had peace and was built up; and walking in the fear of the Lord and in the comfort of the Holy Spirit it was multiplied."[16] Given the violence directed toward disciples for their unwavering allegiance to Jesus over and against all other authorities, Luke's suggestion that the church is at peace certainly appears puzzling. But the interlocking dynamics of the preceding stories reveal that Luke's description of a new and alternative community serves as the model for peace.

First, the growing community of disciples begins to proclaim the gospel to the nations, thereby not only resisting provincial exclusion but

15. See Gilbert, "The List of Nations in Acts 2." In this pioneering essay, Gilbert traces Roman employment, both literary and architectural, of geographic catalogues as articulation of its ideology of dominance in the world.

16. For a brief remark on this Lukan summary, see Marshall, *The Acts of the Apostles*, 176–77.

also shattering its boundaries. When Philip filled with the Spirit proclaims the gospel in Samaria, the Jerusalem community welcomes Samaritan converts into fellowship (Acts 8:4–25). Peter and John by their visit to the Samaritans symbolize the embrace of the Jerusalem community and the reception of Peter and John by the Samaritan believers symbolizes Samaritan embrace of their former rivals in Jerusalem. In other words, Spirit inspired witness proves salvific not only for disenfranchised individuals but reconciles entire communities marked by a history of division.[17] When Saul carries on his murderous rampage against Christians, he encounters the living Jesus and becomes the primary missionary, apologist, and church planter to the Gentiles. Given Saul's earlier approval of Stephen's death, the transformation of Saul from persecutor to apostle unto the Gentiles affords the church plenty of reason to celebrate a time of peace. Second, the church at peace also fulfills Lukan expectations for an alternative community. The apostles choose seven men (among them Stephen and Philip) filled with the Spirit to address an internal ethnic dispute. These men restore peace between feuding Hebraic and Hellenistic Jews over community meals (Acts 6:1–7).[18] Luke's narration of Philip's mission to the Samaritans and the ensuing evangelism of the Ethiopian eunuch break further barriers. Community with Samaritans brings an end to ethnic exclusion and hostility. The conversion of a eunuch provides an outcast with new possibilities for community. Thus it is through a singular use of the word "peace" that Luke's summary in Acts 9:31 not only celebrates the unity of a new community, but also the emergence of an ever enlarging inclusive community. Finally, Luke emphasizes that this state of the mission is neither accidental nor the result of mere human effort. The coming of the Spirit on the Day of Pentecost set the foundation for an inclusive community. The Spirit compels witnesses such as Peter and John, the Twelve, Stephen, and Philip to invite respondents not only to personal salvation but entrance into this alternative community. And, of course, the inclusion of outcasts, gender, ethnic enemies, and a former persecutor not only transforms the lives of the respondents but also the

17. I have heard numerous Pentecostals preach and teach a different purpose for the Samaritan encounter with the Holy Spirit. Peter and John come from Jerusalem to lay hands upon the Samaritan believers due to Philip's lack. Moreover, these Pentecostals also emphasize the empowering element of Spirit-reception. Such a view tends to be individualistic instead of reconciliatory as noted above.

18. The summary statement in Acts 6:7 indicates that the church resolves this issues and moves forward.

community.[19] Under the sensitive leadership of Apostles willing to follow the leading of the Spirit, the emerging community welcomes new respondents thereby increasing its scope as a welcoming and inclusive community of peace.

Luke follows his summary statement in Acts 9:31 with another critical story. In a dramatic narrative, Luke tells of Peter's passionate resistance to the rousing of the Spirit for an evangelistic mission to a Gentile household. Ironically, it was Peter who delivered the inaugural sermon of inclusivity on the Day of Pentecost to people representing all tongues: "For the promise is for you, for your children and for all who are far away, everyone whom the Lord our God calls" (Acts 2:39). After wrestling with God, Peter finally surrenders his exclusionist biases: he goes to the house of Cornelius. Peter explains his struggle to Cornelius and begins to proclaim the gospel. With an enlarged understanding of God's impartiality (Acts 10:34), Peter commences his preaching as the "good news of peace by Jesus Christ, he is Lord of all" (NIV, Acts 10:36). He follows with a summary of Jesus' sacrificial death and resurrection and the expansion of this message thus far. Now, at the household of Cornelius, Peter testifies to Jesus' commandment to preach to all people, "to everyone who believes in him" (Acts 10:43).[20] While Peter speaks these words, listeners welcome the message, receive the Holy Spirit, and are baptized into the community of Jesus Christ.

Note two implications for the topic at hand. First, Luke follows up the previous summary of the church at peace with a synopsis of the apostolic message as the good news of peace. Through Peter, the first preeminent voice of the gospel, Luke declares that the gospel is tantamount to the triumph of peace. For Luke, Peter's response to the guidance of the Spirit and his embrace of Cornelius' household represents a peace between Jew and Gentile, which to this point had not been realized. Second, readers recall the anticipatory words from the beginning of the Third Gospel. Earlier hopes for the messianic rule highlighted as "the way of peace," and "peace on earth," and the message "peace to this house" find their fulfillment in Peter's declaration of the "good news of peace by Jesus Christ

19. Concerning gender, note Luke's retroactive emphasis via Jesus' radical inclusion of two women in Luke 7–8.

20. In fact, a close reading of the Gentile Pentecost reveals that Luke's purpose includes not only the conversion of Cornelius and his household, but also the "conversion" of Peter.

who is Lord of all." By telling of the inclusion of Cornelius, Luke declares to readers the migratory success of the gospel from its Jewish roots to Samaritans and now to Gentiles.[21] In a world littered with heavy-handed propaganda declaring an idyllic and illusory *pax Romana*, the church counters with *pax Christi* based upon an alternative model. The church pronounces Jesus as Lord and invites searching individuals and communities to experience the loving embrace of Jesus and his followers. The gospel provides a way for anyone looking to replace hatred and hostility with love and inclusion under the radical Lordship of Jesus Christ.

CONTEMPORARY POSSIBILITIES

First, all individuals and traditions fall prey to a canon within a canon. In other words, no matter how much a movement desires to follow the Scriptures, it is impossible to embrace its message in totality. With this in mind, individuals and traditions must remain committed to theological exploration and the ensuing implications for the Christian life. Luke's message of the Spirit-inspired gospel of peace calls Pentecostals to consider a more holistic approach to their witness.[22] According to Luke, following Jesus is akin to the way of peace. Spirit-inspired witnesses consistently call prospective candidates to embrace God's message of peace.

Second, while Pentecostals delight in Spirit-inspired witness, their gospel proclamation tends to be overly individualistic. Undoubtedly, Luke recounts the stories of numerous individuals who respond favorably to the message proclaimed by Jesus and his witnesses. Similarly, Pentecostals readily celebrate through worship, preaching, and testimony the salvation of a sinner. However, Luke envisions not only individual peace with God, but the establishment of a new community marked by peaceful reconciliation. Luke's utilization of the peace motif does not center primarily

---

21. Following the conversion of Cornelius, Peter defends his actions in Jerusalem (Acts 11:1–17). The Jerusalem community welcomes his news of the Gentiles (Acts 11:18). Only a short time later, Jewish leaders at the Jerusalem Council decide to embrace Gentile converts without a host of Jewish requirements (Acts 15). Under the direction of the Holy Spirit (Acts 15:28), the church succeeds in addressing another threat to its unity; delegates take the decisions of the council to Antioch and receive a joyous reception. Luke writes that the delegates from Jerusalem "are sent off in peace" (Acts 15:33) and return home.

22. See the encouraging efforts by the Pentecostals and Charismatics for Peace and Justice (www.pcpj.org).

upon an inner or spiritual peace based upon individual reconciliation with God, but upon reconciliation of people with histories of separation and/or conflict. I call upon Pentecostals to express the gospel not only as a radical personal conversion but as a radical community of faith.

Third, Pentecostals love to pontificate about Pentecost as the consummate symbol of inclusivity. Pentecostals invest a great deal of academic and ecclesial energy on the meaning of Pentecost. An unending flood of sermons, articles, books, and theses point to Pentecost as the foundation for the breaking of racial, ethnic, and gender barriers. For example, Robert Beckford returns to the birth of the movement: "Azusa street teaches us that the Spirit of God is a force for challenging social structures that discriminate in the world today . . . [a] socio-political happening with profound effects for ecclesiology."[23] Paul Alexander pushes further. The glossolalia of Pentecost represents more than words; Pentecost initiates an eschatological community marked by intentional diversity. He argues: Pentecostals must strive to be "a radical prophetic community that can withstand the fierce gales of nationalistic pride and witness to the conviction that the holy Christian ethnos is not only transracial, transgender, and transcultural, but also transnational."[24] While the way of Christ need not erase national identity, response to the gospel demands the de-sacralization of nationhood. For Luke, Pentecostal unity of the Spirit symbolizes the establishment of a new and holy community with ultimate allegiance to King Jesus. As Pentecostals ponder the implications of a more encompassing Pentecost, I believe the Spirit will open eyes to see contemporary barriers and divisions in need of reconciliation through the gospel of peace.

Fourth, a fresh reading of Luke-Acts should encourage Pentecostals to revisit their own pacifist heritage. I hesitate to include this in the discussion since it is impossible to defend pacifism on the basis of Luke-Acts alone. However, Pentecostals must give careful attention to Luke's alternative socio-political platform. If Luke's promotion of pneumatological inclusivity requires the rejection of power that expresses any presumptions of special ethnicity or nationhood, and if the gospel provides the answer to hatred, conflict, and hostility, pacifism deserves a further hearing. The current culture of violence and the celebration of triumphant revenge,

23. Beckford, "Back to My Roots", 2.

24. Alexander, "Historical and Contemporary Pentecostal Critiques of Nationalism," 2. See also Alexander's recent *Peace to War*.

whether in media or film, leave little room for non-violence and embrace except as signs of weakness.[25] Yet as Jesus and his followers (Peter and John, the Twelve, Stephen, James, Paul, and others) suffered for the gospel, Pentecostals are able to recount their own stories of persecution and martyrdom due to radical allegiance to Christ. Proclamation of the gospel of peace requires willingness to suffer persecution and possible martyrdom. The Spirit of Jesus calls for disciples not bent on conquest but marked by radical commitment to nonviolent reconciliation.[26]

Finally, Pentecostals must revisit their counter-cultural worldview. As people of the Spirit, early Pentecostals took great pleasure in their counter-cultural worldview. Whether through preaching, witness or prophecy, Pentecostals longed to hear and proclaim the word of the Lord. However, is it possible that the breadth of Spirit-inspired speech begins to wane over time? Is it reasonable to conceive of current Spirit-inspired speech as a limiting reflection of the core doctrines and values of the community? If so, fresh biblical insight and instruction should go hand in hand with inspiration. In other words, as the people of God engage the Scriptures afresh, God speaks. As Pentecostals engage the Lukan story, I believe they will receive fresh revelation from God. Indeed, the ensuing essays demonstrate the ongoing centrality of forgiveness and reconciliation to authentic Pentecostal life and witness. May we open our ears to hear what the Spirit is saying to the church. Lord Jesus! Fill us with your Spirit that we may be agents of reconciliation and proclaim the way of peace, Amen!

BIBLIOGRAPHY

Alexander, Paul. "Historical and Contemporary Pentecostal Critiques of Nationalism." In *That Which We Have Received We Now Pass On: Sprit, Word, and Tradition in Pentecostalism*. Papers presented at the 34th Annual Meeting of the Society for Pentecostal Studies, Regent University, 2002. Virginia Beach, VA: Society for Pentecostal Studies, 2005.

25. See also my earlier and related paper "Spirit and Peace" where I address these motifs with greater emphasis upon pacifism and potential for Pentecostal/Anabaptist dialogue.

26. See Mittelstadt, *Spirit and Suffering in Luke-Acts*.

———. *Peace to War: Shifting Allegiances in the Assemblies of God.* The C. Henry Smith Series 9. Telford, PA: Cascadia, 2008.

Beckford, Robert. "Back to My Roots: Speaking in Tongues for a New *Ecclesia*." The Bible in Transmission, Summer 2000. www.biblesociety.org.uk/exploratory/articles/beckford00.pdf.

Borgman, Paul. *The Way According to Luke: Hearing the Whole Story of Luke-Acts.* Grand Rapids: Eerdmans, 2006.

Bovon, François. *Luke the Theologian: Fifty-five Years of Research (1950–2005).* Waco, TX: Baylor University Press, 2006.

Cadbury, Henry J. *The Making of Luke-Acts.* New York: Macmillan, 1927.

Fitzmyer, Joseph A. *The Gospel according to Luke (X-XXIV): Introduction, Translation, and Notes.* Anchor Bible 28A. New York: Doubleday, 1985.

Gilbert, Gary. "The List of Nations in Acts 2: Roman Propaganda and the Lukan Response." *Journal of Biblical Literature* 121 (2002) 497–529.

Johnson, Luke Timothy. *The Literary Function of Possessions in Luke-Acts.* Society of Biblical Literature Dissertation Series 39. Missoula, MT: Scholars Press, 1986.

Kilgallen, John. "'Peace' in the Gospel of Luke and Acts of the Apostles." *Studia Missionalia* 38 (1989) 55–79.

Kurz, William. "Narrative Approaches to Luke-Acts." *Biblica* 68 (1987) 195–222.

———. "Narrative Models for Imitation in Luke-Acts." In *Greeks, Romans and Christians: Essays in Honor of Abraham J. Malherbe*, edited by David L. Balch, Everett Ferguson, and Wayne A. Meeks, 171–189. Minneapolis: Fortress, 1990.

———. *Reading Luke-Acts: Dynamics of Biblical Narrative.* Louisville: Westminster, 1993.

Marshall, I. Howard. *The Acts of the Apostles: An Introduction and Commentary.* The Tyndale New Testament Commentaries. Grand Rapids: Eerdmans, 1980.

Mittelstadt, Martin. "Spirit and Peace in Luke-Acts: Possibilities for a Pentecostal/Anabaptist Dialogue." In *Pentecostal/Charismatic Intersections: What Does the Spirit Have to Say Through the Academy?* Papers presented at the 38th Annual Meeting of the Society for Pentecostal Studies, Eugene Bible College, 2009. CD-ROM. Virginia Beach, VA: Society for Pentecostal Studies, 2009.

———. *Spirit and Suffering in Luke-Acts: Implications for a Pentecostal Pneumatology.* Journal of Pentecostal Theology, Supplemental Series 26. London: T. & T. Clark, 2004.

Stronstad, Roger. *The Charismatic Theology of St. Luke.* Peabody, MA: Hendrickson, 1984.

Swartley, Willard. *Covenant of Peace: The Missing Peace in New Testament Theology and Ethics.* Grand Rapids: Eerdmans, 2006.

Tannehill, Robert C. *The Narrative Unity of Luke-Acts: A Literary Interpretation.* 2 vols. Foundations and Facets. Philadelphia: Fortress, 1986–1990.

Literary Perspectives

2

Pentecostals, Postmodernism,and *The Shack*

Robert Berg

In his bestseller, *Life of Pi,* Yann Martel narrates the amazing story of a boy who survives a shipwreck and 227 days in a lifeboat on the open sea with a live Bengal tiger. The two men sent to investigate find such a story hard to believe. They are after *the truth,* that is, a reasonable explanation in accordance with what they have seen and thus think possible. Such people, says the narrator, are committed to a "dry, yeastless factuality" and as a result "miss the better story."[1] Martel calls his readers to be freed from "mere believability" to a life open to the realm of God. And Pentecostals, "postmoderns," and *The Shack's* William P. Young say amen.

PENTECOSTALS

Pentecostals have always been people of story. For generations now, we have participated in testimony services, when the saints enthusiastically share what God has done in their lives since the last gathering. This past week, Jesus healed my niece's fever, protected me from a car accident, provided money for groceries, filled me with the joy of the Holy Spirit.

1. Martel, *Life of Pi,* 63–64.

Those without the sight of faith can always find a perfectly reasonable explanation for all such incidents. To them, Pentecostals represent the sort of pre-Enlightenment religion that sooner or later would succumb to the advance of reason. So for many years, Pentecostals have been patronized much as the young Pi was by his elder interrogators, much as the man born blind healed by Jesus was by his interrogators (John 9). "But such things don't happen"—"We've never seen such things"—"It makes no sense." I recall in my college years reading Harvey Cox's *The Secular City,* and wondering if indeed religious faith would have little place in our increasingly secularized culture." But in his survey of the Pentecostal explosion around the globe, *Fire From Heaven,* Cox has documented how wrong he was. As it turned out, Pentecostals had a better story. And they have testified to this better story.[2]

Actually, it is not possible to speak of *the* Pentecostal story, given the staggering diversity of the movement. And the story, like all stories, has changed over the years, even among its North American family. In many ways, we are quite different from the first Pentecostals of a century ago. We are now in the mainstream of American society and of evangelicalism. Most of us value some of the changes. We were embarrassed by some of the emotional excesses and doctrinal peculiarities. But we rue some of the changes. On the upward path toward respectability, we have lost some of our identity. In part, this was because everybody else grew more like us, especially in their "contemporary" Sunday service. But in large measure, we were the ones who grew more like our evangelical relatives.

We were told by our more intellectually mature colleagues that we "based our doctrine on experience." As if these more thoughtful friends did not base their doctrine on their experience—or lack of it. As if anyone could formulate one's beliefs in a pristinely objective manner apart from personal experience. The blatant acknowledgment in our culture that this is true, in fact, is one of the signs of a transition from what has been called the modern.

POSTMODERNISM

Pentecostals should be able to appreciate the transition in the twentieth century from a "modern" to a "postmodern" culture in the West. To say the least, the term "postmodern" can mean many different things. For the

---

2. Cox, *Fire From Heaven.*

narrow purposes of this essay, I mean by "modern" the mindset that re-sulted from the Enlightenment, in which reason is the ultimate arbiter of what is true. Those who cling to religion and "the supernatural" are at best primitives on their way to extinction. Modern individuals want answers to difficult questions, and if they set their minds to it, they can ascertain the true answers. And the answers are not subject to variables like per-sonal experiences or biases. By "postmodern" I mean the absence of this confidence in reason—or anything else—as the fundamental criterion by which things are evaluated. In recent decades, more people have come to believe that there are a variety of "truths" and that some of these truths are outside the cognitive realm.

A number of recent scholars have argued that evangelical Christianity has adopted fundamental perspectives from modernism.[3] Evangelicals "have often uncritically accepted the modern view of knowledge despite the fact that at certain points the postmodern critique is more in keeping with Christian theological understandings."[4] The modern view holds that universal truths are attained by objective scientific investigation and can be stated in propositions verifiable by human reason.

"The essential difference between modernism and postmodernism at the theological level consists in what might be termed a 'propositional' as opposed to a 'vocative' understanding of Scripture. Propositional lan-guage is always flattened, confined to a third person. It is always 'about' something else. Propositional language adjudges and describes. It relates one set of impersonal terms to another."[5] Vocative language, in contrast, uses the second person. "While the Bible of course contains numerous 'descriptive' statements about the nature of God, the defining moments in which he 'reveals' himself involve interpersonal encounter and sec-ond-person address."[6] A typically "modern" assessment would consider the Bible a gristmill for a thoroughly logical systematic compilation of the facts recorded therein. A "postmodern" approach is more intuitive than cerebral, more immediate than analytical, and—to use scientific

---

3. Grenz, *A Primer on Postmodernism*; Downing, *How Postmodernism Serves (My) Faith*; Smith, *Who's Afraid of Postmodernism?*; Raschke, *The Next Reformation*.

4. Grenz, *A Primer on Postmodernism*, 167.

5. Raschke, *The Next Reformation*, 137.

6. Ibid., 138.

terminology—more aligned with the uncertainties of quantum mechanics than the certainties of Newtonian mechanics.[7]

Perhaps now it is clearer why I suggest that Pentecostals should appreciate the transition from a modern era to a postmodern era. A modern approach to God and the Bible was precisely what the early Pentecostals found intolerable. Many found the churches they had attended to be Christian only in creedal formulation; without the moving of the Holy Spirit, they were like those Paul described as "having a form of godliness but denying the power thereof" (2 Tim. 3:5).[8]

THE SHACK

In 2006, the wife of Paul Young suggested that he write a story that reflected some of the things he had gone through in recent years as a Christmas gift to his children. When others read it, they said that it deserved a larger audience. The result is the novel, *The Shack*.[9] The main character is Mack, who has been devastated since his youngest daughter was kidnapped and murdered by a serial killer. Mack finds a note from God in his mailbox inviting him to the shack where his daughter was killed. The bulk of the tale, then, is Mack's weekend of what might be called divine therapy with the members of the Trinity. By the end of the story, Mack has a new perspective of God and his own life.

The book has had phenomenal success. It was the best selling trade paperback in the country for nearly a year, and remains at number two even at this writing.[10] Ask those who have read the book or peruse the entries on various websites and you will marvel at the effusive comments. Many have found the book transformative. They seem to share Mack's experience in the shack, and sense that they understand and relate to God more deeply as a result. On the other hand, critics have charged that on a

---

7. Jencks (ed.), *The Post-Modern Reader*, 34; Cox, *Fire from Heaven*, 301. A postmodern approach does not necessarily reject the validity of propositions, just that propositions have major limitations (e.g., they are formulated by groups holding power, and they do not move humans in the way that stories do).

8. John H. Brooks urged the necessity of "come-outism" (cited by Blumhofer, *Restoring the Faith*, 29).

9. All references to *The Shack* will remain in the main text.

10. You can tell that your book is extremely successful when others write books about it—in Young's case two books by the same name: Olson, *Finding God in the Shack*; and Rauser, *Finding God in the Shack*.

variety of subjects, *The Shack* is misleading at best, and in the judgment of some, downright heretical in its view of God, the Bible, salvation, and the church.

Since Young's view of forgiveness has been roundly faulted, our present task is to ask what *The Shack* has to say about it. I will work with Young's definition of forgiveness: "release from judgment" (225), "letting go of another person's throat" (224), or "'removing your hands from around his neck" (227). Specifically, then, what does Mack learn about forgiveness from his weekend with God?

Experiencing Forgiveness

The first thing that Mack learns is that he needs to experience forgiveness. Mack has been living since childhood haunted by issues of forgiveness, or more accurately, lack of forgiveness. His "'overly strict church-elder father was a closet drinker" (7). So his father was respectable in the eyes of the church and community, but Mack knew what he was like at home: a "vicious mean beat-your-wife-and-then ask-God-for-forgiveness drunk" (8). When thirteen-year-old Mack dares to speak of such hidden things to "a church leader," it is not so much to report on his father as to tearfully confess that he had not done anything to prevent his father from beating his mother unconscious at times. When his father hears about this from his church friend, he ties up Mack to a tree behind their house and for two days beats him "with a belt and Bible verses" (8). Mack runs away, but not before he puts "varmint poison in every bottle of booze he could find" and leaves a note for his mother: "Someday I hope you can forgive me." We learn nothing more about the remainder of the lives of Mack's father and mother.

One can hardly overemphasize the importance of these experiences for Mack. They enlighten all that will follow in *The Shack* and must be kept in mind when evaluating Mack's perspectives and God's interaction with Mack. Many critics of *The Shack* point out the negative view of the church seen in the novel.[11] But we must allow a novelist to create a plausible narrative world. Given what has happened to him, how could this young boy not grow up to be bitter toward the God who allowed this to happen and toward the church that helped to bring it about? Although he is never again mentioned, the "church leader" in whom Mack confides

---

11. Some critics see the deficient view of the church as part of a broader "subversive quality." See Challies, "A Reader's Review of *The Shack*."

is symbolic. The church is supposed to be a place of safety, refuge, and comfort. Instead, the church betrayed Mack's trust and well-being.

Mack continues to wonder whether he can ever be forgiven. Could his mother ever forgive him? Is Mack's question related to the poison he used against his father or to the fact that he leaves without saying good-bye, apparently never to see her or even communicate with her again? The reader surmises that Mack's mother dies without Mack ever having had the chance to hear "I forgive you" from her.

Early in the novel, readers learn that Mack had hurt his wife Nan "something fierce" (10) in the early years of their marriage. Her love, in spite of his actions, "saved his life."[12] The impression is that she has already forgiven Mack a great deal. When Mack receives God's invitation, he conceals from Nan his plans to go. During his weekend with the Trinity, Papa confronts Mack with the real reason why he had not told her: his fear of the emotions that would result.[13] "What if she doesn't forgive me? Mack knew that this was indeed a deep fear that he lived with" (189). Maybe this most recent betrayal of confidence would be the last straw.

After the devastating loss of Missy, Mack also feels guilty for not preventing the kidnapping and murder; as her father, he was responsible for protecting his little girl and he had failed her. He repeatedly plays over in his mind "the if-only game" (64–65): if only he had not taken his kids on that trip, if only he had left a day earlier . . . He is haunted by nightmares in which he helplessly screams in a vain effort to save Missy. In a conversation with Sophia, a personification of divine wisdom on the order of Proverbs 7, Mack reveals his fear. "'Has she forgiven me?' he asked. 'Forgiven you for what?' 'I failed her,' he whispered. 'It would be her nature to forgive, if there were anything to forgive, which there is not.' 'But I didn't stop him from taking her. He took her while I wasn't paying attention . . . ' his voice trailed off." The fact that he was saving his two other children after their boat had capsized didn't seem to matter. Mack was haunted by the thought that his baby girl hated him for abandoning her to an unthinkable fate. The words of Sophia that follow are also revealing. "Only you, in the entire universe, believe that somehow you are

---

12. Young uses this same language in the dedication of the book to his wife: "thank you for saving my life."

13. Papa is the intimate term Nan uses for God the Father and what the Father is called in *The Shack*.

to blame. Missy doesn't believe that, nor Nan, nor Papa. Perhaps it's time to let that go—that lie" (168).

So, along with his questions about whether he could be forgiven by his mother, Nan, and Missy, Mack had been unable to forgive himself. In these cases, he desperately needs to receive forgiveness. But Mack also needs to grant forgiveness. *The Shack* does not describe the actual kidnapping and murder of Mack's daughter. But readers experience with him the horror and panic of losing a child and the gradual realization that a monster has stalked this innocent child, abused her and taken her life. And this was the deed of a serial killer, one who had done the same thing to little girls before; he had gotten away with it again.

But it is only on the last day of the weekend that Papa confronts Mack's anger toward the man. "Papa," he cried, "how can I ever forgive that son of a bitch who killed my Missy? If he were here today, I don't know what I would do. I know it isn't right, but I want him to hurt like he hurt me . . . if I can't get justice, I still want revenge" (224). Many readers, unlike God, probably share his sentiments (if not his language). Papa, though, patiently calls on Mack to grant forgiveness even to the perpetrator of such evil. Eventually, Mack does indeed express his forgiveness for his daughter's murderer, much to Papa's joy.

More complicated still are the two cases in which Mack needs both to receive and grant forgiveness. The first of these cases is his father. We have already described the abuse Mack's father inflicted on him, and how Mack runs away after leaving poison in his father's liquor bottles. Readers remain ignorant of the effects of this action. Perhaps it made the father sick. Or perhaps Mack killed his father, no small thing to have to live with. In any case, intermingled with the hate and bitterness Mack feels toward his father, there is guilt. So in a scene toward the end of the novel, in which Mack is given the ability to "see" things humans normally cannot, he is allowed to meet his father. Upon first seeing him, Mack is flooded with a "wave of emotions, a mixture of anger and longings . . ." (215). But quickly Mack was running to his father, who was on his knees. Mack takes his father's face in his hands "so he could stammer the words he had always wanted to say: 'Daddy, I'm so sorry! Daddy, I love you" (215). God takes great joy in their tearful embrace. Some may object to this scene, since it seems to say nothing about the father asking for Mack's forgiveness for his contemptible behavior toward his son. But the story is not about the father, it is about Mack.[14] The scene allows Mack to both receive from and grant forgiveness to his father. Mack is finally free of a burden he had carried since the day he ran off from home.

Even more consequential is the case of God. Mack's early impressions of God were molded by his relationship with his father. In contrast to Jesus, God the Father is "brooding, distant, and aloof" (10). At various times, his long held resentment bursts forth. "Well, I'm here, God. And you? You're nowhere to be found! You've never been around when I needed you—not when I was a little boy, not when I lost Missy. Not now! Some 'Papa' you are!" (78–79). Note the two key elements: Mack's brutalization as a child, and the brutalization of his beloved Missy. God had allowed both to occur. Mack's resentment is ultimately confronted in a scene where Mack is made to "judge" God. Sophia presses Mack: "Isn't that your just complaint, Mackenzie? That God has failed you, that he failed Missy? That before the Creation, God knew that one day your Missy would be brutalized, and still he created? And then he allowed that twisted soul to snatch her from your loving arms when he had the power to stop him. Isn't God to blame, Mackenzie? Finally, then, Mack responds: 'Yes! God is to blame!'" (161). Mack has been unable to forgive God and, though some will find the entire idea objectionable, Mack needs to "forgive God." A better way to put this, of course, is that Mack must get past his misperception that God has wronged him. But the point is that Mack must experience this. Using the definition of forgiveness mentioned earlier, Mack must release God from Mack's judgment (even though it is a false judgment).

Readers can view the other side of the coin in a similar way. Mack must also experience God's forgiveness. According to Young, Mack has already been forgiven of all his evil actions and attitudes (225). But he certainly has not realized or experienced a "release from judgment." Mack had thought that he was supposed to observe laws and commandments in order to please God and avoid punishment (202–3). As a result of his weekend with God in the shack, Mack is able to release God from his own judgment, and to come into a realization of the release from judgment that God provided in Jesus' death on the cross.

---

14. Told in this way, the story reflects how one can forgive someone who cannot actually accept the forgiveness, such as a parent who has died.

Understanding Forgiveness

The second crucial thing that Mack learns is that he *needs to understand forgiveness*. Over the weekend at the shack, the Trinity gives Mack quite a schooling on a wide variety of theological topics. But one of the most important things that Mack has to learn is what forgiveness is all about. As I have pointed out, Mack must come to the point of relinquishing his "hold on the throat" of both God and the man who murdered his daughter. In this process, God must correct some of Mack's misperceptions of what it means to forgive. Among other things, Mack thinks that forgiveness (1) means forgetting the wrong that was committed, (2) is failing to do justice to the wrong done, (3) is an act for the offending party, (4) necessarily involves reconciliation with the offending party. This misperception of forgiveness goes hand in hand with his misperception of God as angry, demanding, and as difficult to please as his own father. The whole weekend is meant to correct these misperceptions. "That's why you're here, Mack," [Papa] continued. "I want to heal the wound that has grown inside of you, and between us" (92). For Papa to do this, she must disabuse Mack of his faulty thinking.

Two conversations prove pivotal. In one, Papa explains the significance of Jesus' death on the cross: "'through his death and resurrection, I am now fully reconciled to the world.' Mack replies: 'The whole world? You mean those who believe in you, right?' 'The whole world, Mack. All I am telling you is that reconciliation is a two way street, and I have done my part, totally, completely, finally'" (192).

The second conversation occurs in a climactic scene when Papa is leading Mack to forgive Missy's killer. Papa clarifies that since God knows everything, God does not "forget" human sins in the usual sense of the word; rather, "forgetting for me is the choice to limit myself . . . because of Jesus, there is now no law demanding that I bring your sins back to mind. They are gone when it comes to you and me, and they run no interference in our relationship" (224). Papa goes on to say that forgiveness does not establish relationship. "In Jesus, I have forgiven all humans for their sins against me, but only some choose relationship . . . When Jesus forgave those who nailed him to the cross they were no longer in his debt, nor mine" (225). Mack, as one might expect, cringes at the thought of forgiving the monster who killed Missy. But Papa shows him that forgiveness is first for the healing and liberation of the forgiver, and forgiveness releases both forgiver and forgiven from a terrible burden, acknowledged or not.

When Mack asks whether he would have to allow this man to play with his other daughter, Papa explains: "Unless people speak the truth about what they have done and change their mind and behavior, a relationship of trust is not possible. When you forgive someone you certainly release them from judgment, but without true change, no real relationship can be established" (225).

The Shack provides the reader with numerous insights into forgiveness. It is true that forgiveness is not forgetting a wrong committed, but the choice not to release the hold on the offender's throat. It is also true that forgiveness is both for the one wronged and the one committing the wrong. A refusal to forgive is toxic to all aspects of human life and rarely "gets back" at the one who did the wrong in the first place.

But what of the claim that God has forgiven everyone their sins? Isn't this universalism and contrary to orthodox Christianity? Young has publicly denied that he believes in universalism, and I take his word for it. But does *The Shack* reflect such a view?[15] Mack (representing Young) thinks that God demands that humans keep laws and takes pleasure in catching them when they do not. "Honestly, don't you enjoy punishing those who disappoint you?" (119). Is Papa's answer unbalanced and dangerous?

Young makes a clear distinction between being forgiven and being in relationship. This is central to the climactic scene where Papa calls Mack to forgive Missy's killer. Papa insists that forgiving this man does not establish a relationship. So what are the implications for God's dealing with humans? Young thinks that God has forgiven all people their sins. "I am now fully reconciled to the world" (192). But this does not mean that all people automatically are in right relationship with God. Despite the fact that Papa refers to Missy's killer as "my son," he has yet to be "redeemed" (224) and transformed into one of God's sons and daughters (182). Many roads that humans take do not lead to God, but God takes any road to reach a human life (182). The emphasis is on God's gracious act of forgiveness, as it is in the Bible; the initiative is with God, not with humans. When we were enemies we were reconciled to God through the death of his Son (Rom. 5:10a).

God's nature is the key issue. As Papa tells him, "The real underlying flaw in your life, MacKenzie, is that you don't think that I am good" (126).

---

15. Wayne Jacobsen, who collaborated with Young on *The Shack*, indicates that Young came into the project with universalist tendencies, but interaction with his colleagues resulted in his revising his views. See Jacobsen, "Is THE SHACK Heresy?"

The God of *The Shack* loves and intends good for all his creatures, but does not insist on his way. This God genuinely allows humans to respond or not respond to his forgiveness; God "submits" to human will because love does not force a response (145–146, 190). To establish a relationship with God, a human must repent, that is, confess and speak the truth. But such repentance does not result in forgiveness because God's forgiveness is granted freely, and so is prior to any human actions or attitudes. Young's language here may imply that there is no hell. God "does not need to punish sin" since it is its own punishment, and it is not God's "purpose" to punish sin but to cure it (120). And after all, "[w]hen you forgive someone you certainly release them from judgment . . . " (225). It would seem to follow that when God in the cross of Jesus forgave all humans their sins, God released all of us from judgment. Without any forthcoming judgment, the concept of a "judgment day" is apparently made moot. But I do not think that Young's concern is to make a case against any sort of divine judgment.

Young's concerns regarding forgiveness, I think, are two-fold. First, Young wants to correct a mistaken impression that God the Father is an angry, vengeful, and legalistic power who is appeased only by the loving sacrifice of his Son, Jesus. A number of times Papa tells Mack that Mack has a flawed picture of God. "I'm not who you think I am, Mackenzie" (96). "I'm not like you, Mack" (97). "I am not who you think I am" (119–20). God is not punishing Mack for his failing Missy (164) nor for what he did to his father (71). Jesus is quite clear that what you get with the Son, you get with the Father (John 14:9). Father and Son share a nature of love and forgiveness portrayed in a parable such as the Prodigal Son. Mack has had his fill of divine judgment and so what he gets in his weekend with God is an outpouring of love and forgiveness. Does *The Shack* lack a theological balance between grace and judgment? Yes. But the same could be said of the Apostle Paul, who "neglects" the doctrine of repentance and divine judgment, for example, in Colossians.[16] Both writers are concerned in their particular contexts to "comfort the afflicted"; neither aims to cover all the theological bases.[17] In *The Shack*, God's concern is to help Mack to unleash the baggage of his dreadful experience of his natural father.

16. The only time the Greek root *kri-* (related to judging) is used is in Col 2:16, where Paul insists that they not submit to the judgment of false teachers.

17. In 1 Corinthians, Paul must afflict the comfortable (1 Cor 4:8–21).

Most significantly, God has forgiven humans their sins. The reason that God can do this is because Jesus, God's Son, died a sacrificial death (192). One of Mack's misperceptions is that the sacrificial love demonstrated on the cross was that of Jesus, while God the Father—much like his own father—is wrathful and judgmental (163–65). In a question that sounds facetious but is actually quite serious, Mack asks Papa, "Weren't you always running around killing people in the Bible?" (119). Mack is surprised to see the nail marks of the crucifixion on Papa, since he thought that the Father had abandoned the Son, based on Jesus' citation of Psalm 22, "My God, my God, why have you forsaken me?" (95–96). But Papa's statement that "(w)hen you forgive someone you certainly release them from judgment" (225) apparently applies to both humans and God. Papa uses the perfect tense: "In Jesus, I have forgiven all humans for their sins against me" (225). God's forgiveness, then, is not contingent on human repentance.

The second concern in Young's view of forgiveness is to show how much more complex forgiveness is than most people realize. For one thing, forgiveness in human experience is often more a gradual process than an instantaneous event. Mack declares his forgiveness of Missy's killer; he releases his throat and his desire to see the man suffer. But a relationship of trust, even if the man repents, may well take many years of conscious effort on Mack's part. He may stay angry with him for a long time.[18] Mack may have to consciously choose to be forgiving of Missy's killer every day for many years before Mack realizes that he has forgiven the man completely (227).[19]

Young is even more concerned that we grasp the purpose of forgiveness. Divine forgiveness is not primarily an entrance ticket into heaven when you die. Instead, forgiveness is the power to transform human life, to effect nothing less than cosmic change. As Papa says: "Mackenzie, don't you see that forgiveness is an incredible power—a power you share with us, a power Jesus gives to all whom he indwells so that reconciliation can grow?" (225). At the end of the story, God allows Mack to choose whether to "remain with us" or to return to his other home and his family. Mack wonders if what he does is important enough to return to. The divine

---

18. Presumably this is not the case when God forgives us, but Young does not address this question.

19. Recent study in forgiveness tends to support Young's perspective. See, for example, Worthington, *Forgiving and Reconciling*.

answer he gets reflects Young's deeper interest in forgiveness. "Every time you forgive, the universe changes . . . " (235). So forgiveness is just as much about the reign of God in this life as escaping God's wrath in the next.

Forgiveness, then, is a necessary step toward relationship, and according to *The Shack*, God's purpose in forgiving is to bring everyone into relationship with God and others. The model is the relationship among the persons of the Trinity, where there is no authority but rather mutual submission. Mack is then astounded when he is told that God "is submitted to you in the same way" (145). Why would God be submitted to God's creatures? "Because we want you to join us in our circle of relationship. I don't want slaves to my will; I want brothers and sisters who will share life with me" (146).

ASSESSING *THE SHACK*

A reader's theological position will influence how she assesses Young's presentation of forgiveness. Calvinists will find the idea of God "submitting" to our choices unacceptable because "the Bible makes it clear that redemption has already been accomplished. The redemption of God's children was accomplished once and for all when Jesus died on the cross. All that awaits now is the application of that redemption to the children of God."[20] So the Calvinist two steps are (1) Jesus dies for the children of God (that is, the elect), and (2) the application of redemption to the elect. Young's two steps are those affirmed by Arminians: (1) Jesus dies, providing forgiveness for all humans, and (2) individuals accept or reject God's bona fide offer of a relationship with him. Pentecostals are passionately Arminian. It is what has propelled our missionary efforts since the first days of the movement. So although Pentecostals have usually avoiding dancing, they should prefer the Arminian two-step to the Calvinist two-step.

I propose that Pentecostals read *The Shack* for what it is: a testimony. I noted early in this essay that Pentecostals know about testimony services. The folks who testify in these settings are not trained theologians, and I can recall hearing some statements that might have been corrected in an academic setting. But their testimonies reflected how much they loved Jesus and were filled with God's Spirit.

20. Challies, "A Reader's Review of *The Shack*."

I heard Paul Young "testify," and he is a man who loves God.[21] He wrote *The Shack* for his family to provide some insight into his long spiritual and emotional journey. What happened in the life of Paul Young over a decade occurs in a weekend for Mack in *The Shack*. And its astounding popularity makes it clear that a great host of Christians identify with his story. Possibly *The Shack* has such an impact because it is the work of a brilliant wordsmith and such works touch readers profoundly. But as various reviewers have noted, Young is not a brilliant wordsmith.

The Shack has been so successful because it captures in story form the spiritual and emotional challenges that scores of Christians experience. And the reason that Young did this with such effectiveness is that he was telling his own story; *The Shack* is his testimony. It is at times brazenly honest enough that some have taken offense. The language is too raw. The liberties taken when speaking to Almighty God, some say, are sacrilegious if not blasphemous. But there is a great deal of pain in the world. And it is Young's frank expression of questions, doubt, and pain—for some, even the experience of "the Great Sadness"—that so many Christians find refreshing. Are there not vivid examples in the Bible when the prophet or the psalmist in his suffering cries out wondering where God is and why there is no answer to his pleas for deliverance?[22] Indeed, Paul Young's honesty has encouraged many readers of *The Shack* to share their own struggles more openly with others. For years, they have secretly wrestled with issues they felt they could not talk about; perhaps they would not be forgiven. So while some have criticized Young for having a deficient ecclesiology, his experience seems to ring true for quite a few readers.

Pastors can learn much from the popularity of *The Shack*. The lesson is not that you will be popular if you avoid preaching about judgment and hell.[23] Most people believe that there should be consequences for conduct. Readers may wish for Missy's murderer to repent and convert,

21. I find this consistent throughout Young's commentary following publication of the book. I heard him say as much in a review session at College of the Ozarks (September 11, 2008). He regularly "testifies" to the theme of *The Shack* as a kind of wrestling with his own personal journey.

22. For example, Pss 13, 22, 88, 102. Note that both the psalmist and Young ultimately reaffirm their trust in God at the end of the literary unit, whether a psalm or a novel. Olson (*Finding God in the Shack*, 133) suggests that *The Shack* is an interpretation of the Book of Job.

23. Pastors may find that preaching on those topics is unpopular, but my point here is about Young's concerns in *The Shack*.

but they do not want him to avoid being held accountable if he does not. I suggest that Pentecostals in a postmodern period take away the following variation on James Carville's advice to Bill Clinton: "It's about relationships, stupid."[24] The Bible is about relationships. God desires for us to be in right relationship with him, and in right relationship with others. This is precisely how Jesus summarized the Law: love God and love others.[25] The kingdom of God is about transformed lives in transformed relationships. So I'm not impressed with the claims that Young is misrepresenting Scripture. Forgiveness is a process, initially a free act of God through Jesus' death and resurrection to release us from the penalty of our sin. Some have derided *The Shack* as a touchy-feely relationship tale, popular because it has been gutted of theological substance. Frankly, I find such claims an insult to the scores of Christians who testify to being brought closer to God by reading *The Shack*.

The more "modern" a Christian is, the more likely he or she is to find fault with *The Shack*. That is, the more a person conceives of Christian faith as the affirmation of rationally configured and objectively accurate doctrines, the more that person will reject Young's portrayal of the nature and behavior of God. Take the well known author and apologist, Norman Geisler. Many Pentecostals follow the lead of such evangelicals on issues of faith; after all, he has been involved in the writing of eighty books. Geisler claims that *The Shack* is nothing less than a "rejection of traditional Christianity."[26] He joins others in charging that Young denies the biblical teaching on repentance, divine judgment, and hell.

But Pentecostals demonstrate the loss of their identity when they follow Geisler's apologetic path. Geisler is affronted by the following passage:

> In seminary (Mack) had been taught that God had completely stopped any overt communication with moderns, preferring to have them only listen to and follow sacred Scripture, properly interpreted, of course. God's voice had been reduced to paper, and even that paper had to be moderated and deciphered by the proper authorities and intellects. It seemed that direct communication with God was something exclusively for the ancients and uncivilized while educated Westerners' access to God was

24. Originally "It's about the economy, stupid!"
25. Mark 12:28–31.
26. Geisler and Roach, "The Shack: Helpful or Heretical?"

> mediated and controlled by the intelligentsia. Nobody wanted
> God in a box, just in a book. Especially an expensive one bound
> in leather with gilt edges, or was that guilt edges? (65–66)

Geisler finds such language an offensive rejection of the authority of the
Bible. But, again, readers must allow Young to create a credible narrative
world. Recall that Mack's most vivid memory of the Bible from his youth
is the scripture citations by his father as he brutally beat Mack for two
days. At this point in the story, he is mulling over the possibility that
God has actually invited him to a meeting. If God is no longer communicating with humans (except through Bible study), the invitation is a
hoax. Geisler may well be offended because the description of the "proper
authorities," who mediate the "properly interpreted" Scripture is a bit too
close to home.[27]

Pentecostals ardently believe in (and experience!) such divine communication today, and thus have more in common with Young than with
Geisler.[28] Pentecostals would be put off a bit if they knew what Geisler
actually thought of them. He believes that what he terms the "supernatural" gifts of the Holy Spirit described by Paul in the New Testament are
no longer in operation. Gifts such as speaking in tongues and prophecy
were "apostolic sign gifts" bestowed uniquely for the formative period of
the Christian church; the Spirit no longer grants these gifts because they
are no longer needed.[29] Speaking in tongues in churches today is a totally
natural phenomenon and is merely "gibberish" rather than real languages.
More than once in his *Systematic Theology*, Geisler compares such tongue
speaking to that found in pagan religions.[30] The "biblical truth" that he
refers to, then, includes the truth that those who speak in tongues today
are not doing so by the Holy Spirit. So Pentecostals should not be quick
to say "Amen" to Geisler's apology for the Bible; his attack on *The Shack* is
also an attack on them.

Norman Geisler serves then as a representative of Christian moderns. He has a handle on orthodox Christianity. He knows with rational

---

27. Ibid. Although he has authored scores of books, he shows little sense of literature. He charges, for example, that it is a "lie" to portray God as a black female because
God is not black or female and does not have a physical body. It would seem that Jesus'
parables depicting God as a bodily human also would qualify as lies.

28. Though such communication does not have the authority of the Bible.

29. Geisler, *Systematic Theology*, 194, 663.

30. Ibid., 195, 666.

objectivity what is true, and can judge Paul Young's viewpoints in *The Shack* and Pentecostal practice as errant. In contrast, postmodernism resists any such claim to be a virtually omniscient arbiter of the truth. Postmoderns do not necessarily claim that there is *no* truth, but that every attempt at formulating truth is colored by individual and group perspectives. The danger in claiming an evangelical Christian absolute truth is that Geisler's version of it may turn out to brand a Pentecostal reader a pagan.[31] He thus is very much like the professionals who interrogate Pi after his astounding adventure with a Bengal tiger on the high seas. "We know that the things you speak of do not happen," say the moderns. Paul Young and postmoderns will not submit to such claims of authority.[32] Nor should Pentecostals; we have a better story.

BIBLIOGRAPHY

Blumhofer, Edith Waldvogel. *Restoring the Faith: The Assemblies of God, Pentecostalism, and American Culture.* Urbana: University of Illinois Press, 1993.

Challies, Tim. "A Reader's Review of *The Shack*." Challies.com . . . Informing the Reforming. http://www.challies.com/sites/all/files/files/The_Shack.pdf (accessed April 19, 2010).

Cox, Harvey Gallagher. *Fire From Heaven: The Rise of Pentecostal Spirituality and the Reshaping of Religion in the Twenty-first Century.* Reading, MA: Addison-Wesley, 1995.

———. *The Secular City: Secularization and Urbanization in Theological Perspective.* New York: MacMillan, 1966.

Downing, Crystal L. *How Postmodernism Serves (My) Faith: Questioning Truth in Language, Philosophy and Art.* Downers Grove, IL: IVP Academic, 2006.

Geisler, Norman L. *Systematic Theology.* Vol. 4: *Church, Last Things.* Minneapolis: Bethany House, 2005.

Geisler, Norman L., and Bill Roach. "*The Shack*: Helpful or Heretical?" Dr. Norman Geisler's Web site. http://www.normangeisler.net/theshack.html (accessed April 19, 2010).

Grenz, Stanley J. *A Primer on Postmodernism.* Grand Rapids: Eerdmans, 1996.

31. Of course, Roman Catholic truth and Orthodox truth would also fall under the judgment of this particular statement of truth.

32. Many young adults today will not even listen to Christians' rational proofs because they deem the church so negatively. While 76% of pastors think that churches accept and love people unconditionally, only 20% of outsiders think so, and 87% of 16–29-year-old un-believers think Christians are judgmental. See Kinnaman and Lyons, *Unchristian*, 28, 185.

Jacobsen, Wayne. "Is THE SHACK Heresy?" Life Stream Blog: Wayne Jacobsen's Notes from the Journey. http://lifestream.org/blog/2008/03/04/is-the-shack-heresy/ (March 4, 2008; accessed April 19, 2010).

Jencks, Charles, editor. *The Post-Modern Reader*. New York: St. Martin's, 1992.

Kinnaman, David, and Gabe Lyons. *Unchristian: What a New Generation Really Thinks about Christianity—and Why It Matters*. Grand Rapids: Baker, 2007.

Martel, Yann. *Life of Pi: A Novel*. Harcourt: San Diego, 2001.

Olson, Roger E. *Finding God in The Shack: Seeking Truth in a Story of Evil and Redemption*. Downers Grove, IL: InterVarsity, 2009.

Raschke, Carl A. *The Next Reformation: Why Evangelicals Must Embrace Postmodernity*. Grand Rapids: Baker, 2004.

Rauser, Randal. *Finding God in the Shack*. Carlisle, UK: Paternoster, 2004.

Smith, James K. A. *Who's Afraid of Postmodernism?: Taking Derrida, Lyotard, and Foucault to Church*. The Church and Postmodern Culture. Grand Rapids: Baker, 2006.

Worthington, Everett L. *Forgiving and Reconciling: Bridges to Wholeness and Hope*. Downers Grove, IL: InterVarsity, 2003.

Young, William Paul. *The Shack: A Novel*. Newbury Park, CA: Windblown Media, 2007.

3

Art Imitates Life

Literary and Life Lessons about Death and Forgiveness

Marilyn Quigley and Diane Awbrey

One of the key elements of Pentecostal experience is the value of personal testimony in reflecting on the work of the Holy Spirit in the believer's life. Having an experience, telling the experience, and reading about experience often inform each other. Literature teachers tell students that stories are an excellent place to explore emotions, ideas, and relationships in a "safe" environment. The characters are not going to be hurt by the reader's response to the situation, and the reader will benefit from thinking about personal issues in someone else's context. Testimony works in much the same way. When one person tells the church about how the Holy Spirit is working in his or her life, the listeners can take inspiration, hope, and faith from that story and seek similar victories in their own life stories.[1] One intersection of literature and life is narrated in this essay, closely

---

1. See Ellington, "The Costly Loss of Testimony."

highlighting the way in which I (MQ)[2] faced a setting similar to one in a story about unforgiveness I had frequently taught. Through my faith in the power of the Holy Spirit to overcome my own inability to pardon, my story reveals a personal struggle that parallels a poignant fictional narrative.

THE STORY: LIFE FADING INTO DEATH

The theme of forgiveness in literature is nowhere more obvious than in a beautifully crafted story called "The Jilting of Granny Weatherall" by Katherine Anne Porter.[3] Granny, as her name implies, has weathered much in her long life of almost eighty years and now is surprised to realize that the day of her death has arrived. Porter deftly ushers the reader into the mind of this dying woman whose family and priest have gathered around the bed to bid her farewell.

As can be the case in one's dying hour, important memory-videos from her life flicker into Granny's awareness as she slips in and out of consciousness, confusing the present with the past and fusing the past with the future. Granny has been a religious woman, and now she says, "God, for all my life I thank Thee. Without Thee, my God, I could never have done it. Hail, Mary, full of grace."[4] The reader learns that "Granny felt easy about her soul . . . . She had her secret comfortable understanding with a few favorite saints who cleared a straight road to God for her. All as surely signed and sealed as the papers for the new Forty Acres. Forever . . . ."[5] In the words of Stephen Timson, "Granny has worked out her scheme for salvation believing that the strength and determination she has exhibited in her efforts to control her earthly fate will also lead to her redemption."[6]

But as peaceful as Granny seems about her soul, something is not at peace inside her. In masterful stream of consciousness prose that borders on the poetic, Porter gradually brings into focus something Ellen Weatherall has tried to forget since she was twenty years old: a humiliating

2. Marilyn Quigley is the first person storyteller in this chapter. She and Diane Awbrey collaborated to produce the final product.

3. First published in 1930 in a collection called *Flowering Judas*. All subsequent citations are taken from X. J. Kennedy and Dana Gioia, *Literature: An Introduction to Fiction, Poetry, Drama, and Writing*.

4. Porter, "The Jilting of Granny Weatherall," 82.

5. Ibid., 84.

6. Timson, "Katherine Anne Porter," 71–80.

offense in front of friends and family that oriented the rest of her life toward pursuit of perfection to prove herself worthy. On a day sixty years before, a day with "a fresh breeze blowing and such a green day with no threats in it," something happened so that "a whirl of dark smoke rose and covered [the day]."[7] Thinking back, she likens that day to hell, a day when she had "put on the white veil and set out the white cake" for a man who never came to the wedding.[8] The reader learns that "for sixty years she had prayed against remembering [George] and against losing her soul in the deep pit of hell, and now the two things were mingled in one and the thought of him was a smoky cloud from hell that moved and crept in her head when she was . . . trying to rest a minute."[9] Thus, memories of both the horrible day and one who made the day unbearable have become through the years synonymous with hell. But Ellen's plans after death do not include hell.

To avoid the region below, Ellen Weatherall has worked hard at trying to forget George, and now to solidify her efforts and control her imminent eternal destiny, she announces her success with an order: "I want you to find George. Find him and be sure to tell him I forgot him."[10] (The irony of her instructions is lost on this confused woman in her final struggle.) As Granny's minutes on earth dwindle, the priest administers last rites. Granny struggles to realize that, indeed, she is leaving the world, stepping into a cart and reaching for the reins. But as much as she has tried to control her life and her family for the past sixty years, she cannot control this journey, for the man seated beside her holds the reins. She has no need to look at his face, "for she [knows] without seeing," understands that the driver is Death himself. "So, my dear Lord, this is my death and I wasn't even thinking about it. My children have come to see me die," she thinks.[11]

Granny suddenly realizes that her time has come, but she is not ready, insisting, "I'm not going . . . I'm taken by surprise. I can't go."[12] Her lack of preparedness pointedly refers to projects and tasks uncompleted rather than to spiritual readiness: she has meant to change her will con-

7. Porter, "The Jilting of Granny Weatherall," 82.

8. Ibid.

9. Ibid.

10. Ibid., 83.

11. Ibid., 85.

12. Ibid.

cerning some property, to finish an altar cloth, to give away some wine. Earlier she reminded herself that she should go through the box of letters in the attic—some of them hers and George's—so that her children will not find them. Those important things still not done, she pleads, "Oh, my dear Lord, do wait a minute."[13] Her protestations, however, may suggest to the Christian reader something more important than property, letters, and gifts: perhaps Granny's subconscious, spiritual self is rapping on the door of her consciousness even as she steps up into Death's cart. Her queue of undone tasks, including a long resistance to forgiving George, may symbolize her underlying suspicion of spiritual disarray.

The reader then sees Granny taking a "long journey outward" looking for someone. . . whom? Her Maker, Judge, and Savior, perhaps? No, she is searching for her long-dead daughter Hapsy. Granny wonders what will happen if Hapsy does not meet her. Thus, at Granny's first foray into the "endless darkness," this old woman is more interested in finding her daughter than in finding God, perhaps a telling detail. Then Granny tries to find the bottom of death but cannot come to the end of it. As her consciousness rises to look down on her own small body curled within itself, she stares in amazement at her form as a small point of light. She sees her body as a "deeper mass of shadow in an endless darkness" and knows "this darkness [will] curl around the light and swallow it up."[14] Ready or not, Granny will be enveloped by death.

Like those who asked Jesus for a sign, Granny Weatherall demands, "God, give a sign." That Granny is looking for a sign of hope that a bridegroom awaits becomes apparent in this sentence: "Again no bridegroom and the priest in the house."[15] She desires a sign that *this* time the bridegroom will appear, will come from somewhere out in eternity to meet her. She wants a sign that, indeed, the departed saints have done their road-paving job for her. However, Granny does not find the heavenly bridegroom as she goes out into the darkness of death. This grief, then, so overwhelms her that it wipes away all other sorrows in her life. And what is her response? One might expect such a woman taking her last breaths to soften, to plead and beg, to repent of the stony bitterness that has permeated her heart for sixty long years.[16]

13. Ibid.

14. Ibid.

15. Ibid.

16. Laman, "Porter's."

However, rather than meet this excruciating blow with repentance, she hardens her unforgiving heart, grits her teeth, and with her dying breath utters harsh words: "Oh, no, there's nothing more cruel than this—I'll never forgive it."[17] So she stretches and with a deep breath blows out the waning light of her life. In one final act of control, she chooses death. She seems to prefer experiencing hell rather than offering herself the gift of heaven that could come with forgiving one who does not deserve it.

THE MEANING: VARIATIONS ON THEME

"The Jilting of Granny Weatherall" models the short story in its finest attire. Certainly the topics of death and eternity are plentiful in the arts, literature especially. Several writers have used the metaphor of a coach, carriage, or cart heading out toward eternity, some driven by Death. Specifically, Emily Dickinson's "Because I Could not Stop for Death," and Alexander Pushkin's "The Coach of Life" come easily to mind. Not many writers, however, have focused on those few seconds when, as in a well-constructed fade of two video scenes, death and life must briefly overlap. Like Dickinson, Porter couples the masterful unveiling of the dying person's thoughts and emotions with the moment when Death drives up and stops. But unlike many authors, Porter inserts the dire consequences of unforgiveness into those final seconds.

According to the ancients, good literature must accomplish two goals: delight the reader and provide instruction. Porter's story certainly entertains as from the opening words it grabs the imagination, then sustains the intellect, and never releases its emotional grip until the final sentence as the reader watches Granny float out into the darkness: "She stretched herself with a deep breath and blew out the light [of life]."[18] As to Porter's theme in this piece, what is it? Critics agree that the title refers to two jiltings, not just the one by her fiancé but another finally by her God. A story, of course, can present more than one life-truth. Some might believe Porter to be illustrating that one's beliefs can let her down, especially if they assert that anything besides personal repentance can clear a straight road to heaven. Other readers might find the theme that God cannot be trusted to reward a person for faith and hard work in overcoming the exigencies of life. Perhaps one might argue Porter's

17. Porter, "The Jilting of Granny Weatherall," 85.
18. Ibid.

point to be that faith in the afterlife, in God himself, is futile in the end. An even more obvious theme could be that salvation cannot be earned through hard work or religious participation. One critic asserts that the sign Granny wants is assurance that her daughter Hapsy will be waiting; however, instead of "trusting Hapsy to wait for her, Granny engages in a futile contest with an absent male god." [19] In short, a central theme is not always readily apparent and obvious to all readers.

Neither must the theme of a story be a truth the author *herself* ascribes to as a personal philosophy. She may see the theme as true only for *that* story. More often, though, theme can be stated as a universal truth. Also, though more than one theme can exist in a story, critics agree that the *central* theme is the one which pulls together more threads from the story's warp and woof, from beginning to end, than any other. In "The Jilting of Granny Weatherall" the idea of forgiveness—really, the lack thereof—is woven throughout this story, which ends with Granny's final words "I'll never forgive it." Once forgiveness is isolated as a possible key, the reader can find a truth about Granny's situation that pulls together more story threads than any other: because Granny has never forgiven the first bridegroom, she does not become the bride of Christ. From that story-specific reality, the reader can universalize a truth about life and death: one who refuses to forgive offenses in life will not find Christ waiting as the "bridegroom" with whom to spend eternity.

TRUTH: THE NECESSITY OF FORGIVENESS

Porter may have drawn upon her own Catholic faith and her knowledge of Matthew 6:14–15: "For if you forgive men when they sin against you, your heavenly Father will also forgive you. But if you do not forgive men their sins, your Father will not forgive your sins" (NIV). Does Porter's theme for "Jilting" represent a universal truth accepted by most Christians? Believers like psychologist Geoffrey Sutton might not interpret this Scripture as literally as do others but see it as Jesus' using "hyperbole and extreme language." In other words, only belief in Christ as the sacrifice for sin is necessary to assure salvation. Sutton concedes, "On the other hand, I think there are many people who must hear strong words if they are to understand how serious God is about the destructive power of sin in the Kingdom." Sutton believes the Matthew account is a

---

19. Laman, "Porter's," 281.

tautology: forgiven people equal people who forgive others; people who forgive others equal forgiven people.[20]

Though finding the meaning Jesus intended for his words in Matthew 6 is not the sole purpose of this discussion, relating Porter's theme to spiritual truth is important here. Without doubt, Scripture insists upon Christians forgiving their malefactors. But, one might say, forgiveness is hard, especially for something like public humiliation and betrayal. How can God refuse us eternal life, if indeed He will, for failing such a difficult test? In fact, is forgiveness something people can achieve just by willing it to happen? Poor Granny—she obviously had tried to forgive, hadn't she? Was it *her* fault she failed? But let's look carefully at the well-chosen words of this careful writer. Porter says Granny tried to *forget* George, never that she even attempted to *forgive* him. Even now at the final moments of her life the very thought of him is "a smoky cloud from hell."[21] This hellish black aura which has accompanied all thoughts of George symbolizes the church's teaching that lack of forgiveness is yoked with an afterlife in utter darkness. Pentecostal believers might see such reminders as faithful pressure from the Holy Spirit to align oneself with Scripture, to ask Him to begin the work of forgiveness, something Granny never has done. Throughout life, Ellen Weatherall has desired and achieved many things, but a heart soft with forgiveness has never been one of them. Even if Granny were *able* to forgive her former fiancé, the fact is that she never tried to do so.

At the end of her long days on earth, Granny still wants several things: to be in control of her life tasks and end-of-life timing, to see her long-dead daughter, to have a straight road already cleared to God, and to forget George. But Granny does *not* want to forgive the man who broke her heart and embarrassed her. She has no desire to give absolution, as it were, in spite of two important merciful gifts in her life: the priest gives *her* absolution, and life has not deprived her of a husband who loved her and gave her fine children. Even so, Ellen will not forgive George because the "something not given back" to her was quite likely the chance to experience life with the love of her life, the man who betrayed her.

---

20. Geoffrey Sutton, interview by Marilyn Quigley, Spring 2009.

21. Porter, "The Jilting of Granny Weatherall," 82.

LIFE REFLECTS LITERATURE: A PERSONAL TESTIMONY

Literature mirrors life, and sometimes life reflects a particular narrative. Porter's story, like all interpretive literature, evolved no doubt from the author's observations or particular experiences. Good writers begin with some essence of what they have seen and lived out; then they write narrative, from which truth and theme bubble to the surface. Good readers recognize life truths in good fiction. For instance, they know this world is full of Granny and Grandpa Weatheralls who try hard to *forget* offenses, believing that if they can only put them out of their minds, then their spiritual lives and eternal welfare will be just fine. But like Granny, they are sure to discover that forgetting is almost impossible and that *forgiving is not a work human beings can actually accomplish.*

I found myself face to face with that truth a few years ago. Most people, given long enough life, will find themselves looking down on at least one deathbed scene similar to Granny's. An elderly man or woman lies waiting to leave this earth as tearful family are gathered around the bed.

One night in June several summers ago, I was in that situation—unexpectedly gazing down at my dying mother-in-law as she lay struggling. Seven family members stood helplessly around her bed in the early hours of morning as the oxygen tube did little to ease her deep pulls for breath. A sudden turn for the worst had occurred the night before after pneumonia seemed to have cleared. A Christian since she was eleven years old, a Sunday school teacher for twenty-seven years, a woman whose conversations were most often of things spiritual—Mom, now ninety-three, had come to her dying hour. The tiny light in her nursing home room pushed back the darkness just enough to envelop us into her final struggle.

Suddenly, like Granny Weatherall, Mom came to the realization that THIS must be it. With rounded eyes, she looked into my face and asked, "Am I dying?" I answered in the affirmative as I named those who had gone before, those she could expect to see in a short time—her long-dead husband, her sisters. And like Granny, Mom surely was focusing on the Bridegroom awaiting her. How many times had she said, "I'm ready to go and see Jesus"? In those final moments, like her literary counterpart, she abruptly focused on preparation for the journey: "What if I'm not ready to go?" Her eyes looked directly into mine rather than at one of her sons. It would seem a strange question from one who had claimed Christ as Savior for all but the first eleven years of her long life, one who had always felt "easy" about her soul and had a comfortable understanding of God's salvation plan. This woman of the Book, who had prayed in tongues as second nature, now wondered if she were ready to go. But I knew—and so did most of the people in the room—why she asked the question.

In the case of Granny Weatherall, the priest was ready to administer extreme unction. We had not called our minister, so I would need to be that "cleric" for my mother-in-law. I went around to her pillow and knelt down to speak privately into her ear. "Would you like me to pray that God will forgive you for any sins?" Yes, she would like that. And so I asked Him to pardon her of anything she had done and make her ready for heaven. Amen. Now she could die in the peace that accompanies forgiveness, and we could await the Death Angel and the King, anticipated soon in the room.

"But I'm afraid YOU are holding something against me," she whispered.

I stared at that small, frail little lady, a look of fear and pleading in her eyes.

Yes, Dear God, I *was* holding something against this woman whom I had loved many years but who had recently betrayed my trust and her word that she would help keep peace in my family. I had even stopped all interaction with her for a time, hoping she would ask my forgiveness. Yes, I was still angry and had begun speaking to her again only a week earlier, even though she had not asked my forgiveness even then. And now, these still were not words of repentance, not really. But I recognized that they might be as close as she was able to come, even though she could have quoted Matthew 6:14–15 perfectly by heart. She believed that only if *she* forgave would she be forgiven. It never would have occurred to Mom that this passage could be interpreted any other way.

Between the moment of her question and my answer, only five seconds passed at most. But within that brief span, uncountable thoughts raced to and fro, each jousting for position, each demanding to be heard and clamoring for judgment in its favor. *Must I tell her I hold nothing against her?* Seventy times seven! *But she doesn't deserve grace.* Well, nobody does. *She must not put me in this untenable position. Let her ask me for forgiveness. We have so much to discuss; then I'll forgive.* But she's dying. *She can't hold her tongue or keep a promise. A gossip.* Does that matter in the light of life and death? Let God be her judge. How can I refuse peace to a dying woman? *Does God want me to tell a lie? Can I forgive her in a few seconds—impossible!* I had planned to tackle this huge task of restoring a broken relationship at a rather slow pace over the coming months. Now those months had melted into moments.

Without telling the exact details of the hurt I experienced because of my mother-in-law's behavior, this story needs some background. I have struggled with whether or not I should relate any of it because she is not here to explain her point of view. My husband Ed and I believe that, could she look down from above and give permission, she would do so. In her heart she was a good woman who wanted her life, mistakes and all, to count for the Kingdom.

With all of her many positive attributes, she occasionally would tell one family member disparaging details about another. A few months earlier, she had given me some information that I knew could be hurtful if disseminated among the family. I asked that she not tell it to anyone. She agreed. Not long afterward, she "let it slip" in the presence of my husband, who was momentarily distracted and did not really hear it. The next day I visited her and for a second time asked sincerely that she keep the information to herself.

Then, not long afterwards, visiting with my husband, she hinted at the situation. This time he heard it clearly and came home with questions. I readily told him. Then Ed went to her and forcefully demanded that she never tell anyone else. I went to her one more time, asking her to keep the information to herself. At one point she apologized but later managed to hint just enough to send yet another person to me wondering what she meant. When finally everyone in the immediate family knew, I faced her in fury. And I convinced myself I was justified in that fury. I did let the sun go down on my wrath, unfortunately (Eph 4:26). The suns of some six weeks had set before I felt able to visit and exchange conversation in a kind tone, only two days before her final hour.

At this juncture the reader is no doubt asking, "What could the information be?" Everyone to whom I've told this story has confessed to that "want to know" urge that grows as the story continues. Wanting to know the "dirt" on others is, of course, human nature. I will be the first to admit that learning that a secret exists inflames my "want to know" brain cells. And it is my willingness to listen and perhaps believe the worst that fuels an informant with the "need to tell." I have also found myself with information and a "need to tell" urge, which unfortunately has at times overpowered my "don't say it" inner voice. My mother-in-law was not the only Christian to fall into the gossip trap. The need to tell can come from another need: to be the center of attention, if even for a short moment. And the inordinate need to feel important can come from many deficits in one's life, some of which are beyond a person's control. But these truths still do not scratch the itch that wants to know exactly what my mother-in-law discovered that I wanted to keep hidden.

One has only to think about any number of sins, pseudo-sins, and man-made holiness issues that cause "sanctified" believers to see themselves as beyond such behavior. We Pentecostals, because the infilling of the Spirit should aid us in living holy lives, often generate a list of improprieties, unbiblical philosophies, and slippery-slope behaviors that we add to the list named in Scripture, (and we leave off some that the Bible clearly warns against). Furthermore, we tend to remember others' past failures long after God has forgiven and forgotten them. We also classify sins and, strangely, have been known to consider smoking, dancing, and drinking of any kind and amount worse than gossip, obesity, and deceit. Divorce and remarriage would probably slightly outweigh an adulterous affair, which would trump stealing and watching sexually explicit movies, worse of course than enjoying violent films. Bearing and raising a child outside of marriage might actually be worse than a secret abortion. Illicit sex, including both fornication and adultery, often make the worst-sin list, but lack of generosity to the poor and refusal to forgive or to keep one's promises raises almost no eyebrows. Verbal abuse of a spouse or child probably would not make the top ten, but alcoholism and pornography would, right along with being seen entering a bar. Gossip? Is that on anyone's list of sins anymore? In Pentecostal Circles, many of the Seven Deadly Sins are no longer sin and definitely not deadly.

The point is that different people in every family have different lists. My mother-in-law had hers, and she once told me that if she had ever done X, she would *never* forgive herself. People who cannot forgive themselves often have trouble believing God can forgive them or anyone else, and they frequently obsess about the shortcomings of others, even if those are one-time failures in the past and long forgiven. Scripture teaches that love in the body of Christ should cover sin, indiscretions, and poor decisions. For example, Peter writes,

> Therefore, since Christ suffered in his body, arm yourselves also with the same attitude, because he who has suffered in his body is done with sin. As a result, he does not live the rest of his earthly life for evil human desires, but rather for the will of God.

> For you have spent enough time in the past doing what pagans choose to do—living in debauchery, lust, drunkenness, orgies, carousing and detestable idolatry. They think it strange that you do not plunge with them into the same flood of dissipation, and they heap abuse on you. . . . Therefore be clear minded and self-controlled so that you can pray. Above all, *love each other deeply, because love covers over a multitude of sins.* . . . If anyone speaks, he should do it as one speaking the very words of God. If anyone serves, he should do it with the strength God provides, so that in all things God may be praised through Jesus Christ. (1 Peter 4:1–11; NIV, emphasis mine)

Mom had done the opposite, choosing to expose rather than cover.

Now in that final hour, perhaps with only moments left on earth, she was asking me to eliminate anger that I had allowed to balloon beyond my ability to deflate. It was one thing for me to pray that *God* would forgive her—which I had readily done—and yet another to forgive her myself. Even worse, I had not reached the place of *wanting* to forgive. Rage feels justified and gleans some kind of satisfaction, poison though it is, through wallowing in that justification. It is for good reason that God warns about continuing a grudge beyond even one sunset.

So standing there in the dim light, I knew time had run out. This woman who had hurt me deeply (but with whom so many times during our forty years' acquaintance I had laughed, cried, prayed, and chatted) needed to die in peace. I had no *feeling* urging me toward forgiveness. Yet I knew that I *wished* I *wanted* to forgive her. And so I said something that was not true, "No, Mom, I'm not holding anything against you." Those words could be said only in faith that sometime later, some green day with a fresh breeze blowing, they would indeed be true.

She sighed and turned to the hard work of dying with pneumonia. Pulling and pulling for breath after breath, she lay struggling as we sang hymns. It might take hours, the nurse said, because the oxygen tube was in her nose. But no one had the courage to shorten her anguish by pulling out that little plastic piece. I stood wishing my husband or his brother would do it but knowing neither could. Then, eyes wide as if a sudden realization had come to her, Mom reached up and pulled it out herself. In one final act of control, she willed death to come quickly, willed the light of her life to diminish, brought about a quicker meeting with her waiting Bridegroom.

Within seven minutes, she breathed her last. We stood transfixed, staring at her face gradually turning from pink to gray even as her rising soul, perhaps, was looking down at her body and her beloved family. Unlike Granny Weatherall, my mother-in-law in her final moments had wanted forgiveness from God and her daughter-in-law. She was not jilted by the Son of God. No doubt His bright light at that moment swallowed up the darkness of death as her soul floated out into eternity to be forever with her Lord. Death was not an endless, bottomless darkness but a vehicle, a "carriage" if you will, heading toward her reward for trusting her salvation to Christ.

A few minutes later I walked out into the pre-dawn summer morning to continue the rest of my own life. I knew I had for a long time loved that little woman now immobile on her deathbed, and my heart was heavy with the sadness of permanent loss. But I also knew the anger against her was not gone just because she was. I also understood I had told her a lie. Yet—and some would say strangely—I felt peace.

FORGIVENESS: AN EXPECTATION

How could I be at peace when a lie was still warm on my lips and something akin to rage lurked in my heart? First of all, she was my husband's mother, and I cared about her. I felt that her home-going moments mattered more than my being honest concerning the strong negative feelings I had no ability in that moment to dispel. I realized that Scripture considers people to be more important than rules and laws. For instance, Jesus and his hungry disciples one day trudged through ripened grain. Although well aware of His Father's injunction against working on the Sabbath, Jesus said nothing when the men began to pick and eat. Since the rabbis considered picking grain as work, Jesus might have reprimanded the disciples. When the Pharisees later asked why he had allowed them to do "that which is not lawful . . . on the Sabbath," Jesus answered by reminding them of two occasions on which both David and the priests had profaned the Sabbath blamelessly by placing their physical wellbeing above the law (Matt 12:1–8). Similarly, although I could not improve my mother-in-law's physical wellbeing, at the very least I could attend to her emotional wellbeing—even though it took a lie. God's laws, including His law against falsehood, are designed *for the good of people*; the spirit of the law supersedes the letter of the law. Sometimes the choices in life are not between right and wrong, good and bad; they are between bad and worse, between the not-so-good and the despicable.

Scripture, of course, is replete with injunctions against lying. However, studying the context of those verses reveals the overarching assumption that falsehoods intended to hurt someone, to bring undeserved gain to the liar, to deceive for dark purposes, to bring death or to kill hope—those falsehoods are disallowed. Quite the opposite is the lie intended to bring hope and peace in the face of death. My belief is that to provide the precious jewel of peace in the dying hour, I had to tell an untruth.

But had I told a lie? The answer to that question rests not so much in the definition of a lie as in understanding the definition and process of forgiveness.

First, what constitutes forgiveness? C. S. Lewis in *Christian Behaviour* reminds that Christians are to love their neighbors as they love themselves "because in Christian morals 'thy neighbour' includes 'thy enemy,' and so we come up against this terrible duty of forgiving our enemies." He continues "'Love your enemy' does not mean 'feel fond of him' or 'find him attractive.'"[22] Actually, I may hate what my enemy does. But to love my neighbor, my enemy (or someone who has behaved toward me as an enemy would in hurting or harming me), I must wish for her exactly what I wish for myself. I may dislike things I do and want to change them, but I do not hate myself, resent myself, or wish myself any ill. I hope the best for myself, as I must hope the same for my enemy. In this situation, I could hold nothing against a woman whom I cared for in the same way I cared about myself. Thus, I had failed the above forgiveness test even as I contemplated how to answer her.

However, understanding the process of forgiveness allowed me to speak words not yet true as though they were true. Although I could not have articulated that night what I am attempting to do now, an earlier "forgiveness" transformation had helped me develop an understanding of how the Holy Spirit works in changing the human heart.

To explain, I must regress to several years before the night of Mom's death when my husband and I had been deeply hurt by the words and behavior of a couple who in more than one way could not have been closer to us. Their negative statements to friends and neighbors concerning our plans had come as a complete surprise, overwhelming us with disbelief at first. Then, for me, the anger had boiled up, fueled by my unrelenting

---

22. Lewis, *Christian Behavior*, 492.

focus on the problem for several days. My husband talked to the man, who understood that his wife was out of line, but he gave no indication that she would change—or ever want our friendship again. Furthermore, she did not want to speak to me about what they had said and done.

After three days of anguish and anger, I realized that lack of forgiveness was beginning to eat me alive from the inside. On my way to work that morning, I felt almost frightened at my intense negative thoughts about the couple. As I drove toward the bridge near my home, an inner voice said I should just forgive the woman and try to patch up the situation. My problem was that I had no desire to forgive and forget; I just wanted to nurse my rage and wallow in my right to do so. I think I said as much to God. That could have been the end of it. After all, did we need their friendship? Truth be told, yes, we did. A permanent rift with this couple would have had unacceptable results for many people. Furthermore, my biblical knowledge told me I *must* forgive. "But I don't even want to forgive her," I thought. That reality brought me to the truth that forgiveness would never come unless I first *wanted* to forgive. I knew I was not to that point and could not easily get there. But as I crossed a bridge, I said, "I *wish* I wanted to forgive, Lord. That's the best I can say. If you want me to forgive, then *you* will have to make it happen." I handed over my thoughts and my wrath and my hurts, completely, and drove on. Strangely, I did not think of the problem most of the day.

About nine hours later, as I crossed that same bridge on my way home, I realized the most amazing thing: I held absolutely no anger toward the couple. I couldn't believe it. Where had the rage gone? God only knew. Nothing about what they had done had changed. They still were completely out of line. But something had changed inside ME. I began to talk to them as if nothing had happened. Gradually, they warmed up. That was over thirteen years ago, and we are now best of friends with this couple. About a year after "crossing the bridge," she gave me a gift, and I recognized it as her olive branch. I have never discussed the situation with her and have no need to do so.

So that night as Death was approaching the room, my previous experience had allowed me to affirm to Mom a "fact" that was not yet true. The Holy Spirit knew that within my affirmation was a wish that I *could* hold nothing against Mom, words spoken as the first step in a process toward those words becoming fact. I rested on a faith that God would again take me down the forgiveness road and lead me to the destination where He wanted me to live. At that moment I had no map, no plan, no guide except the memory of another time, a successful forgiveness journey. Because faith is the "substance of things hoped for, the evidence of things not seen," I forgave my mother-in-law by faith (Heb 12:1 KJV). Statements of faith are not lies; conversely, statements based only on emotion are not necessarily true.

Following Mom's death, the next week was filled with plans, travel, and a funeral in another state. I listened to my mother-in-law almost "canonized" by a former pastor and sincere friends. I listened with a mixture of feelings such as I had never experienced.

After the funeral as I had the task of going through all Mom's old pictures and journals, I felt *positive* that somewhere in time, at some dock along the river of my life, I would come to harbor no resentment against that woman. I was also positive that I, myself, could not bring that to pass; but I had faith in the Holy Spirit to do it for me. My only job would be to cooperate with Him. The first step in that cooperation was to place a smiling picture of Mom above my computer where I would look at her every day. (There she still sits, looking joyful on her eighty-fifth birthday wearing, ironically, the suit in which she was buried.)

I had a feeling that the deeper the hurt, the harder to heal, so I placed no timetable on the Spirit and no demands upon myself. That release from the calendar and from personal work on the problem served to relax me in the journey. I would not expect inner changes soon, would accept whatever improvements I might notice, and never castigate myself for harsh thoughts. However, I determined not to dwell on such thoughts, not to nurse them or "wallow" in my right to do so. Whenever I was in prayer and Mom popped into my mind, I asked God to continue His forgiveness work. But I did not put the situation on a prayer list so that I prayed about it every day. *Trying* to forgive, I believe, can thwart the process whereas relaxing in the faith that forgiveness is the Holy Spirit's task erases anxiety.

As the days and months passed, I often thought of her. In the early days, the thoughts were negative. As I looked at her picture, I might ask, "*How* could you have tried to hurt someone dear to me?" She would just smile back, frozen in that happy moment posing for the photographer with her family around her. Since she gave no answer, I would turn the question over to the Holy Spirit and quickly go on to other tasks. Or I might even look at her picture and realize that I could not remember the good things, only the way it all had ended. Sometimes that made me sad. As the months turned into a year and then two, I thought of her fewer and fewer times. I might glance at her picture sometimes with no thought whatever as I was concentrating on something else. Then as time passed, I noticed more and more good memories replacing the bad ones. I didn't try to second guess whether I actually was making progress or not. Nor did I worry about my eternal fate, should I die without my emotions having changed. Why? Because I had done everything within my power to stay on the forgiveness path, and the whole situation now lay in the hands of God. I was no longer responsible for occasionally recurring feelings. God would not hold me accountable for the emotions that still sometimes surfaced.

The truth that many have discovered is this: the smallest sincere attempt at forgiveness is the only requirement, the turning of the key in the vehicle to start the forgiveness journey. The tiniest spark of an attitude that says "I want to *want* to forgive" will result somewhere down the road in God's ultimate work of removing hatred and ill will from the heart and emotions. Only God can enact what humans cannot do in their own power: forgive grave offenses. God *will* engage His Holy Spirit to begin the process at the slightest sincere invitation. However, God will not insert the key in the ignition. The forgiveness road is often long and beset with emotional switchbacks. But the Holy Spirit is faithful to accompany the sincere travelers and guide them to the place of forgiveness. I knew I was on the journey.

At some time on the trip—I don't know exactly when—I began to think of reasons mom might have been unable to keep her tongue from gossip. I now know the Holy Spirit began to help me connect some dots. She was the youngest of nine children, no doubt the center of a family's attention as a baby and for the rest of her life perhaps. Also, her husband had doted upon her and was often at her beck and call. Beyond that, she had taught a large Sunday school class of women for twenty-seven years as a much admired and beloved teacher, the center of attention. Mom, a capable woman, had loved being wanted, needed, and admired throughout most of her life. But self-esteem had moved out when Old Age moved in. Like Granny Weatherall, she no longer controlled anything or felt needed by anyone. Though we visited often and called, long and lonely hours stretched between visits. On the periphery of everything, she must have met a need by being the bearer of information and center of attention if only for a few moments each time she told her secret. My comprehension of that psychological truth helped replace some of my anger with understanding. I continued the journey realizing my heart had softened to a large extent but not entirely.

When did I realize that I had forgiven my mother-in-law? It happened six summers after she died when I began the task of turning old VHS videos into DVDs.

Sit with me as I begin to play old tapes, taking a sentimental journey back into our family history. There we all are on the deck celebrating a birthday. Ah, there's my niece toddling as a two-year-old. My sons. Darling! My husband quips, "Wow, did I have a wife who looked that young?" I feel like hitting him with the remote! Now the video has switched to Christmas, and we are gathering around the table for dessert. There she is—Mom laughing and telling a funny story from her childhood. "We were riding in the sleigh when something broke and we tipped over in the snow and . . . " Now she suddenly appears in another Christmas video, wearing a flattened wig. I laugh as I remember the fun we had teasing her about her "helmet" that she decided looked better than her own hair. In one scene after another she is as natural as if she were sitting in the room talking to me.

Suddenly I stop and arrest a thought that just buzzed through my mind: "I wish I could just sit down and have a nice conversation with her one more time." I rewind that thought. Yes, that's exactly how I feel. I still love this woman who was so much a good part of my life for so many years. I start to cry (as I am doing now). The anger is gone, probably long gone and I just haven't notice before. So my tears flow as I think of Mom, now with her God and happy to give Him all her attention. She has no more need of being front and center. But perhaps she is being made to feel important in her eternal home. Maybe that's one delightful truth about heaven: whatever need we have or had will be met in a wonderful way.

Is she looking down as I watch the movies and remember her? And if she is and could speak about her final days on earth, what would she say? I let my imagination—perhaps guided by the Holy Spirit—fill in her words.

"Marilyn, I'm so sorry about what I said. I have no idea what possessed me to hurt the very people I love. I think I had lost so much there at the end that I wanted to bring some attention to myself. It seems so silly now. My gossip was a sin. But I don't even feel guilty about it because here, of course, there is no guilt—all is forgiven. I've followed along with your lives as much as I've been allowed, and I see that what I said didn't cause any real upset in the long run. I'm glad for that. And I'm SO grateful that all my sins, that last one and many others, have been forgiven through the blood of Jesus.

"Thank you for your final gift of forgiveness at my bedside. I couldn't have passed away with any peace if I thought you held something against me. And I wish I'd called earlier to talk it over with you. Anyway, you know I always loved you. Thanks for all you did for me during my life, and I look forward to having a good talk with you again—soon maybe, as up here there are no calendars.

"Oh, and don't worry about writing your piece for people to read about what I did. And in good Pentecostal fashion, I tell the story because I hope my testimony will benefit others. Up here, there's no pride, embarrassment, or hurt feelings.

"And I've been reading along over your shoulder. Too bad about that Granny Weatherall. I'm glad I didn't have her fate. When I went out into eternity, there was the Bridegroom, waiting . . . just as I always knew He would be."

CONCLUSION

My transformation from lack of forgiveness to peace may not have occurred so completely without the connection I made between Granny Weatherall and my husband's mother. Until I faced my dying mother-in-law's question, I had not personally confronted the eternal consequences of Granny's inability to forgive or receive forgiveness. Because Mom and I both acknowledged the infilling of the Holy Spirit in our lives, forgiveness was for us a necessity—for me an act of faith, for her an act of mercy. This experience showed me the faithfulness of the Holy Spirit in one's dying hour to help us take those steps necessary before death. Granny Weatherall's inability to forgive stands in stark contrast to the Holy Spirit's work at my mother-in-law's deathbed to rescue her from the fate of Mrs. Weatherall.

BIBLIOGRAPHY

Ellington, Scott. "The Costly Loss of Testimony." *Journal of Pentecostal Theology* 16 (2000) 48–59.

Laman, Barbara. "Porter's 'The Jilting of Granny Weatherall.'" *Explicator* (Summer 1990) 279–81.

Lewis, C. S. *Christian Behaviour.* In *C. S. Lewis: Five Best Books in One Volume.* Grand Rapids: Baker, 1969.

Porter, Katherine Anne. "The Jilting of Granny Weatherall." In *Literature: An Introduction to Fiction, Poetry, Drama, and Writing,* edited by X. J. Kennedy and Dana Gioia. 11th ed. New York: Pearson Longman, 2009.

Timson, Stephen. "Katherine Anne Porter and the Essential Spirit: The Pursuit and Discovery of Truth in 'The Jilting of Granny Weatherall.'" *Kyushu American Literature* (1986) 71–80.

Historical Perspectives

4

The Azusa Street Revival and Racial Reconciliation

An Afro-Pentecostal Perspective

Renea Brathwaite

This movement is in its infancy. If you keep your hearts pure and open, God will give you the old apostolic power. It depends on whether we keep clear of the entanglements about us.

—Father L. C. Ebey of Hermon, CA in *Apostolic Faith Los Angeles* (November 1906)

Racial reconciliation has been a very controversial issue and the election of America's first biracial president has done little to quell the storm. This should not be surprising since the institution of slavery has not only left a deep stain upon the American consciousness, but has also bequeathed an imposing legacy of unresolved economic and social inequities. This is true in wider society and, unfortunately, in the North American Pentecostal movement.

Despite the fact that North American Pentecostalism ostensibly began as a multiracial, multiethnic movement in 1906, when the Pentecostal Fellowship of North America (PFNA) formed in Indiana in 1948, no predominantly black denominations were invited to become members. It would take another forty-six years for this matter to be addressed during the so-called Memphis Miracle. The Memphis Miracle was actually the culmination of a series of five meetings that sought to reverse the trend of isolation between the races and was an attempt to atone for prior misdeeds.[1] The first meeting was on July 31, 1992 in Dallas, TX; the second was January 4–5, 1993 in Phoenix, AZ; the third was October 25–27, 1993 at the PFNA annual meeting in Atlanta, GA; and the fourth was January 10–11, 1994 in Memphis, TN. The late Bishop Ithiel Clemmons of the predominantly black Church of God in Christ (COGIC) and Bishop Bernard E. Underwood of the mostly white International Pentecostal Holiness Church (IPHC) were the chief architects of these meetings and the vision for reconciliation.

The actual miracle took place in the Dixon Meyers Hall of the Cook Convention Center in Memphis, Tennessee, during the scholars' meeting held on the afternoon of October 18, 1994. A young, black attendee gave a glossolalic utterance, which Dr. Jack Hayford, then head of the International Church of the Foursquare Gospel, interpreted as a call for unity: that the Holy Spirit was "flowing the two streams [black and white

1. Here and throughout this essay, I hesitate to use the term *race*. The term, in reality, is an inexact, phenomenologically driven, socio-linguistic fiction. Genetic science has shown that the differences within a so-called racial type can be as great as or sometimes even greater than those across supposed racial lines. In addition, racial typologies have proven to be arbitrary, based almost exclusively on those relatively minor genes that determine skin color and hair type. Furthermore, the whole system of classification tends to either presuppose or promote a crass and inherently racist form of biological determinism. Yet, the use of race as a descriptor stubbornly persists. Reasons for this are complex and lie outside the scope of this essay. One might consider Graves, *The Race Myth* as a good starting point for discussion. But the conundrum remains: *How can we speak meaningfully of racial reconciliation when race does not exist and any appeal to race only further hypostatizes the fiction of race, a fiction that inherently opposes reconciliation?* Surely, an essential part of dealing with racism must be the deconstruction of the racialism that makes racism possible. However, racialism and its consequent racism have has generated a potent self-fulfilling prophecy by creating the necessary conditions for supposed differences to become enshrined in history, culture, language, politics, economics, and law. In this essay, I warily employ the term *race* and associated words (black, white, etc.) as shorthand for ethnicity or cultural group. Even then, I do this with a North American point of view in mind, since construals of what constitutes race differ greatly.

sections of the movement] into one."[2] After this, Rev. Donald Evans of the Assemblies of God (AG) came forward to the stage with a towel and basin and asked permission to wash the feet of Bishop Clemmons. As he washed Bishop Clemmons's feet, he wept and asked forgiveness on behalf of whites for their racist attitudes toward blacks. Thereafter, Bishop Blake (COGIC) asked to wash the feet of Thomas Trask, the general superintendent of the AG, and repented on behalf of blacks for their animosity toward whites. This all occurred in a highly emotionally charged atmosphere filled with deep contrition and weeping. The following day, the members of the PFNA agreed to dissolve the organization, and along with previously excluded groups, they formed the integrated Pentecostal and Charismatic Churches of North America (PCCNA).[3]

Watching the spectacle unfold is profoundly moving, yet some important critical questions also arise. Why did such a supposedly multiracial movement so quickly separate along racial lines? Why would it take a group, such as the PFNA, over forty years to remedy its error? What would a participant of the earliest Pentecostal revivals have thought of this display in Memphis or indeed the need for it? Even more fundamentally, was the early Pentecostal movement truly as integrated as some have alleged? The answers to these questions are certainly complex and I cannot hope to fully address them all. Instead, I focus on a few important aspects of the last question and leave the others, pressing though they are, for another discussion. Specifically, this chapter attempts to examine the racial legacy of the Azusa Street mission and revival of 1906–1908 through the events that occurred there, through its newsletter, Apostolic Faith, and through the subsequent writings of its African American leader, William J. Seymour.[4] In them there is a remarkable contrast. In the beginning there is such hope and a theological vision of a

2. It seems rather ironic that the young African American who gave the glossolalic message remains anonymous to this day.

3. For more information and eyewitness analysis, see Underwood, "The Memphis Miracle"; and Synan, "Memphis 1994: Miracle and Mandate." See also Rosenior, "Toward Racial Reconciliation." There has been consternation in some quarters that the *Memphis Miracle* seemed to have been engineered and portrayed as an exclusively black-white affair with little attention given to other ethnic groups. For example, see Solivan, *The Spirit, Pathos, and Liberation.*

4. This chapter depends heavily on the primary sources and quotes frequently on them. It is important that readers interact with the breadth of literary output from the mission.

post-racial, Spirit-filled Christian community. However, only eight years later, Seymour denies any leadership role for women and the very few non-blacks left in the mission. What went wrong? What can those who are interested in Pentecostal racial reconciliation, or racial reconciliation generally, learn from this story?

THE BIRTH OF A DREAM

The Azusa Street revival was a spectacular event and ranks as one of the more important moments in the history of twentieth century Christianity. When William Seymour agreed to move from Houston to Los Angeles to pastor a small African American church in 1905, he probably had no idea of the historic nature of his decision. Seymour had been in Houston for a short while and had been attending Bible classes held by the flamboyant Charles F. Parham. Because of the existing Jim Crow laws, he could not enter the classroom with whites as a fellow student. He did, however, listen through a half-opened door and was exposed to Parham's novel theory concerning baptism in the Holy Spirit. Parham believed that Spirit baptism, an experience described in the book of Acts as one of spiritual empowerment, was rightly evidenced by glossolalia (speaking in languages the recipient did not know).[5] Seymour believed Parham's teaching on the evidentiary value of glossolalia sufficiently for it to become a focal point of his ministry, even though he had not received the experience. Unfortunately, the church Seymour was to have pastored in Los Angeles rejected his message and he found himself in the unfortunate position of having to procure alternative living arrangements and an alternative ministry venue. So for a while he lived with Edward Lee and held prayer meetings in Ruth and Richard Asberry's house on 214 Bonnie Brae Street, where on April 9, 1906 he and his small band of followers received an answer to their prayers. The following account was written in the Apostolic Faith (December, 1906):

> Then they felt led of the Lord to call Bro. Seymour from Houston,
> Texas to Los Angeles, the saints in Los Angeles sending his fare.
> It was as truly a call from God as when He sent His holy angel to

---

5. For more information, see S. Parham, *The Life of Charles F. Parham*. See also Goff, *Fields White unto Harvest*. The experience of Alfred G. and Lillian Garr in India would add a significant nuance to Parham's theory. See Garr, "Tongues, the Bible Evidence"; McGee, "Garr, Alfred Goodrich, Sr."; and McGee (ed.), *Initial Evidence*.

tell Cornelius to send for Peter. He came and told them about the baptism with the Spirit, and that every afternoon at three o'clock they would pray for the enduement of power. He told them he did not have the Pentecost but was seeking it and wanted all the saints to pray with him till all received their Pentecost. Some believed they had it, and others believed they did not have it because the signs were not following. Hardly anyone was getting saved.

There was a great deal of opposition, but they continued to fast and pray for the baptism with the Holy Spirit, till on April 9th the fire of God fell in a cottage on Bonnie Brae. Pentecost was poured out upon workers and saints. Three days after that, Bro. Seymour received his Pentecost. Two who had been working with him in Houston came to Los Angeles just before Pentecost fell. They came filled with the Holy Ghost and power. One of them had received her personal Pentecost, Sister Lucy Farrow, and said the Lord had sent her to join us in holding up this precious truth. She came with love and power, holding up the blood of Jesus Christ in all His fullness.

And the fire has been falling ever since. Hundreds of souls have received salvation and healing. We can truly say that the revival is still going on. The Lord God is in Los Angeles in different missions and churches in mighty power, in spite of opposition.

The fire did in fact fall and news of the strange events hit the front page of the *Los Angeles Times* on April 18, 1906. The article was an attempt at ridicule, but according to some insiders, it only served to further promote the incipient movement, especially after the devastating earthquake in San Francisco the following day. Frank Bartleman, an early participant, observes, "All classes began to flock to the meetings. Many were curious and unbelieving, but others were hungry for God. The newspapers began to ridicule and abuse the meetings, thus giving us much free advertising. This brought the crowds. The devil overdid himself again."[6]

Because of the swelling crowds, Seymour and his fledgling congregation moved to 312 Azusa Street and there for three years people came from far and near to receive their Pentecost. Many believed that this experience of glossolalia qualified them for missionary work in the lands in which their supernaturally given language was spoken. Thus, in a remarkably short time, the mission on Azusa Street also became a missions agency sending independent Pentecostal emissaries to other parts of the

6. Bartleman, *Azusa Street*, 48.

United States and the rest of the world.[7] Currently, according to the World
Christian Database, there are approximately 92 million Pentecostals, 204
million Charismatics, and 305 million Neo-Charismatics.[8] Many of these
people can either trace their roots to the Azusa Street revival or have been
significantly impacted by those who can.[9]

THE DREAM MATURES

To hear Bartleman tell it, the saints at Azusa had found the solution to
the "race problem." Perhaps referring to W. E. B. DuBois's concern that
America's central problem of the twentieth century was the problem of
the color line,[10] Bartleman notes, "Soon the meetings were running day
and night coming. The place was packed out nightly. There were far more
white people than colored people. The 'color line' was washed way in the
blood."[11] Though Bartleman centered his analysis in this quote on a chris-
tological foundation, the Apostolic Faith newsletter seems to possess a
far grander theological scheme with respect to its understanding of racial
and social equality.

First, Seymour and the mission leaders took seriously the ethical and
social dimensions of Christian teaching. As former Holiness believers,
they subscribed to a belief in the necessity of sanctification in Christian

7. See "The Lord Sends Him." Here is an account of a young missionary named
Thomas Mahler, who received Spirit baptism at Azusa Street and of whom it was proph-
esied that he would suffer martyrdom in Africa.

8. World Christian Database.

9. Creech ("Visions of Glory") disagrees with the notion of the centrality of the Azusa
mission. He insists that it "played only a limited substantial role in the institutional,
theological, and social development of early Pentecostalism" (408). Yet his analysis fails
to adequately account for the power of symbols to transcend and inform these other
categories. On the other hand, respected writers such as Hollenweger, (Pentecostalism)
and Anderson (Spreading Fires) challenge the view that Azusa Street was the source of
world Pentecostalism. On the other end of the spectrum see Synan, The Pentecostal-
Holiness Tradition, 92–106. He places the Azusa Street revival at the epicenter of the
North American Pentecostal movement, calling it the "American Jerusalem," a description previously given by Bartleman in Azusa Street, 63. This writer takes the view that
the Azusa Street revival is crucial for explaining North American Pentecostalism and
some sectors of the global Pentecostal movement through the direct action of missionaries sent from Azusa Street (such as John G. Lake to South Africa) and indirectly
through the influence of later organizations owing their existence to the revival.

10. DuBois, The Souls of Black Folk, 19.

11. Bartleman, Azusa Street, 54.

life. "Sanctification," the Azusa mission doctrinal statement reads, "is that act of God's free grace by which he makes us holy."[12] Furthermore, sanctification was for them a requirement for reception of Spirit baptism, for "the Baptism with the Holy Ghost is a gift of power upon a sanctified life."[13] "If we are sanctified and have clean hearts, living pure, holy lives and having perfect love in our souls," one wrote, "O let us receive the baptism with the Holy Ghost."[14] This life was defined by an overwhelming love for God and others, a love which manifests itself in humility in interpersonal relationships. Note how these themes are combined in the following quote from the newsletter:

> It is sweet to have the promise of Jesus and the character of Jesus wrought out in our lives and hearts by the power of the Blood and the Holy Ghost, and to have that same love and that same meekness and humility manifested in our lives, for His character is love. Jesus was a man of love . . . Yes, He was a man of love. He was the express image of the Father, God manifest in the flesh. Dear loved ones, we must have that pure love that comes down from heaven, love that is willing to suffer loss, love that is not puffed up, not easily provoked, but gentle, meek, and humble. We are accounted as sheep for the slaughter day by day. We are crucified to self, the world, the flesh and everything, that we may bear about in our body the dying of the Lord Jesus, that our joy may be full even as He is full.[15]

Second, and more importantly, they saw their view of racial and social equality as proceeding directly from God's nature. This manifests in a number of ways. To begin with, they believed that God did not see people according to racial or other distinctions. One writer exhorts,

> We must give God all the glory in this work. We must keep very humble at His feet. He recognizes no flesh, no color, no names. We must not glory in Azusa Mission, nor in anything but the Lord Jesus Christ by whom the world is crucified unto us and we unto the world. Azusa Mission stands for unity of God's people

---

12. "The Apostolic Faith Movement," 2.

13. Ibid.

14. "Sanctification and Power," 4.

15. "The Character of Love," 4.

everywhere. God is uniting His people baptizing them by one Spirit into one body.[16]

Participants believed that in the shadow of the cross and with the outpouring of the Spirit, human distinctions disappeared.

In addition, the Azusa leaders were convinced that, by the Holy Spirit, God speaks to all, through all, and as all. Such a view comes across clearly in their belief that

> [t]he gift of languages is given with the commission, "Go ye into all the world and preach the gospel to every creature." The Lord has given languages to the unlearned Greek, Latin, Hebrew, French, German, Italian, Chinese, Japanese, Zulu and languages of Africa, Hindu and Bengali and dialects of India, Chippewa and other languages of the Indians, Esquimaux, the deaf mute language and, in fact the Holy Ghost speaks all the languages of the world through His children.[17]

This idea is also reflected in the following:

> It is noticeable how free all nationalities feel. If a Mexican or German cannot speak English, he gets up and speaks in his own tongue and feels quite at home for the Spirit interprets through the face and people say amen. No instrument that God can use is rejected on account of color or dress or lack of education. This is why God has so built up the work.[18]

That the Holy Spirit would deign to speak to the peoples of the world in their own languages and through human instruments underscores both the equality and intrinsic worth of every human being. And, especially in this last quotation, the success of the Azusa Street revival is attributable to the fact that the leaders and attendees there subscribed to this egalitarian ideal. This was a place for all people.

Moreover, for the Azusa Street faithful, the ministry of the Holy Spirit was through all and for all. This is illustrated in the story of a Mexican Indian and two white women. The Indian apparently came to the Azusa Street meetings and heard a German woman speaking glossolalically in his native dialect. So overcome was he that he praised God in what little English he knew and then proceeded to pray for a young white woman

16. "Beginning of a World Wide Revival," 1.

17. Untitled, *Apostolic Faith (Los Angeles)*, September 1906.

18. "Bible Pentecost."

named Mrs. S. P. Knapp, who, according to the report of her father Frank Gale, was instantly healed of consumption. This kind of spiritual interchange no doubt confirmed to those present that God dealt equally with all. The logical conclusion is that God must therefore see all equally and thus true Christians must do the same.

Given this rich theological mosaic, it follows that all God's people should worship and serve together in a common body, regardless of ethnicity, language, or any other human particularity. And this is what they practiced at Azusa Street. Observe the following descriptions:

> This is the Nazareth of Los Angeles. Some have come from long distances to this spot, directed of the Lord, and the humble have always been greatly blest. The work began among the colored people. God baptized several sanctified wash women with the Holy Ghost, who have been much used of Him. The first white woman to receive the Pentecost and gift of tongues in Los Angeles was Mrs. Evans who is now in the work in Oakland. Since then multitudes have come. God makes no difference in nationality, Ethiopians, Chinese, Indians, Mexicans, and other nationalities worship together.[19]

> This meeting has been a melting time. The people are all melted together by the power of the blood and the Holy Ghost. They are made one lump, one bread, all one body in Christ, There is no Jew or Gentile, bond or free, in the Azusa Mission.[20]

> It is a continual upper room tarrying at Azusa Street. It is like a continual camp-meeting or convention. All classes and nationalities meet on a common level . . . The altars are filled with seekers.[21]

The "conversion" of white Holiness leader Gaston B. Cashwell is a quintessential moment in Azusa Street race relations. According to his own testimony in the Apostolic Faith, he arrived in Los Angeles from North Carolina after having read Frank Bartleman's tantalizing reports in the Way of Faith newsletter. He describes his tearful departure from his wife in vivid detail, but then he mentions quite cryptically, "As soon as I reached Azusa Mission, a new crucifiction [sic] began in my life and

---

19. "The Same Old Way," 3.

20. Untitled, *Apostolic Faith (Los Angeles)*, December 1906, 1.

21. "Beginning of a World Wide Revival," 1.

I had to die to many things, but God gave me the victory. The first altar call I went forward in earnest for my Pentecost. I struggled from Sunday till Thursday."[22] Why does he seem so evasive, and what would have occasioned this immediate "new crucifixion"?[23] According to his associate, Luther R. Graham, Cashwell wrestled with racial prejudice. Though he had previously worked with blacks in his meetings, the level of integration between blacks and whites and the prominent role blacks played in the mission profoundly disturbed him. Even the thought that blacks would have to pray for him to receive the encounter with the Spirit he had traveled over 3,000 miles to experience made "chills go down my spine."[24] He nonetheless persevered, endured the radical reordering of his social scheme, submitted to prayer at the hands of Seymour and some other young black men, and experienced his baptism in the Holy Spirit.

The metanarrative operative at Azusa Street was that God was at work to bring equality and racial harmony to the Body of Christ. The faithful recognized that differences among peoples do exist (language, etc.), yet these differences did not rise to the level of creating barriers to acceptance and aptness for service. So what happened to distort this vision? What went wrong?

THE DREAM WITHERS

Perhaps the question is incorrectly stated and should read "What was happening to distort this vision?" At the level of the meta-narrative racial equality was lauded, but there were indications that a subversive counternarrative was "always already" at work. To start with, the integration at Azusa Street was probably not as profound as it first appears. Upon more careful analysis, Bartleman's account of the color line being washed away, as quoted above, contains some troubling elements. At one level, he seems to be innocently reporting that, on account of the free publicity offered by the disparaging press and the fallout from the San Francisco earth-

22. Cashwell, "Came 3,000 miles for his Pentecost," 3.

23. Cashwell was not the only person to describe his journey toward Spirit baptism in this way. See Charles H. Mason's account in Mason (ed.), *The History and Lifework of Elder C. H. Mason*, 26–30. He too wrestled with his first impressions concerning the Azusa Street mission, though his difficulties centered on the biblical fidelity of the practices he found there.

24. Synan, *Oldtime Power*, 97–98. Synan's report is based on a personal interview he conducted with Luther Graham in Tennessee in 1966. See also Beacham, *Azusa East*.

quake, more people came to the meetings. And since Los Angeles was a majority white county (about 96% to 4% black and other), it stood to reason that more whites than blacks would attend the revival.[25] Even this charitable reading raises a significant question: was the racially mixed nature of the early Azusa Street meetings merely a function of arithmetic and probability and not because of any purposeful design? This seems very likely; however, it does not properly account for why many whites stayed for as long as they did. But a more suspicious reading evokes even darker responses. Imagine a white man, a part of the still oppressive majority, declaring the dissolution of racial distinctions just after he observes that the mission had become majority white? "There were far more white people than colored people. The 'color line' was washed way in the blood."[26] Rather than being a merely a joyous declaration of the power of Christianity to unite the races, does this not at least seem like an ominous assertion of superiority, especially from the perspective of the blacks who had already been faithfully attending the mission?

But there are even more troubling hints within the mission's paper itself that a counter-narrative was at work. Although the official position of the Apostolic Faith newsletter extolled the virtues of racial equality and reconciliation, its language was not entirely devoid of racial stereotyping. These brief examples show the racially charged nature of some of the language:

> There are 50,000 languages in the world. Some of them sound like jabber. The Eskimo can hardly be distinguished from a dog bark. The Lord lets smart people talk in these jabber-like languages. Then He has some child talk in the most beautiful Latin and Greek, just to confound professors and learned people.[27]

Concerning a visionary or other extracorporeal experience, one article reported,

25. According to the University of Virginia's Geospatial & Statistical Data Center, in the decade between 1900 and 1910, the population of Los Angeles County nearly tripled from 170,298 to 504,131. Of these, in 1900, 163,975 were white and 6,323 were black and in 1910, 483,478 were white, 9,424 were black, and 11,229 were recorded as other. Statistics available at http://fisher.lib.virginia.edu/collections/stats/histcensus [last accessed 14 October 2009].

26. Bartleman , *Azusa Street*, 54.

27. Untitled, *Apostolic Faith (Los Angeles)*, April 1907, 4. This article first appeared in another newsletter, *Banner of Truth*.

> They were taken in the Spirit to the heathen in Africa, and found themselves surrounded by those poor idolators [sic], and they were given the interpretation, at this time of what they said. They appeared to read to them from John 14, and found themselves opening up the chapter to their benighted listeners, with the earnestness of all their souls.[28]

Another article proclaimed, "The great majority of the girls have been admitted to 'Mukti' in times of famine during the past ten years, and when they entered they were simply raw heathen."[29] One woman testified, "I shall never forget that night. I was about two hours receiving words in different languages and songs in the Spirit. O what a great joy it is to me to know that I can go with the language and songs and the love of God to the dying, famishing heathen. How I treasure the privileges and gifts. O how precious to be born in this age."[30] Reporting a divine commission, another Azusa Street attendee wrote:

> Eight years ago, in A. B. Simpson's missionary school at Nyack, New York, I heard the Macedonian cry to go to Jerusalem, but it is to the Arabs. I am told there are more Arabs than Jews there, and God has been speaking to me and asks me if I would be willing to go with Him to the wild Arab of the desert. Anywhere with Jesus I will gladly go.[31]

It is true that some of the comments were either reprints from other newsletters or letters sent in to the Apostolic Faith. It is also true that our contemporary ear is more sensitive to some of the language because the postcolonial discourse has chastened us.[32] However, even at that time, these comments bore the marks of an entrenched Eurocentrism and paternalism. The editors of the newsletter could have easily exercised the choice to modify the language they found; but they did not and this fact demonstrates that they were too deeply entrenched in their cultural paradigms to realize how the racially and ethnically charged portrayals stood at odds with their ideals. Consequently, despite its attempts to put forth a radically new vision of a postracial Spirit-filled community, the Azusa

28. "From Other Pentecostal Papers," 3.

29. "Pentecost in Mukti, India," 4.

30. Untitled, *Apostolic Faith (Los Angeles)*, December 1906, 3.

31. Leatherman, "Pentecostal Experience," 4.

32. See Said's *Orientalism* as an example of one of the early voices in postcolonial discourse.

Street mission nonetheless struggled in the quagmire of the racist context in which it found itself. Even if the above arguments from the various texts are not convincing, the events that plagued the mission from very early on should suffice to make the case.[33]

The first was Seymour's relationship with Parham and the disastrous results of Parham's visit to the mission in October 1906. As mentioned before, as a black man in the South subject to Jim Crow laws, Seymour could not attend Parham's class like his white counterparts could; he had to listen to lectures through a cracked door. This set a certain tone for the Seymour/Parham relationship. However, the fuse that would ignite the racism implicit in this action lay in the future.

Because Seymour initially saw Parham as the leader of the move-ment, when the events of Azusa Street revival began to unfold, he re-quested that Parham come and give his apostolic blessing in person. After a delay, Parham finally arrived at the Azusa Street Mission.[34] Far from being the congenial affirmation Seymour sought, the visit became an emotionally charged conflict. Parham did not approve of the spiritual demonstrations he found during the services. He later wrote, "I found hypnotic influences, familiar-spirit influences, spiritualistic influences . . . mesmeric influences, and all kinds of spells, spasms."[35] Even more scath-ingly he complained,

> Men and women, whites and blacks, knelt together or fell across one another; frequently, a white woman, perhaps of wealth and culture, could be seen thrown back in the arms of a big "buck nigger" and held tightly thus as she shivered and shook in freak imitation of Pentecost. Horrible awful shame![36]

---

33. This thesis directly challenges the view that the Azusa Street revival was able to create a truly racially integrated community. Rosenior typifies this view when he writes, "Although American Pentecostalism had been forged in the fires of discrimina-tion, racial hatred, lynchings, Jim Crow segregation, and the overall racism of the early years of the twentieth century, Pentecostals in their infancy had managed to create an interracial Christian movement, something which up to that time was unheard of in American Christianity" ("Toward Racial Reconciliation," 29).

34. Parham was busy trying to take over the apparently more successful, though factious Zion City, which had been founded by Alexander Dowie (see Goff, *Fields*, 129–34).

35. S. Parham, *Life of Charles F. Parham*, 168.

36. Ibid., 246.

His reaction was the exact opposite of Cashwell. Cashwell had come, confronted with his racism and began the process of recovery. Parham would not be so convinced. He viewed the events of Azusa Street as nothing more than wildfire and fanaticism and cast them in a very racist light.[37] But he did not merely voice his disapproval, he tried to assert his authority over the mission; and when that failed, he opened a nearby rival mission. Seymour's handling of the matter in the December issue of the Apostolic Faith is particularly telling. In the article he unequivocally rejects the leadership of Parham. Jesus, not Parham was the Projector of the Azusa Street mission and revival.[38] There never was reconciliation between the two men.

The second event that demonstrates how race factored greatly in the mission involves Clara Lum, a young white woman who worked with Seymour in the leadership of the mission and served as managing editor for the newsletter. The episode began with Seymour's marriage to Jennie Evans Moore on May 13, 1908. Moore was a black leader in the mission and one of the first to receive the baptism in the Holy Spirit while the revival was in its infancy at the house on Bonnie Brae Street. In response, Clara Lum abruptly left the mission to work with former Azusa Street mission member, Florence Crawford in Portland, Oregon. Speculation abounds concerning her reasons for sudden departure. Some argue that Lum felt that Seymour's marriage would distract him from his primary task of leading the mission. Others ascribe a more personal reason, suggesting the possibility of some sort of love triangle. In fact, this was the position of Ithiel Clemmons. Based on his interview with Charles Mason, the founder of the COGIC and an Azusa Street alumnus, Clemmons reports that Seymour had gone to Mason, asking Mason whether or not he should pursue a romantic relationship with Lum, who had made her romantic aspirations known. Mason counseled Seymour against the idea, ostensibly reasoning that his ministry and the young movement were not ready for such a scandal. Consequently, Seymour turned his attentions to Moore.[39] Feeling the sting of rejection, Lum left the mission and took

---

37. See further C. Parham, *The Sermons of Charles F. Parham*, 72–73. He wrote of Azusa-like revival meetings that he saw people crowded at the altar, "laying across one another like hogs," and "black and whites mingling . . . this should be enough," he says, "to bring a blush of shame to devils."

38. "Pentecost with Signs Following," 1.

39. Clemmons, *Bishop C. H. Clemmons*, 50.

with her the mission's financial lifeline: its national and international mailing lists. She also took with her the expertise necessary for the running of the newspaper.[40] Even more disastrous to the mission, as early as May 1908, Crawford and Lum began producing the paper and started giving Portland as its address. The Azusa Street revival, cut off from its supporters and its public, began its descent into relative obscurity within the now burgeoning Pentecostal movement. Seymour realized the imminent danger Lum's actions posed to his ministry and traveled to Oregon with the intention of persuading the postmaster to compel Lum to return his lists. His efforts were in vain and in the last known Apostolic Faith paper published in Los Angeles in November 1908, he laments, "It was a sad thing to our hearts for a worker to attempt to take the paper."[41] What could have happened had Mason given Seymour different advice and he had pursued a marital relationship with Lum? What message would that have sent to the Pentecostal movement? If Seymour had truly believed his teaching about racial equality and reconciliation, why had he not acted upon those beliefs in a clearly demonstrative way? Any number of defenses may be postulated and the fact is that, given the paucity of materials available from this period in Seymour's life, a fully satisfactory answer may never be forthcoming. What seems clear is that Seymour's actions show that despite the egalitarian rhetoric, Azusa Street was still encumbered by the pernicious legacy of racism.

The third event that demonstrates the mission's struggle was the debacle involving Seymour and William H. Durham, a white minister from the Chicago area. Durham had come to Los Angeles and stayed from February to March, 1907. There, at the mission, Durham had received the baptism in the Holy Spirit. Of Durham and fellow preacher "Brother Blake" an article in the Apostolic Faith joyfully recalled, "They both were baptized with the Holy Ghost and went back filled and saturated with the power of God, speaking in tongues and magnifying God."[42] Durham sent a thank you letter back to the mission, saying of Seymour, "He seems to maintain a helpless dependence on God and is as simple-hearted as a little child, and at the same time is so filled with God that you feel the love and power every time you get near him."[43] In September 1907, the

40. Alexander, *Limited Liberty*, 41.

41. Quoted in Nelson, "For Such a Time as This," 218.

42. Untitled, *Apostolic Faith*, February–March, 1907, 1.

43. Durham, "A Chicago Evangelist's Pentecost," 4.

paper reports, "The Lord is using Bro. Durham as a river that overflows its banks and waters the thirsty ground."[44] However, the second visit was not so congenial. While Seymour was on a preaching tour, Durham left his post as pastor of the North Avenue Mission in Chicago and went to live in Los Angeles in February 1911.[45] At Azusa Street he promulgated his "Finished Work of Calvary" doctrine at the Azusa Street mission with some success.[46] Up until that point most Pentecostals, especially those coming from a Holiness background, had understood sanctification as a second definite work of grace, with baptism in the Holy Spirit a gift of power upon the sanctified life. Durham dismissed this idea entirely. For him, sanctification was not a crisis, but a process involving the appropriation of Christ's work on the cross to the believer's life. Not only was the doctrine foreign to the majority of the Azusa Street membership, Durham's manner was derogatory and highly polemical. For ten weeks Durham held sway over the Azusa Street mission until, at the urging of the mission's board, Seymour returned. Seymour appealed to Durham to tone down his rhetoric, but Durham refused. Eventually, Seymour reluctantly locked him out of the mission. This led to a split, with Durham taking a number of the Azusa Street mission's white members with him.[47] Though not racially motivated, Durham's actions still served to drive a deeper wedge between blacks and whites at Azusa Street. Thereafter, the mission would cater to a primarily black constituency.

THE DREAM DIES

If one adds to the previous indignities the other racially involved separations led by Elmer K. Fisher and William Pendleton and the fact that in 1913 the organizing committee of the Arroyo Seco Camp meeting refused Seymour any active role in its program even though it had used the Apostolic Faith name and Azusa Street fame in its promotions, then one

---

44. Untitled, *Apostolic Faith*, September 1907, 1.

45. Nelson suggests that his departure had been "unfriendly." Nelson, "For Such a Time as This," 247.

46. See Riss, "Finished Work Controversy," 638 for a more detailed discussion of this doctrine. However, for a sustained treatment see Farkas, "William Durham and the Sanctification Controversy."

47. Bartleman, *Azusa Street*, 156.

can perhaps now begin to understand Seymour's reaction in his Doctrine and Discipline.[48]

The compounding effect of these episodes undermined Seymour's ministry and his influence within Pentecostalism would never be the same. Those who had hurt Seymour the most shared three characteristics: they were all white; they had all vied for control over all or a portion of the Azusa Street mission; and they all spoke in tongues. It is not surprising, that each of the three significant changes Seymour made in his thinking was linked to one of these.[49]

However, two final events demand attention and perhaps serve as the final pallbearers for the dream of Azusa as a post-racial, Spirit-filled, Christian community. The first is the formation of the Assemblies of God in April 1914. Anthea Butler has made a strong case for race as a primary factor in the separation of the predominantly white AG from its "mother organization" the predominantly black COGIC.[50] Whatever the reason, however, the result was an institutional split along racial fault lines that crystallized the separation between the races. Significantly, just a month after the AG organizational meeting, the Azusa mission board of trustees voted to exclude non-colored people from its leadership. This might not have been coincidental.

The second important event occurred, not within Pentecostalism itself but within the wider American context: the February 8, 1915 Los Angeles premier of D. W. Griffith's *The Birth of a Nation*.[51] The movie was Griffith's adaptation of Thomas Dixon's novel *The Clansman*. Considered one of the first Hollywood blockbusters, it was a disparagingly racist

48. As early as August 1906, Pendleton took about forty mostly white members with him to the Eight and Maple Mission where he would succeed Frank Bartleman as pastor. Fisher, a former Baptist and a graduate of Moody Bible Institute, had been a trusted co-leader at the Azusa Street Mission. While on a four-month preaching tour of the South, Seymour left Fisher in charge of the mission. He later left the mission, taking a large number of white believers with him to establish the Upper Room Mission. By calling these events "racially involved separations," I am not suggesting that there was *necessarily* any personal acrimony, racism, or impropriety involved. I am suggesting, however, that the movement of people and resources away from the Azusa Street Mission and the fact that these separations were led by whites and involved mostly whites who then either established or worked in rival missions played a role in Seymour's evolution.

49. Nelson, "For Such a Time," 265.

50. Butler, "Walls of Division."

51. The film was first released as *The Clansman* in Los Angeles and then re-released under the more famous title on March 3, 1915.

portrayal of post-civil war America. According to the revisionist plot, the true patriots and heroes of this period were the dispossessed Southerners who reluctantly but courageously established the Ku Klux Klan to protect their women, children, and way of life from lecherous, shiftless, and lazy Negroes and the Northerners who supported them. Ironically, life followed art. The film fostered a rebirth of the Klan throughout the South and spawned several episodes of racial turmoil in many cities.[52] Shortly after the release of *Birth of a Nation*, Seymour published *Doctrines and Disciplines of the Azusa Street Apostolic Faith Mission*, which announced his new stance on race relations within the context of the mission. Although with the documents currently available it is perhaps impossible to declare a definitive cause and effect association, the close timing and proximity of these events and the language Seymour used in the document indicate some kind of a relationship.

In the profoundest of ironies, the same Seymour who had printed in his paper, "No instrument that God can use is rejected on account of color or dress or lack of education," and "God recognizes no flesh, no color, no names," now forbade non-colored members from holding key leadership positions in the mission.[53] The mission of which it was said, "The color line is washed away in the blood" was now guilty of discriminatory practices. "The Apostolic Faith Mission," Seymour wrote, "shall be carried on in the interests of and for the benefit of the colored people."[54] He reasoned that it was "not for discrimination, but for peace. To keep down race war in the Churches [sic]."[55] Douglas J. Nelson portrays this act as an attempt at legal self-preservation, which seems reasonable, even forgivable, given the stark political realities and the vulnerability that Seymour and all African Americans experienced.[56] Nonetheless, it still probably taints Seymour's legacy as a person who sought racial reconciliation. Instead of affirming his egalitarian principles in the face of opposition, he capitulated to the forces that had always been at work to undermine the experiment and lofty ideals of the Azusa Street mission. The harsh exigencies of a Jim Crow America stymied the initial faltering steps toward reconciliation and caused a retrenchment to previously established racial lines. Thus,

---

52. For a recent analysis see, Stokes, *D. W. Griffith's The Birth of a Nation*.

53. "Gracious Pentecostal Showers Continue to Fall," 1.

54. Seymour, *Doctrines*, 48.

55. Ibid., 12.

56. Nelson, "For Such a Time," 263–65.

the opportunity for the Azusa Street revival to be a prophetic witness to the possibility of a postracial, Spirit-filled Christian community died.

And Seymour died not long after.

CAN THESE DRY BONES LIVE?

Given this history, it is not strange that it did not occur to white Pentecostals that they should invite black Pentecostal denominations to join them when forming the PFNA some forty years after the height of the Azusa Street revival. They had already retreated to their separate social spheres with lost memories of missed opportunities. Likewise, it is not surprising that such a state of affairs could continue for forty-five years before it was addressed during the events that culminated in the Memphis Miracle and the disbanding of the PFNA and the formation of PCCNA. The question now remaining is whether Pentecostals have learned anything from their abysmal failures at racial reconciliation in the Pentecostal movement.

If the Pentecostal movement is serious about its desire to create a post-racial, Spirit-filled Christian community as a prophetic witness to the reality of the power of God to engender forgiveness and to reconcile humanity, its members and leaders must realize that a triumphalistic or rose-colored view of Pentecostalism's past, while appearing as an aid to progress, only obscures the truth and interferes with the critical work necessary for creating a new future. Nostalgia for the "good old days" will not suffice because, as I have attempted to show, the old days were not that good after all, at least not with respect to racial reconciliation.

Racial interaction is not racial reconciliation. It can be a distraction and is an insultingly poor substitute that only makes the real task harder. More explicitly stated, staging racially-mixed events without the deep work of forgiveness and reconciliation is a superficial masquerade that simultaneously a) allows the real wounds of disharmony and prejudice to putrefy, and b) tranquilizes those involved.[57] Resultantly, unwary participants in this charade think that the "race problem" (What race problem?!) has been resolved, when in reality it has only been submerged and transformed into something even more insidious and all the more

---

57. Very often, a look behind the scenes at the organization and leadership of such events betrays the fact that age-old power structures and presuppositions remain unchanged. By this assertion I am not discounting the value of symbolic action. In fact, rightly motivated and substantiated actions, even if symbolic, can have a positive effect.

difficult to eradicate. No longer is it on the surface where it can be named, confronted, and exorcised; it is now the subliminal (and even institutionalized) fabric from which human relationships are sown.

The differences between supposed races have nothing to do with the color of skin and everything to do with the cultures from which various ethnicities emerge. Pentecostals must address the underlying cultural and social differences that are the true hindrances to reconciliation. Are Pentecostals willing to live out the implicit meaning of speaking in tongues? Namely, are they willing to perform the ultimate act of self-forgetfulness by speaking each other's languages and thereby affirming each other's worth before God?

Sustaining racial equality in North American Pentecostalism calls for more than just a sound, but utopian, theology. In fact, as Azusa Street experiences illustrate, racial prejudice is very deeply ingrained; and not even a move of the Holy Spirit is sufficient in itself to remove the animosity and the stain. The damage to both oppressed and oppressor is too deep and has endured for too long to expect a quick Holy Ghost fix. As Acts 6, Acts 10, and Acts 15 demonstrate, racial reconciliation will require profound personal, organizational, and structural change (metanoia), not just symbolic or token acts. It will involve changes in our concepts of power and its appropriate use and our definitions of rights, responsibilities, and, yes, ownership.

This is the beginning.

"Son of man, can these bones live?" I said to him, "Sovereign Lord, you know." Then he said to me, "Prophesy over these bones, and tell them: 'Dry bones, hear the word of the *Lord*. This is what the sovereign *Lord* says to these bones: "Look, I am about to infuse [Spirit] into you and you will live" Ezek 31:2–5 (NET Bible).

BIBLIOGRAPHY

Alexander, Estrelda Y. *Limited Liberty: The Legacy of Four Pentecostal Women Pioneers.* Cleveland: Pilgrim, 2008.
Anderson, Allan. *Spreading Fires: The Missionary Nature of Early Pentecostalism.* Maryknoll, NY: Orbis, 2007.
"The Apostolic Faith Movement." *Apostolic Faith (Los Angeles)* (September 1906) 1.

Bartleman, Frank. *Azusa Street*, Plainfield, NJ: Logos International, 1980. Reprint of *How Pentecost Came to Los Angeles*. Los Angeles: F. Bartleman, 1925.

Beacham, Doug. *Azusa East: The Life and Times of G. B. Cashwell.* Franklin Springs, GA: LSR, 2006.

"Beginning of a World Wide Revival." *Apostolic Faith (Los Angeles)* (January 1907) 1.

"Bible Pentecost." *Apostolic Faith (Los Angeles)* (November 1906) 1.

Butler, Anthea. "Walls of Division: Racism's Role in Pentecostal History." Paper presented to the annual meeting of the Society for Pentecostal Studies, Wheaton College, Wheaton, IL, November, 1994.

Cashwell, G. B. "Came 3,000 Miles for His Pentecost." *Apostolic Faith (Los Angeles)* (December 1906) 3.

"The Character of Love." *Apostolic Faith (Los Angeles)* (November 1906) 4.

Clemmons, Ithiel C. *Bishop C. H. Mason and the Roots of the Church of God in Christ.* Bakersfield, CA: Pneuma Life, 1996.

Creech, Joe. "Visions of Glory: The Place of the Azusa Street Revival in Pentecostal History." *Church History* 65 (1996) 405–24.

Du Bois, W. E. B. *The Souls of Black Folk.* New York: New American Library, 1903.

Durham, William. "A Chicago Evangelist's Pentecost." *Apostolic Faith (Los Angeles)* (February–March 1907) 4.

Farkas, Thomas G. "William H. Durham and The Sanctification Controversy in Early American Pentecostalism, 1906–1916." PhD diss., Southern Baptist Theological Seminary, 1993.

Fox, Charles R. "William J. Seymour: A Critical Investigation of his Soteriology, Pneumatology and Ecclesiology." PhD diss., Regent University, 2009.

"From Other Pentecostal Papers." *Apostolic Faith (Los Angeles)* (May 1907) 3.

Garr, A. G. "Tongues, the Bible Evidence." *Cloud of Witness to Pentecost in India* (September 1907) 40–47.

Goff, James R. *Fields White Unto Harvest: Charles F. Parham and the Missionary Origins of Pentecostalism.* Fayetteville: University of Arkansas Press, 1988.

———. "Initial Tongues in the Theology of Charles Fox Parham." In *Initial Evidence: Historical and Biblical Perspectives on the Pentecostal Doctrine of Spirit Baptism,* edited by Gary B. McGee, 57–71. Peabody, MA: Hendrickson, 1991.

———. "Charles Fox Parham." In *The New International Dictionary of Pentecostal and Charismatic Movements,* edited by Stanley M. Burgess, 955–56. Grand Rapids: Zondervan, 2002.

"Gracious Pentecostal Showers Continue to Fall." *Apostolic Faith (Los Angeles)* (November 1906) 1.

Graves, Joseph L., Jr. *The Race Myth: Why We Pretend Race Exists in America.* New York: Penguin, 2005.

Hollenweger, Walter J. *The Pentecostals: The Charismatic Movement in the Churches.* Minneapolis: Augsburg, 1972.

———. *Pentecostalism: Origins and Developments Worldwide.* Peabody, MA: Hendrickson, 1997.

———. "An Introduction to Pentecostalisms." *Journal of Beliefs and Values* 25 (August 2004) 127–34.

Leatherman, Lucy M. "Pentecostal Experience." *Apostolic Faith (Los Angeles)* (November 1906) 4.

"The Lord Sends Him." *Apostolic Faith (Los Angeles)* (September 1906) 2.

Lovett, Leonard. "Black Origins of the Pentecostal Movement." In *Aspects of Pentecostal-Charismatic Origins,* edited by Vinson Synan, 123–42. Plainfield, NJ: Logos International, 1975.

MacRoberts, Iain. *The Black Roots and White Racism of Early Pentecostalism in the USA.* New York: St. Martin's, 1988.

Mason, Mary, editor. *The History and Lifework of Elder C. H. Mason Chief Apostle and His Co-Laborers.* 1924.

McGee, Gary B. "Garr, Alfred Goodrich, Sr." In *The New International Dictionary of Pentecostal and Charismatic Movements*, edited by Stanley M. Burgess, 660–61. Grand Rapids: Zondervan, 2002.

———, editor. *Initial Evidence: Historical and Biblical Perspectives on the Pentecostal Doctrine of Spirit Baptism.* Peabody, MA: Hendrickson, 1991.

Newman, Joe, Race and the Assemblies of God Church. Youngstown, NY: Cambria Press, 2007.

Nelson, D. J. "For Such a Time as This: The Story of Bishop William J. Seymour and the Azusa Street Revival." PhD diss., University of Birmingham, 1981.

Parham, Charles Fox. *The Sermons of Charles F. Parham.* Edited by Donald W. Dayton. New York: Garland, 1985. Originally published as *The Voice of One Crying in the Wilderness.* Kansas City, MO: Charles Fox Parham, 1902.

Parham, Sarah E. *The Life of Charles F. Parham: Founder of the Apostolic Faith Movement.* Higher Christian Life 35. New York: Garland, 1985. Originally published Joplin, MO: Hunter, 1930.

"Pentecost in Mukti, India." *Apostolic Faith (Los Angeles)* (September 1907) 4.

"Pentecost with Signs Following." *Apostolic Faith (Los Angeles)* (December 1906) 1.

Riss, R. M. "Finished Work Controversy." In *The New International Dictionary of Pentecostal and Charismatic Movements*, edited by Stanley M. Burgess, 638–39. Grand Rapids: Zondervan, 2002.

Robeck, Cecil M., Jr. "William J. Seymour and the 'Biblical Evidence.'" In *Initial Evidence: Historical and Biblical Perspectives on the Pentecostal Doctrine of Spirit Baptism*, edited by Gary B. McGee, 72–95. Peabody, MA: Hendrickson, 1991.

———. "Seymour, William Joseph." In *The New International Dictionary of Pentecostal and Charismatic Movements*, edited by Stanley M. Burgess, 1053–57. Grand Rapids: Zondervan, 2002.

———. *The Azusa Street Mission and Revival: The Birth of the Global Pentecostal Movement.* Nashville: Thomas Nelson, 2006.

Rosenior, Derrick R. "Toward Racial Reconciliation: Collective Memory, Myth and Nostalgia in American Pentecostalism." PhD diss., Howard University, 2005.

Said, Edward W. *Orientalism.* New York: Pantheon, 1978.

"The Same Old Way." *Apostolic Faith (Los Angeles)* (September 1906) 3.

"Sanctification and Power." *Apostolic Faith (Los Angeles)* (November 1906) 4.

Seymour, William Joseph, editor. *The Azusa Street Papers: A Reprint of the Apostolic Faith Mission Publications Los Angeles, California (1906–1908).* Foley, AL: Together in the Harvest, 1997.

———. *The Doctrines and Disciplines of the Azusa Street Apostolic Faith Mission of Los Angeles, Cal.* Los Angeles: W. J. Seymour, 1915.

Stokes, Melvyn. *D. W. Griffith's The Birth of a Nation: A History of "The Most Controversial Motion Picture of All Time."* New York: Oxford University Press, 2008.

Synan, Vinson, editor. *The Century of the Holy Spirit: 100 Years of Pentecostal and Charismatic Renewal, 1901–2001.* Nashville: Thomas Nelson, 2001.

———. "Memphis 1994: Miracle and Mandate." Pentecostal/Charismatic Churches of North America. http://www.pccna.org/about_history.htm (accessed October 10, 2009).

———. *Oldtime Power: A Centennial History of the International Pentecostal Holiness Church.* Franklin Springs, GA: LifeSprings, 1998.

————. *The Pentecostal-Holiness Tradition: Charismatic Movements in the Twentieth Century*. Grand Rapids: Eerdmans, 1997.

————. "William Seymour." *Christian History* 65 (2000) 17–19.

Underwood, B. E. "The Memphis Miracle." Pentecostal-Charismatic Theological Inquiry International. http://pctii.org/arc/underwoo.html (accessed October 10, 2009).

Untitled. *Apostolic Faith (Los Angeles)* (September 1906) 1.

Untitled. *Apostolic Faith (Los Angeles)* (December 1906) 1.

Untitled. *Apostolic Faith (Los Angeles)* (December 1906) 3.

Untitled. *Apostolic Faith (Los Angeles)* (February–March 1907) 1.

Untitled. *Apostolic Faith (Los Angeles)* (April 1907) 4.

Untitled. *Apostolic Faith (Los Angeles)* (September 1907) 1.

Valdez, A. C., Sr., and James F. Scheer. *Fire on Azusa Street*. Costa Mesa, CA: Gift, 1980.

Wacker, Grant. *Heaven Below: Early Pentecostals and American Culture*. Cambridge: Harvard University Press, 2001.

Walling, Aaron. "An Evaluation of the Apostolic Faith." *Assemblies of God Heritage* 19 (Summer 1999) 10–15.

World Christian Database. Center for the Study of Global Christianity, Gordon-Conwell Theological Seminary. http://www.worldchristiandatabase.org/wcd/ (accessed May 5, 2010).

5

I'm Sorry, My Brother

A Reconciliation Journey[1]

Lois E. Olena

Graduation day 1951 stood just two weeks away for Robert ("Bob") Harrison. Though Bob Jones University had rejected his application due to the color of his skin, Bob found a home at an Assemblies of God (AG) school, Bethany College, in Santa Cruz, California. Knowing Bethany's president, Bob's grandmother—the Rev. Cornelia Jones Robertson—marched her grandson-of-promise into the president's office, where Harrison was welcomed as Bethany's "first negro."[2]

Harrison's music and preaching ministry blossomed at Bethany. He represented the school all across the state and conducted numerous evangelistic services. Nearing graduation, his anticipation intensified as

1. This chapter is adapted with permission from, "I'm Sorry, My Brother," in *We've Come This Far: Reflections on the Pentecostal Tradition and Racial Reconciliation*, edited by Byron D. Klaus (Springfield, MO: Assemblies of God Theological Seminary, 2007) 130–52.

2. Harrison, *When God Was Black*, 19.

89

he readied for one last matter of business—his interview for ministerial credentials with the Northern California-Nevada District of the AG. In spite of the fact that the AG had many years prior ordained his grandmother, Harrison was soon to face the most painful rejection of his life— the denial of credentials to him because of his race.[3] As he stood before the District credentialing committee, the superintendent looked Harrison "square in the eye and said, 'I'm sorry, my brother (sic), but it is not the policy of our denomination to grant credentials to Negroes.'"[4] Stunned and hurt, Harrison left the interview, rejecting the superintendent's offer to return his $2 credentialing fee. Not until 1957 would the District grant him a ministerial license, and only in 1962 would he receive General Council ordination.

Why the delay? What attitudes and events within the Assemblies of God with respect to the credentialing of African Americans contributed not only to Harrison's1951 rejection, but also to the long delay on his road to ordination? This paper puts Harrison's situation within the historical context of the AG struggle over racial issues. I will show how various mounting pressures from many venues facilitated a context in which Harrison was able to serve as a catalyst for change, helping to carry the movement beyond its paralysis to a point of action with respect to ministry to, by, and with African-Americans.[5]

AG CREDENTIALING "POLICY"

At some point after his licensing in 1957, Harrison saw himself as the first African-American granted a ministerial license by the AG.[6] However, as

3. The Rev. Robertson, an Azusa Street revival participant, "was one of the first blacks to be ordained by the Assemblies of God. She founded and served Emmanuel Pentecostal Church and House of Prayer in San Francisco for more than 30 years and established a mission in the nearby Barbary Coast area" (Gohr, "For Such a Time as This", 6).

4. Harrison, *When God Was Black*, 29. Perhaps Bob Harrison's inclusion of (sic) in his quote is because he considered the superintendent's reference to "brother" an inappropriate notation in light of his rejection.

5. The focus of this paper is not Harrison's full biography, though the numerous AG Archive and *Pentecostal Evangel* resources listed in the "Sources Consulted" section of this paper will direct the reader to significant biographical information. Harrison's autobiography, *When God Was Black*, and Glenn Gohr's article, "For Such a Time as This: The Story of Evangelist Bob Harrison," provide excellent overviews of Harrison's life and ministry.

6. Harrison, *When God Was Black*, 92.

Howard Kenyon has pointed out, ever since the early years of the movement, the AG had received black ministers into fellowship.[7] What happened, then, between the time of ministry by those Kenyon mentions
(1915–1937) and Harrison's moment of humiliation before the credentialing committee?

A key turning point toward the ambiguous "policy" the Northern
California-Nevada AG superintendent spoke of to Harrison in 1951 was
a General Presbytery (GP) ruling in 1939. At the 1939 GP meeting, the
question of ordaining a "man of the colored race" arose.[8] Though this
man was educated and "qualified Scripturally for ordination . . . [with]
a fine work in the Bronx" among "educated people," had been "brought
up in Glad Tidings Tabernacle (New York)" and knew "nothing but the
Assemblies of God fellowship,"[9] the GP, after much discussion and an
adjournment, ruled the following afternoon that the GP

> express disapproval of the ordaining of colored men to the min-
> istry and recommend that when those of the colored race apply
> for ministerial recognition, license to preach only be granted to
> them with instructions that they operate within the bounds of
> the District in which they are licensed, and if they desire ordina-
> tion, refer them to the colored organizations.[10]

7. Kenyon, "Black Ministers in the Assemblies of God," 10. Ellsworth S. Thomas,
pastor in Binghamton, New York, was the first minister granted credentials by the AG,
in 1915. Kenyon's excellent article recounts the important contributions of numerous
African-American ministers (Pastor G. T. Haywood, Pastor J. Edward Howard, missionaries Isaac and Martha Neeley, evangelist and pastor Bruce Gibson), as well as the
support shown to black ministers by (white) pastor Robert Brown of Glad Tidings in
New York City.

Gibson, ordained in 1933, left the AG on good terms in 1937 to work with "the
colored organization" (most likely COGIC). The AG reinstated him in 1952 upon
his desire to return. NJ-NY District Superintendant R. J. Bergstrom spoke in 1952 of
Gibson as "carrying on a fine work in the Bronx," recommending him for reinstatement
"inasmuch as we have other ordained colored Brethren working in our District" (R.
J. Bergstrom, Cross Reference Sheet to Letter, AG Archive, 26 February 1952.) It is
interesting to note that the unnamed "man of the colored race" referred to in the 1939
General Presbytery case also had "a fine work in the Bronx."

8. Kenyon identifies this man as a "Brother Ellison." The Eastern District Secretary,
Newton Chase, had "advised the national headquarters that the Eastern District was
willing to refer Ellison to the 'colored' organization." However, Robert Brown—who
had earlier endorsed two other blacks, Ellsworth S. Thomas and J. Edward Howard—
had referred Ellison to the credentialing committee "without the committee knowing
he was black!"

9. General Presbytery Minutes. "Ordination of Colored Brethren."

10. General Presbytery Minutes. "Ordination of Colored Brethren."

Without any national policy on the issue, the GP's ruling—though a "delicate attempt to balance things on the floor"—was, as Cecil Robeck points out, also a "vote for the status quo."[11] Districts could license capable candidates and yet at the same time those unwilling to ordain blacks would not be forced to do so. The status quo would be challenged and the Assemblies of God as a whole would continue to wrestle with racial issues regarding evangelism, missions, credentialing, the establishment of a "Colored Branch/Fellowship," and integration throughout the forties, fifties, and sixties, however, in both formal and informal settings.[12] Not only would various individuals and groups challenge the status quo, but also contradictions in "policy" would arise, such as the reinstatement of Bruce Gibson as an ordained minister in 1952, only one year after Harrison was denied licensing credentials.

When Harrison stood before the credentialing committee of the Northern California District in 1951, then, the "policy" of not credentialing "Negroes" that the superintendent spoke of was actually the result of a complicated series of decisions made by a movement apparently double-minded on racial issues.[13] For example, though there was a willingness in 1943 to evangelize blacks, there was an unwillingness to "tie the hands of the brethren" by a binding resolution. Though there was a willingness to establish a "Colored Branch" in 1945 and repeatedly throughout subsequent years, leaders showed little sign of following through. Though leaders willingly discussed racial issues on numerous occasions, there was a tendency to postpone decisions and actions, defer to (and back and forth between) other ruling bodies or committees, and even (in 1955)

11. Robeck, "The Past: Historical Roots of Racial Unity and Division in American Pentecostalism." Continued AG activity on this matter throughout subsequent decades was because the movement had only ever appealed to the canon of "American law and society" (15) with respect to race relations, instead of appealing to the biblical canon. By this the AG was able to "wash its hands of the issue by simply referring all such racial questions to the Church of God in Christ as its sibling or else explore ways with Church of God in Christ leaders about how the two groups might work together" (15).

12. For a detailed account of the evolution of AG thinking regarding these issues see Olena, "I'm Sorry, My Brother," 132–41.

13. Harrison's issue in 1951 and the struggle regarding the credentialing of African-Americans must be seen in the larger context of the AG struggle with racial issues in general, i.e., issues of evangelism among blacks, receiving churches into fellowship, the nature of the AG's relationship with COGIC, and the dilemma of having to choose between segregation (i.e., the "Colored Branch" option) and full integration. Treating the credentialing issue as separate and outside of this context would make for an artificial and unrealistic handling of the problem.

expunge minutes from the official record. Though some expressed a willingness to have a "Colored Branch" or "Colored Fellowship" ("without
organic relationship," as Gayle Lewis put it) as a movement, the AG was
not ready to commit to complete integration. Though some regions of
the country showed readiness to license blacks, the granting of full ordination remained only a story from the past and a distant hope for the
future for people like Harrison. Such double-mindedness paralyzed the
AG—partially if not fully—preventing it from advancing beyond the attitudes and actions of the surrounding society on these issues.

QUIETLY ORDAINING

With the intensification of the civil rights struggle, however, it appears
pressure mounted on and within the AG to come to grips with the issue some may have considered resolved in 1939. Within the AG, hopeful examples of pro-activity in the context of a history of paralysis do
exist. The efforts of Superintendant Leonard Palmer and Sec. Joseph
Gerhart in the Northern California-Nevada District played an important
role in Harrison's situation.[14] Other examples of pro-activity include the
New York District's choice to "quietly ordain" blacks,[15] the role of Teen
Challenge in breaking down the "color barrier at the grassroots level,"
and the 1959 New Jersey District Council Resolution "inviting Negroes
to join the church, and, if they wish, to enter the ministry."[16]

Though top AG leaders often found themselves unable to resolve
or act upon their many discussions regarding racial issues, it is evident
from General Presbytery and Executive Presbytery minutes and executive correspondence that official efforts to deal with racial concerns certainly intensified toward the end of the fifties. This increased effort in

14. It appears from Bartlett Peterson's June 30, 1961 letter that even though Gerhart
had repeatedly appealed to Zimmerman on behalf of Harrison, that he, too, was torn
about the issue. Peterson interprets some of Gerhart's correspondence as indicating
that "the ordination of this colored brother would pose some real problems within the
district." It is unlikely that Gerhart personally would have any problem with it, because
he was supportive of Harrison. However, he realized that not all those within his district
would agree.

15. Kenyon, "Black Ministers in the Assemblies of God," 11. David Wilkerson began
Teen Challenge in 1958 and received "immediate fame for his work among Spanish,
black, and Anglo youth." Asst. General Supt. Charles W. H. Scott noted in 1970 that
Teen Challenge had played a "major role" in "reaching into the black community."

16. "Church Unit Invites Negroes to Join."

itself indicates a growing realization that the situation for blacks with respect to the AG needed to change somehow, someway, and in a not too distant future.[17]

A handful of outside pressures existed as well. No small motivator was the May 17, 1954 Supreme Court ruling that declared racial segregation in the public schools as unconstitutional. Somehow, the AG would need to begin to resolve its decades-long racial dilemmas given the growing national trends. If the highest court in the country had ruled such, certainly the AG faced the necessity of reexamining its alignment with American law and society.

Tuskegee's interest in the role of the Assemblies of God in desegregation four years later—and the immediate AG executive reply—are telling. As well, Robert Stewart's inquiry in 1957 as to the AG policy on "receiving colored ministers" also provides evidence that (at least desire for) change was in the wind.[18] Moreover, perhaps the words of Selina Kirby regarding the AG's unchristian attitude, her shock that "especially Pentecostal people" could act this way, her forthrightness regarding the AG's race discrimination, her accusation that the fellowship was "worse than the world" because of hatred in people's hearts, etc., echoed in the consciences of AG leadership at the time. Clearly, from his own words, Ralph Riggs struggled with how the AG could best discharge its responsibility toward blacks.[19] Perhaps Kirby's comments regarding the bold steps Wheaton

---

17. Riggs's comment, "It is certainly high time in American living and in our church experience that we come closer together" indicates both his personal commitment to better racial relations as well as his sensitivity to change. However, as Robeck ("The Past") points out, Riggs walked a careful line between those against and those in favor of full integration. To those for integration, he could point to actual attempts to cooperate with COGIC. For those against, he could "safely say that he had intentions which merely recognized a sister organization with a fine ministry in the black community. In this way, Riggs could avoid the pressure to integrate on the one hand the pressure to segregate on the other. In either case he would not extend the Assemblies of God beyond the limits common to American law and society. But Riggs' letter must also be placed within the context of a white dominated and racist society. Conformity to American law and society would have left Riggs blind to his own racial presuppositions" (16).

18. To which Ralph Riggs responded in his October 23, 1957 letter, "I can advise you that our districts are *left to operate on their own discretion* in this matter. Our friends of the northern states do not find any difficulty here, at least to have such brethren to serve as *licensed ministers*" (emphasis mine).

19. Reared in Meridian, Mississippi in the early twentieth century, yet having spent six years as a missionary to blacks in South Africa, no doubt Riggs had mixed impulses.

and Moody had taken came to their remembrance and provided some impetus to look again at the problem in the latter part of the decade.

QUERYING THE MAINLINE

Though apparently double-minded and partially paralyzed, the AG genuinely struggled with respect to racial issues, and—though not quickly enough for folks like Harrison—did increasingly make strides in the right direction. One of the most significant efforts made by AG leadership was their querying of several mainline denominations to determine the nature of the work these organizations were carrying out among "the negroes."[20] An October 3, 1957 letter sent out by Victor Trimmer, National Secretary of the Home Missions Department of the Assemblies of God, notes that the AG was keenly interested in "determining the organic relationship of the negro work" to the respective denominations.[21] Having struggled with the question of a "Colored Branch" now for a dozen years, the AG wanted to know whether the work among blacks by these denominations was characterized as a "branch," or as an "integral part" of the organization.

Responses arrived from the Southern Baptists, National Baptists (the nation's oldest and largest African-American denomination), American Baptists, Methodists, Lutheran Synod, United Lutheran Church in America, Presbyterian Church U.S.A. (PCUSA), and Evangelical United Brethren Church. By May 19, 1958 R. L. Brandt, the new National Home Missions Secretary, presented a nine-page summary of "Negro Work" among these denominations to Gayle Lewis, then Assistant General Superintendent.[22] Brandt's bottom line deduction from the survey was that "by far the majority of denominations contacted have begun, or have had in effect for some years, a policy of de-segregation."[23] Areas sum-

---

20. See Bentley, *The National Black Evangelical Association*. Though the AG was pro-NAE and anti-ecumenical in its stance, they chose to query the more progressive and socially conscious mainline denominations over the NAE on this issue because the NAE did not include black denominations at that time. In 1963, partly as a result of feeling "often not welcome" in sister Christian organizations and associations (1), a National Black Evangelical Association was organized.

21. Trimmer (National Home Missions Secretary), Letter to Mainline and Evangelical Denominations.

22. Brandt, "Survey and Summary of Work among the Negroes," 1–9.

23. Ibid., 1.

marized included membership, ministerial credentialing, and education. The SBC report includes "areas for advance."

As for membership, Brandt noted, "In most instances membership is granted on an equal basis to negroes and whites."[24] The American Baptists reported having four hundred integrated congregations. They had also adopted a resolution in 1957 that membership was open to all regardless of race. The Methodists had some churches that were integrated. The United Lutheran churches had established congregations that were "wholly or almost wholly negro, as well as others that are bi-racial or multi-racial."[25] The PCUSA was represented as working toward a "non-segregated church and a non-segregated society."[26] The PCUSA was also making every effort to "move in the direction of a completely non-segregated pattern in work and worship."[27] The Evangelical Lutheran United Brethren church reported having a number of churches that had "negro members, and the Organization has set forth the idea that the local church should seek to minister to all unchurched people in its community regarless [sic] of color or other conditions."[28]

With regard to integrated ministry, the American Baptists made a formal statement that "Each church shall choose its minister on the basis of character and ability without regard to national background."[29] The Methodists were reported as having "at least two negro ministers of white congregations."[30]

This pattern of inclusiveness and openness without respect to race was also evident in the responses of the mainline denominations with respect to education. The Lutheran Synodical Conference of North America had made a formal resolution dated June 8-10, 1954, that its institutions of higher education were "intended for all students without racial

24. Ibid.

25. Ibid.

26. Ibid.

27. Ibid.

28. Ibid.

29. Ibid.

30. Ibid., 2. The National Baptist Churches called for "real harmony in God's kingdom here on earth," noting that in recent years just playing "one race" had become "increasingly impossible." They called for whites and blacks to work side by side, "Understanding each other. Sharing with each other. Cooperating together . . . Extending the Kingdom of God to all Nations, all kindreds and tongues." This is not surprising, since this denomination was black.

consideration."[31] The PCUSA noted that all of its colleges had "moved into a racially inclusive policy and practice."[32]

> Only the Southern Baptist picture was different. Brandt notes that the Southern Baptist policy regarding "their negro work" was "somewhat individualistic." The Baptists, he points out, "treat it much the same as another mission field, not integrating negroes with whites but providing for ministry among the negroes. Thus there apparently are many negro Southern Baptist churches, but I find no hint that the Southern Baptists are seeking to integrate negroes and whites. They do, however, provide some white leadership for negroes especially along educational lines."[33]

Included in the very detailed report on the Southern Baptist position was a quote from Guy Bellamy, Secretary of the Department of Work with Negroes, who stated, "We have no organic relationship, as they have their own churches, district associations, state and National Conventions. Our work with them is a cooperative work."[34] In intention and outcome, however, a huge difference exists between "ministry *among*" Negroes and "cooperative work" *with* Negroes.

The SBC report lists five phases of their work (teacher-missionaries in Negro colleges, Negro Centers, Negro Institutes, Scholarships for Christian workers, and Summer Student Workers). One portion of their "areas for advance" section of the report calls for a Negro Director of Evangelism

31. Ibid., 1, 5. "Resolution Concerning Schools of Higher Education." Included as the basis for this resolution were such points as the Lutheran Synodical Conference's realization of man's inhumanity to man, the Supreme Court 1954 ruling that racial segregation was unconstitutional, declarations of the Presbyterian Church and SBC that no distinction should be made "solely on the basis of race" in its program of higher education, and the Lutherans' view that exclusion based on race was not "in keeping with both Christian principle and practice."

32. Ibid., 1.

33. Ibid.

34. Ibid., 2. One can easily deduce from Bellamy's language that this Secretary for the Department of Work With Negroes was himself not a Negro. Bellamy provided a detail listing of Negro workers in the department (60), of students enrolled in classes (52,196), preachers in regular classes (8,140), institutes conducted (122), enrollment of mostly ministers (7,722), extension classes held (656), enrollment—many preachers (13,976), professions of faith (1,815), and additions to churches (2,074). He adds, "We are making much progress and moving forward with our work with negroes over our whole Southern Baptist Convention. Six states have the *right, white,* man as Director, or Secretary, of the Department of Work with Negroes, in cooperation with the Home Mission Board" (emphasis mine).

who would serve "under the direction of the Department of Evangelism of the Home Missions Board."[35] Another portion calls for "Widespread cooperation" between "each church, pastor, and members of the convention" such that they would "seek opportunities for helpfulness and sharing of ideas with Negro churches, pastors and people everywhere, to the end that the Gospel might more fully be exemplified by both groups and that the Kingdom be advanced among us all."[36] The SBC saw the "work among Negroes" as soon becoming a "vital part of the missions work of every district association and every Baptist church in the state" if its constituents put it on the "same level" as other mission efforts.

An interesting addendum at the end of the SBC report points out the difference between Evangelical and mainline views on racial issues during this time period. Whereas the mainline churches at this time seem to have been moving more in the direction of integration, the Evangelical churches remained seemingly locked in a paternalistic, white-controlled, outreach-oriented, "non-organic" (i.e., segregated) relationship.

> According to some of the Negro leaders, their being members of a minority race has made it necessary, through the years, to follow white leadership. A white man that loves them and that they believe in, can lead them *farther and much faster than one of their own race.* There are some places where I would recommend Negro leaders (emphasis mine).[37]

Though no official AG response to the mainline survey currently exists in the AG archival material on racial issues, the impact of such a survey should not be minimized. That the AG took the time and, in a sense, humbled itself to reach outside the comfort zone of its own four walls to make the survey in the first place is an indication of the developing importance of the issue. How much the mainline attitudes and trends affected subsequent AG action is not clear. There is no formal indication that the AG was moved by the actions of any of these denominations, as was the case with the Lutheran Synodical Conference.[38] One can only speculate as to the weight the opinions of other denominations had on

35. Ibid.

36. Ibid.

37. Ibid.

38. The declarations of the Presbyterian Church and SBC that no distinction should be made "solely on the basis of race" were influential in shaping the Lutheran position to the point of a formal resolution.

this issue, especially in light of continued referrals and deferrals regarding the credentialing issue among and between executive ruling bodies.

BILLY GRAHAM, CATALYST

If the survey results of the mainline churches on racial issues had questionable impact on propelling the AG to a new *modus operandi* for racial issues (particularly ordination of blacks), the actions of one man certainly appear to have done the job. As Kenyon put it, "Whatever happened to that request [Gerhart's 1957 request for Harrison's ordination], an event outside the Assemblies of God would soon override all the General Presbytery discussions and actions of the previous 2 decades."[39] In 1962, Billy Graham invited Harrison to join his evangelistic team. In attendance as guests on the platform at one of the 1962 Billy Graham crusades not long after Harrison came on board were AG General Superintendent Thomas Zimmerman and the president of Bethany Bible College. Harrison recounts in his book that when they saw him there, "they turned handsprings. They shook hands, they hugged me, they slapped me on the back. 'We're so proud to have our boy on the Billy Graham team,' they chorused."[40] Two days later Zimmerman invited Harrison to headquarters at AG expense. Harrison flew down, was introduced to denominational officials, received a grand tour of the facilities, and then met with the head of the missions department. "You can write your own ticket, Bob, if you'll come and minister under our banner," he said.[41] The AG promised Harrison a large expense account to travel to places like Africa, the Caribbean, the Fiji islands, and elsewhere (Harrison noted to himself that these were all places with a large black population). Though it all sounded great to Harrison, he asked how it could be possible, though, when he was not ordained with the AG. The home missions head "inferred that this might be arranged if I would just come with the organization."[42]

Ultimately, choosing not to "lay sixty years of sin of a whole denomination" on the backs of the current AG leadership, Harrison accepted and not only obtained his ordination in 1962 and subsequent ministry opportunities within the AG, but received permission concurrently to retain his

39. Kenyon, "Black Ministers in the Assemblies of God", 11.
40. Harrison, *When God Was Black*, 92.
41. Ibid., 93.
42. Ibid.

ministry involvement with the Billy Graham team.[43] Harrison recounts his ordination as an emotional moment for him. "The very ones . . ." [who had previously denied him a ministerial license] his mother pointed out, were now the ones congratulating him. But Harrison chose not to look at the past; instead, he looked to the future and saw a "whole new day dawning."[44] He felt he was just the first of many black AG ministers to come, and that this change within the AG would also challenge other "denominations with a Jim Crow clergy" to change.[45]

Perhaps even without realizing it, in opening the doors of his own ministry to blacks, Billy Graham had served as a catalyst to propel the Assemblies of God out of their decades-long paralysis on the ordination question. As Kenyon points out, though Harrison's ordination was not the first in the AG, it was clearly the most visible. In a "very definite sense," says Kenyon, Harrison broke the "color line" within the Assemblies; his "high visibility ordination and ministry effectively ended once and for all the ongoing ambiguities of the General Council on the matter of inclusion of American blacks."[46] The "blessing" Wheaton and Moody had experienced for opening their door to blacks, according to Selina Kirby's 1953 letter, now waited just around the corner for the AG. Throughout the sixties and seventies, the AG took great strides to reach and accept the blacks they had previously shunned. They opened black churches, gave scholarships to qualified black students, included black history in their educational material, and met with Harrison and other black leaders in order to work together to find ways to "come to grips with the challenge of the black community."[47]

Though Harrison already had solid evidence of a powerful preaching, music, evangelistic, pastoral and missionary ministry, with his ordination breakthrough, his contribution to the AG would increase exponentially. Beginning in 1964, numerous *Pentecostal Evangel* articles about and by Harrison describe that "whole new day" Harrison spoke of. He conducted revivals across the United States and around the world, preached at the General Council in Long Beach, California (1967), corre-

43. Ibid., 94.
44. Ibid., 95.
45. Ibid.
46. Kenyon, "Black Ministers in the Assemblies of God," 11.
47. Harrison, *When God Was Black*, 95.

sponded and met repeatedly with Zimmerman and other AG officials[48] as
to how best reach America's blacks, helped prepare black-friendly guidelines for AG publications (1970), was named Consultant on Inner City
Evangelism (1972)—aligning his efforts with Foreign Missions, Home
Missions, and AG educational endeavors, pioneered a black church in
Oakland's inner city (1987), was appointed as National Representative
of Black Ministries (1990), and played a significant role in the formation of the National Black Caucus (1993)[49] and the National Black
Fellowship (1998). As well, Harrison continued to write articles motivat-
ing AG leadership and constituency to reach America's cities (1988), re-
claim black America (1991), minister to her poor and oppressed (1993),
and overcome prejudice (1998).

48. The *Pentecostal Evangel* ran articles about some of these meetings, in 1969,
1970, 1981, and 1983. Records of other such meetings (such as one in 1972 to describe
Harrison's ministry and relationship with headquarters and 1980, effectively to reach
America's blacks) are available in the AG Archives. An AG news release (November,
1972) describes Harrison's service as a consultant for and participant in inner city
evangelism and in overseas crusades for the AG. Another release (November, 1973) announces his involvement, along with other black AG pastors, in the cause of strength-
ening AG inner city ministries.

Proceedings of the Home Missions Consultative Committee (June 11–12, 1968)
describe the need, current efforts, and future plans to "get into the Negro community."
The Committee's subsequent report to the EP proposes a conference "involving negro
ministers for the purpose of counsel and the charting of a course of ministry among
the black people of our cities," the development of a scholarship program for "Negro
ministerial students" at AG schools, revision of departmental publications to make AG
literature "more acceptable by including representatives of other racial groups besides
Caucasian," and the effort to "establish rapport with independent Negro congregations." The report encourages district leadership to "make discreet contacts with Negro
churches who might desire Assemblies of God fellowship and recognition." The issues
raised in the 1968 proceedings are offered as recommendations in the 1969 meeting of
the Home Missions Committee. Upon the heels of these Home Missions meetings, the
first "Conference on Ways and Means of Reaching the Black Community" (December
15, 1969) was held. This meeting with Zimmerman and top AG leaders, initiated at the
invitation of the EP, was attended by "Seven Pentecostal Negro brethren and one lady,"
whose names are listed in the report.

49. "National Black Caucus Holds Annual Meeting in Springfield." This Caucus
serves as a think tank, rather than an official body that would pass resolutions. The
stated goal of the group included dealing with "issues of our nation and inner cities
regardless of ethnic group. Our black ministers want to be equal partners in the gospel
mandate to reach all peoples" (23). The group also worked on plans for cooperation
between the AG and COGIC, as well as recruitment of black professors and students
for AG colleges, the use of black leaders at District and General Council functions, and
a continued focus on racial reconciliation.

Harrison also came full circle regarding Bethany College. In 1996, he received the Founders Day Award, and in 2002, at the age of 73, returned to Bethany College for a ceremony dedicating a remodeled student union in his honor, as the first African American to graduate from the college. What a telling image to describe the impact Harrison had upon the AG—a remodeled building for future generations! Though in 1951 Harrison was the right man at the wrong time, he worked toward overcoming his hurt by focusing on ministry within the kingdom at large and eventually became the right man at the right time, helping the AG move from a place of "tabling" proposals and resolutions to participating with African-Americans as partners *at* the table.

Not long after changing its position on credentialing of African-Americans, the AG passed a resolution on civil rights (1965) and also began more fully to address the question of social concern and evangelistic strategy with its "Statement of The General Presbytery of the Assemblies of God Regarding Social Concern," (1968). Additional related resolutions were passed regarding racism and the use of black ministers, in 1989 and 1995, respectively.

Though statements are important, follow-through in the form of real action was not always forthcoming. As Gary McGee noted, "At the same time the [1968] Council met, however, America's major cities were seething with racial discontent . . . Yet no agency within the denomination was added to work toward those ends [the 1965 Civil Rights Resolution]. White Pentecostals rarely became involved in any prophetic witness against the injustices of the prevailing culture . . . Twenty-five years would pass before white and black Pentecostals themselves would begin the painful process of repentance and reconciliation."[50]

CONCLUSION: MEMPHIS AND BEYOND

Bob Harrison's decade-long ordeal was the culmination in one sense of a sad and shameful chapter of Pentecostal history.[51] In another sense,

50. Gary McGee, *People of the Spirit*, 349.

51. Regarding the debate over the AG-COGIC "split," Anthea Butler ("Walls of Division") recounts the view that the white Pentecostal bodies were "uncomfortable with the relationship to the Negro Church of God in Christ, and wished to issue their own credentials separately."

Grant Wacker presents two "readings" of the problem—that of Menzies (above) and that "the whites who later organized the Assemblies of God shared minor business arrangements with COGIC but little else" (*Heaven Below*, 227). He sees a "more complex

however, it was just the beginning. Heartening indeed is the trail of effort on the part of the AG since the early sixties. However, the prejudice
and discrimination that took decades—centuries even—to build within
American society would not come down in days, weeks, months, or even
a few years.

The road to racial reconciliation, unity, and cooperation in kingdom business remains a long, hard journey. Ever since the amazing days
of racial reconciliation in 1994 known now as the "Memphis Miracle,"
many continue to ask, "What now?"[52] Some, who perhaps still experience the same sting of rejection, exclusion, or lack of opportunity that
Bob Harrison felt in 1951, remain skeptical. Others, working long and
hard on the long path of reconciliation, call loudly to move beyond "feel
good" meetings and seem more hopeful in the face of continuing signs
of progress.[53]

Whether one chooses to be optimistic or pessimistic is often determined by where one stands in the struggle. Those who stand on the
sidelines often complain the loudest at lack of progress. Those in the
trenches making real efforts know the work is hard but the rewards
worthwhile. And what holds true for racial reconciliation also applies to
other struggles, such as the ones many women feel concerning lack of
leadership opportunities within the Assemblies of God. In many ways the
story of women's struggles is the same as black Pentecostals: strong participation in the early years of the movement, then a pulling back from
being regarded as full partners in the work (perhaps due to the influence
of the NAE), and then some measure of redress within recent years in the
attempt to make real changes within the movement.

---

pattern" of initial "unselfconscious mixing," followed by whites pulling away when they
"stopped to think about what was happening," blacks then following suit, and then the
failure of pentecostal culture "to provide a sustained theology of racial reconciliation
for whites and blacks alike" (227).

52. Maempa, "Interracial Conference Unites Major Pentecostal Denominations,"
24, 26.

53. Morgan, "Pentecostals," 87. For examples, see the efforts of the AG National
Black Fellowship founded in 1998 (nbfag.org), see the AG's 1999 "Spiritual Life Report"
calling for the repair of past racial barriers; the 2000 story of the AG Cornerstone
Church, the "most racially diverse church in our city," revitalizing downtown Fresno;
the 2002/2003 stories of First Christian AG in Cincinnati's efforts at racial reconciliation in their city; the 2004 joint AG-COGIC project of the School of Urban Missions,
and the 2005 Intercultural Ministries report presented at the AG General Council.

What remains, however, is to learn from the past in order to avoid similar mistakes in the present, and to continue to set out specific strategies for the future.[54] AG leadership and constituency must fight the paralysis that often comes from valuing societal norms over Scripture, and must continue to commit to real action—such as its cooperative effort now with the Church of God in Christ for the School of Urban Missions—instead of making empty resolutions, deferring to the "other guy" to take care of business, or postponing decisions indefinitely. May the AG of the future preempt being embarrassed (by people the likes of Billy Graham) into action on issues it knows are biblically right.

BIBLIOGRAPHY

Bentley, William H. *The National Black Evangelical Association: Reflections on the Evolution of a Concept of Ministry*. N.p.: NBEA, 1974.

Bergstrom, R. J. (NY-NJ District Sec.-Treas.). Cross Reference Sheet to Letter (Re: Bruce Gibson's reinstatement). AG Archive, 26 February 1952.

Brandt, R. L. "Survey and Summary of Work Among the Negroes." AG Archive, 1958.

Butler, Anthea. "Walls of Division: Racism's Role in Pentecostal History." Paper presented to the 24th Annual Meeting of the Society for Pentecostal Studies, Wheaton College, Wheaton, IL, 1994.

"Church Unit Invites Negroes to Join." Atlantic City, N.J. Newspaper, 1959. Clipping in AG Archive.

"Conference on Ways and Means of Reaching the Black Community." AG Archive, 1969.

General Presbytery Minutes. "Ordination of Colored Brethren." AG Archive, 1939.

Gohr, Glenn. "For Such a Time as This: The Story of Evangelist Bob Harrison." *Assemblies of God Heritage* (2004) 5–11.

Harrison, Robert. *When God Was Black*. Canoga Park, CA: Bob Harrison Ministries International, 1978.

Home Missions Consultative Committee. "Proceedings (Re: Negro ministry)." AG Archive, 1968.

Kenyon, Howard N. "Black Ministers in the Assemblies of God." *Assemblies of God Heritage* 7.1 (1987) 10–13, 20.

Maempa, John. "Interracial Conference Unites Major Pentecostal Denominations." *The Pentecostal Evangel* (December 11, 1994) 24, 26.

McGee, Gary B. *People of the Spirit: The Assemblies of God*. Springfield, MO: Gospel, 2004.

Menzies, William W. *Anointed to Serve: The Story of the Assemblies of God*. Springfield, MO: Gospel, 1971.

54. See Synan, "The Future."

Morgan, Timothy C. "Pentecostals: Youth are Key in Moving Past 'Feel Good' Reconciliation." *Christianity Today* (November 11, 1996) 87. Available online as "Pentecostals: Youth Leaders Launch Racial Reconciliation Network," http://www.ctlibrary.com/ct/1996/november11/6td087.html (accessed February 9, 2006).

"National Black Caucus Holds Annual Meeting in Springfield." *The Pentecostal Evangel* (1996) 23–24.

"National Black Fellowship Formed." *The Pentecostal Evangel* (1991) 29.

National Black Fellowship of the Assemblies of God. Web site http://www.nbfag.org (accessed February 14, 2006).

Olena, Lois E. "I'm Sorry, My Brother." In *We've Come This Far: Reflections on the Pentecostal Tradition and Racial Reconciliation,* edited by Byron D. Klaus, 130–52. Springfield, MO: Assemblies of God Theological Seminary, 2007.

Peterson, Bartlett. Letter to R. J. Carlson (June 30, 1961). Flower Pentecostal Heritage Center Archive Collection.

Robeck, Cecil M., Jr. "The Past: Historical Roots of Racial Unity and Division in American Pentecostalism." Paper presented at the October 1994 "Memphis Miracle" Meeting. *Pentecostal-Charismatic Theological Inquiry International,* http://www.pctii.org/cyberj/cyberj14/robeck.html (accessed March 3, 2006).

"Spiritual Life Report." 48th General Council, August 10–13, 1999, Orlando, Florida. *AG.org* web site, http://www.ag.org/top/events/General_Council_1999/19990811_sptl_life_rpt.cfm (accessed February 14, 2006).

Synan, Vinson. "The Future: A Strategy for Reconciliation." Paper presented at the October 1994 "Memphis Miracle" Meeting. *Pentecostal-Charismatic Theological Inquiry International,* http://www.pctii.org/cyberj/cyberj14/robeck.html (accessed March 2, 2006).

Trimmer, Victor. Letter to Mainline and Evangelical Denominations (Re: "determining the organic relationship of the negro work to your denomination"). AG Archive, October 3, 1957.

Wacker, Grant. *Heaven Below: Early Pentecostals and American Culture.* Cambridge, MA: Harvard University Press, 2001.

6

From Forbidden Fire to a Different Spirit

A Pentecostal Approach to Interfaith
Forgiveness and Reconciliation

Tony Richie[1]

I recently participated in an especially fruitful interfaith dialogue that produced a cooperative statement containing several descriptive suggestions about the nature of faith. Dialoguers admitted that "religion has often been used, rather misused, to shed blood, spread bigotry, and defend divisive and discriminatory sociopolitical practices." This is sad, but all too true. They also insisted, however, on the "necessity and usefulness" of inter-religious dialogue "for promoting peace, harmony and conflict-transformation" in our world today.[2] This, I think, is also true. I am

1. A shorter version of this paper was presented at the Congress on World Religions (Montreal, Canada, September 14, 2006) on an ecumenical panel addressing interreligious relations after September 11, 2001, and an expanded version appeared as "Healing Fire from Heaven: A Wesleyan-Pentecostal Approach to Interfaith Forgiveness and Reconciliation."

2. "Report from Inter-Religious Consultation." This important dialogue event was

therefore both challenged and encouraged at the present opportunity to wrestle through these issues with religious others by focusing on themes of forgiveness and reconciliation among the religions. I do this from my perspective as a Wesleyan/Pentecostal Christian.

EXPLORING PENTECOSTAL VALUES

Pentecostal Christians share much with most other Christians, but also have some unique perspectives that inform their views on forgiveness and reconciliation among the religions. A selection of their perspectives follows.

Extinguishing the Forbidden Fire of Sectarian Strife

In the context of sectarian strife, full-blown religious and racial prejudice and tension were evident between Jews and Samaritans. Two of Jesus' disciples desired to call fire down from heaven to consume their competitors. Jesus firmly forbade them. Some ancient manuscripts added an explanatory comment from Jesus that "You do not know what kind of spirit you are of, for the Son of Man did not come to destroy men's lives, but to save them" (Luke 9:56, NIV margin). Craig Evans opined that, while the addition "is probably inauthentic," "it certainly captures the essential point of the passage." According to Evans, the episode "portrays a loving and gracious Lord who does not seek vengeance."[3] Jesus wills forgiveness and reconciliation among rival religions, and the Spirit he imparts to his disciples wills in the same way. With its appreciation for pneumatological nuances, Pentecostal theology and spirituality ought to guide in the same direction.

Assessing the Spirit's person and work as counter to interreligious conflict is consistent with the Johannine connection between Jesus' breathing of the Spirit upon his disciples and his commissioning of them for the ministry of forgiveness (John 20:21–23). While Pentecostals tend to focus on how this biblical symbol fits with our focus on distinct works of the Spirit, pneumatological intimacy with the ministry of forgiveness is nonetheless affirmed.[4] Those who receive the Spirit are empowered for

---

organized by the Pontifical Council for Interreligious Dialogue, Vatican City, and the Interreligious Relations & Dialogue of the World Council of Churches, Geneva.

3. Evans, *Luke*, 162.

4. Thomas, *The Spirit of the New Testament*, 171–73.

forgiveness and reconciliation in fulfillment of the atoning work of Christ. Christ imparts the Spirit to facilitate forgiveness among human beings. Thus, Pentecostal accent on pneumatology should lead Pentecostals to become agents of forgiveness operating under the Spirit's anointing. Though John 20:21–23 has been traditionally, and no doubt correctly, interpreted in the context of Christian evangelistic witness, I see no reason to restrict it from interreligious relations as well. Is not the Spirit who empowers for forgiveness pleased whenever and wherever the virtue of forgiveness is honestly applied?

Pentecostals, as Harvey Cox has aptly described them, are enamored with "fire from heaven."[5] Following Scripture, Pentecostals speak of baptism with the Spirit and with fire, and frequently use fire as a metaphor for intense spiritual experience and fervor (cf. Matt. 3:11–12). The destructive fire of sectarian strife is forbidden. Unfortunately, as Pentecostal ecumenist and historian Mel Robeck sadly shows, after the religiously ecumenical and racially open age of the first few years of the modern Pentecostal movement, this understanding was deliberately discarded in a grave act of disobedience to the Spirit's leading.[6]

I call upon Pentecostals to identify religious violence of any kind, by any party, as inconsistent with the Spirit of Christ and of Pentecost, which they claim as their ecclesial heritage in the Christian family of faith. I also call upon Pentecostals to promote procedures or programs of justice and peace among the religions with the same kind of faith and fervor that they pursue Christian evangelism and Pentecostal experience. Only then can they correctly answer the question based upon Jesus' descriptive statement: "What kind of Spirit are we of?"

Extending Divine Healing

Divine healing for the body and deliverance from the oppressive demonic realm remain important and intrinsic values of the Pentecostal faith. I suggest that such healing and deliverance extend beyond the physical and emotional to include the institutional, specifically, wellness and wholeness in human relationships. This welds well with Latino Pentecostal theologian Juan Sepuœlveda's description of the Pentecostal community

5. Cox, *Fire from Heaven.*

6. Robeck, *The Azusa Street Mission,* 313–25. I have argued elsewhere ("Unity of the Spirit") that Pentecostalism has an inherent ecumenical and inclusivist impulse that has been artificially stifled.

of faith as a place of "enormous curative or healing efficacy."[7] The context clearly suggests that he perceives this *curative or healing* power to extend beyond the physical to emotional and social realms. I insist that it includes relations among the world religions as well.[8]

Pentecostal educator and scholar Cheryl Johns concluded that Pentecostals are not only capable of but actually conducive to "conscientization" among marginalized masses of oppressed peoples. Conscientization is "a process whereby persons become aware of the socio-cultural reality which shapes their lives and their ability to transform that reality."[9] Pentecostals are becoming more aware of and more actively involved in social and institutional ministries as an authentic extension and application of healing. Johns states, "Despite its tendencies toward emphasizing personal experience over social witness, there is potential within Pentecostal-charismatic circles for a radical witness of the meaning of Pentecost for the world in which there is exhibited justice, peace, dialogue and authentic self-giving love and in which there is no oppressed-oppressor distinction."[10]

The time has come for Pentecostals to address our social and institutional relationships with other religions.

Pentecostal theologian of religions, Amos Yong, argues that a distinguishing characteristic of Pentecostalism is its multidimensional or holistic view of salvation. Personal, familial, ecclesial, material, social,

---

7. Sepuœlveda, "Reflections on the Pentecostal Contribution," 102.

8. The account of Abraham and Abimelech in Gen 20 is an emphatic example of a dynamic interplay of healing and forgiveness in an interreligious context. Origen points out that Abimelech acted very differently from Pharaoh in a similar situation (Gen 12), even describing Abimelech as pure of heart and virtuous by comparison. Origen argued that God vindicates Abimelech as a representative of "the studious and wise men of the world" and a philosophical, pious, ethical, and moral man. The only reserve is in waiting for the coming of Christ as the promised redeemer. The healing of his harem, which God had struck with barrenness, suggested to Origen soteriological implications. See Sheridan (ed.), *Genesis 12–50*, 85. Another example includes Jesus' healing of the man born blind (John 9:1–41). The healing involved both physical and spiritual blindness. This man of Jewish faith did not know even Jesus' name, but developed faith ultimately through a series of enigmatic encounters with Jesus thereby demonstrating, among other things, God's glory and gracious forgiveness. However, an important element is that the lack of healing, physical or spiritual, of the synagogue investigative panel prevented interpersonal reconciliation, resulting instead in multilayered experiences of expulsion and alienation. See Aker, "John," 61–64.

9. Johns, *Pentecostal Formation*, 13.

10. Ibid., 81.

cosmic, and eschatological facets of salvation are therefore included in a full-orbed Pentecostal soteriology.[11] Yong advances considerably beyond a traditional focus upon individual experience; yet remains consistent with early Pentecostals. In Pentecostal parlance, this implies that *full gospel* believers ought to grapple with how our relations with religious others are affected by our relationship with God. This, I believe, includes attitudes and expressions of forgiveness and reconciliation among the religions.

Possible Directions for Forgiveness and Reconciliation

Pentecostals demonstrate their concern for the personal salvation and social needs of individuals. Involvement in social organizations is an authentic extension of Pentecostal theology and spirituality. Therefore, Pentecostals' concern for personal salvation and social salvation can apply to the social problem of impaired interreligious relations. I wish to apply institutionally what Pentecostals already endeavor to put into practice individually.

My understanding of contemporary theology of religions is shaped by the thought of John Wesley and the subsequent Wesleyan theological tradition.[12] Applying a distinctively Pentecostalized Wesleyan soteriology, Pentecostal New Testament scholar and theologian Hollis Gause wrote of the way of salvation (*via salutis* vis-à-vis *ordo salutis*) as a journey involving justification from sin and adoption into the divine family, repentance for sin, regeneration, and sanctification—all issuing in a Spirit-filled and Spirit-led life of love toward God and others. He particularly stressed "the unity of redemptive experiences."[13] Individual salvation cannot be complete without relational and social application. Experiencing God's love for each of us overflows into our love for each other. This, of course, must now be understood to include relations with religious others. I am not promoting soteriological universalism, but rather advocating for application of Christian themes of forgiveness and reconciliation to interpersonal and institutional relationships.

Christians, including Pentecostals, who expect justification or forgiveness should also forgive others (Eph 4:32; Col 3:13). This applies not

---

11. Yong, *The Spirit Poured Out*, 91–98.

12. See Richie, "John Wesley and Mohammed."

13. Gause, *Living in the Spirit*, Introduction and 125–36.

only individually but institutionally. Pentecostals need to enter into dialogue with representatives of other religious groups, particularly where there is a history of giving and receiving offense. The Christian message and ministry of reconciliation, though firmly focused in evangelistic outreach through the gospel of Christ (2 Cor 5:11–21), ought never to exclude any part of a process that promotes peace between all peoples (Rom 12:18; Heb 12:14).[14]

Although peace may not be attained, forgiveness and reconciliation among the religions may at the least reduce violence. In some way, interreligious forgiveness and reconciliation also encourage cooperative efforts on humanitarian causes. Moreover, I hope that one day, people of various faiths learn to live in mutual respect and appreciation for one another. An attitude of trust must replace the politics of suspicion if we are to experience genuine forgiveness and reconciliation. This interreligious trust will undoubtedly be broadened and deepened through probationary encounters and over a prolonged length of time lead to an enduring trust.

Pentecostals stress the importance of forgiveness in the context of repentance. My Wesleyan-Pentecostal denomination, the Church of God (Cleveland, TN USA), states in its formal *Declaration of Faith* that "all have sinned and come short of the glory of God and that repentance is commanded of God for all and necessary for forgiveness of sins."[15] Its original "Teachings" also stressed "Restitution where possible."[16] These two statements affirm that the doctrine of sin releases no one from culpability and responsibility. The importance of making wrongs right serves as an expression of true repentance. However, I concede that there are limitations in undoing the effects of wrongful actions. Deeds done cannot be undone. Nevertheless, I feel obligated to insist that forgiveness and reconciliation in interreligious relationships requires repentance on the part of all parties implicated. *Repentance (metanoia)* implies not only an

---

14. A worthy investigation involves the sequence of forgiveness and reconciliation. Does forgiveness always or necessarily precede and therefore lead to reconciliation? While this sequence may occur at a personal and/or practical level, theologically and experientially *Christian* forgiveness flows out of having been forgiven *in Christ,* as indicated by the biblical texts in the above paragraph (esp. Eph 4:32 and Col 3:13). See Adams and Stamps, "Ephesians," 1070. Interestingly, when Christians and non-Christians are entering reconciled relationships both sequences may occur simultaneously in the various participants.

15. Conn, *Like a Mighty Army*, 337.

16. Ibid., 139.

awareness of wrongdoing and regret for it, but also a willingness to make radical changes in one's behavior. The test for genuine repentance is demonstrated in transformation of behavior (Matt 3:8).[17] I reject as inadequate any version of interfaith forgiveness and interreligious reconciliation that does not give appropriate attention to the importance of repentance.

We cannot reasonably expect non-Christians to repent in the Christian sense before offering them forgiveness and entering into reconciled relations with them. Rather, I suggest that we and they grant forgiveness in a practical and relational way for any wrongs we have done to each other. At the very least, this requires cessation of sinful behavior. Even better, it leads to benevolent and positive actions toward the religious other. As to what constitutes *sinful behavior* or *benevolent and positive actions*, I am confident that true dialogue in the best tradition of each religion can find common ground when economical and political agendas are interpreted in the light of the values of faith. I am sure that themes of justice and peace will be in the forefront of each faith's value system. I am persuaded that religion can and should be a force for peace rather than a weapon of war.

From a Wesleyan-Pentecostal perspective, forgiveness and reconciliation among the religions is a process whereby forgiveness occurs as a result of repentance and reconciliation occurs as a fruit of forgiveness. In addition, forgiveness and reconciliation are acts of faith that occur in the context of God's grace (cf. Eph 2:8–9). Ultimately, forgiveness and reconciliation will only be successful when Pentecostals allow God to work through them.

I therefore urge Christians in general and Pentecostal Christians in particular to apply our tradition of grace and faith to interreligious forgiveness and reconciliation. Authentic reciprocity is essential for forgiveness and reconciliation. Let us lead the way by seeking forgiveness from others and in turn, being willing to grant forgiveness.

ENGAGING ECUMENICAL VOICES

The desire to develop a distinctively Wesleyan-Pentecostal approach to forgiveness and reconciliation among the religions does not turn inward but outward. Hearing what others think and speak about forgiveness and reconciliation among the religions is essential if Pentecostals are to effectively engage and be engaged by religious others.

17. See Arrington, *Christian Doctrine*, 202.

Integrating Apparently Competing Commitments

One example of integration is the monograph entitled *Forgiveness and Reconciliation,* which was the product of a conference of public policy-makers and theologians at the close of the twentieth century.[18] Following a *foreword* by Archbishop Desmond Tutu, the authors examined the complex interrelatedness and importance of the role of religion and themes of forgiveness and reconciliation, beyond traditional areas of religion *per se* and into other sectors of contemporary life such as political, sociological, anthropological and psychological.

Another example of integration is the work of Rodney L. Petersen. He sought to locate the ontological foundation for forgiveness in Christian theology, look at its language within the context of the church, and sketch ways by which it can cross confessional boundaries.[19] He skillfully surveys the theological history, ideology, and terminology of Christian forgiveness, pushing beyond talk to show how forgiveness looks in the real-life practical experience of human relations. I wish to utilize several of Petersen's ideas for further dialogue.

Petersen argues that forgiveness reaches deeper than a shallow "transactional relation." He refers to the distortion of the divine image in humans to recognize that "each of us individually and corporately is in need of forgiveness and restoration."[20] Petersen stresses the life and teaching of Jesus as "the paradigmatic solution to the pervasive nature of violence" and an ultimate refutation of any attempts to arrive at inexpensive and therefore valueless forgiveness. Jesus demonstrates the kind of power that decisively "breaks the cycle of violence" and makes available the power of the Holy Spirit, "God's power in us and to us" to make forgiveness and reconciliation efficacious.[21] Petersen avoids the degeneration of forgiveness and reconciliation into mere conflict management. He candidly confesses, "forgiveness certainly takes place outside of Christian circles." Further, he does not hesitate to affirm the "universal significance" of the death and resurrection of Jesus of Nazareth for forgiveness. Petersen suggests that in some mysterious way those of other religions

---

18. Helmick and Petersen (eds.), *Forgiveness and Reconciliation.*
19. Petersen, "A Theology of Forgiveness."
20. Ibid., 14.
21. Ibid., 15–16.

"correspond to the true Light" of Jesus Christ.[22] In this way, he opens the door for genuine interfaith forgiveness.

As a Wesleyan/Pentecostal Christian, I find myself unable to experience or even understand forgiveness apart from the Lord Jesus Christ and I am fully persuaded that the Spirit of Christ propels me toward interfaith forgiveness. Accordingly, I inescapably conclude that the Spirit of Christ works in both Christians and non-Christians to inspire forgiveness. This opens me up to all kinds of claims and counterclaims. Some Christians will think that I am compromising Christ. Other Christians will think that I am holding on to a narrow Christology. And some non-Christians may be understandably offended at the subtle suggestion that Christ is somehow at work in them.

Regardless of others' opinions, I take the position that recognizes Christ at work among all to inspire forgiveness, which enlarges the lordship of Christ. Similarly, a position that sells out Christ's absoluteness and uniqueness in favor of interfaith coziness is left with something considerably less than the Christian faith. Therefore, as a Pentecostal Christian, I can affirm that forgiveness is inseparable from Christ and his Spirit, but still contend that "Christian" forgiveness occurs outside of Christianity.[23]

Deeply Practicing Real Religion

Miroslav Volf demonstrated decisively that Christianity, when "deeply practiced," does not foster violence. He insightfully examined the intricacies of forgiveness and justice to arrive at a view in which forgiveness leads to reconciliatory embrace of the other. His theology of forgiveness, reconciliation, and justice rests squarely on the model of God's action in the cross of Christ.[24] He promotes a realistic experience of justice and peace in the present age as the world yearns for fully realized eschaton. In contrast, when Christianity is stripped of its transcendent values and made subservient to some political or economic ideology, it becomes a force based upon violence. Therefore, contrary to contemporary secularizing systems, Volf called for more not less religion as the antidote to interreligious acrimony inherent in global violence.

22. Ibid., 21–22.

23. Yong's *Discerning the Spirit(s)* is the premier example of a Pentecostal approach to signs of the Spirit (or spirits) in world religions.

24. Volf, "Forgiveness, Reconciliation, and Justice."

I believe that all the major faiths, when *practiced deeply*, foster justice, peace, forgiveness, and reconciliation rather than violence. Accordingly, I will examine three concepts that demonstrate how this can occur: fellowship, censorship, and partnership.

Fellowship

C. S. Lewis suggests "in the present state of divided Christendom, those who are at the heart of each division are all closer to one another than those who are at the fringes." He carries this magnanimous sentiment "beyond the borders of Christianity." Lewis exclaims, "[H]ow much more one has in common with a *real* Jew or Muslim than with a wretched liberalising, occidentalised specimen of the same categories."[25] At the heart of all shared devotion and piety is a commonality or connectedness that extends beyond divisions of sectarianism.

In a Christian sense, fellowship (*koinonia*) means more than friendship. It is a sharing together and a participation in divinely ordained unity. This suggests that, when those of other faiths come together for the cause of justice and peace, they may become more than representatives of different faiths who happen to be sitting at the same table talking about the same subject. In a special sense, participants in the same devout and pious impulse toward forgiveness and reconciliation share in what God has placed within them.

Censorship

I had the following pastoral encounter with an ex-member and local leader of the Ku Klux Klan.[26] One of my parishioners, now a committed Christian gentleman, tried to convince me that "the Klan had not been all bad;" in fact, "it did a lot of good," helping people no one else would help. When speaking with him, I felt a pastoral responsibility to challenge these seemingly positive activities of the Klan to ensure that my comments would not show any approval of such an evil organization. Without compromise, I had to contest any implicit affirmation of an empire of hate. If I made an affirmative comment with tacit pastoral approval, it might encourage certain members of this man's family or friends to follow his leadership.

---

25. Lewis, *Letters to an American Lady*. Italics are original.
26. On the KKK see O'Donnell (ed.), *Ku Klux Klan*.

I imagine a parallel relationship between the world religions and the radical groups within them. Religious leaders who share a desire for justice and peace must not give the slightest hint of approval for the actions of terrorist groups. Silence is insufficient. Leaders must act courageously to publicly and clearly condemn everything terrorists do. The slightest suggestion that religious leaders empathize with terrorist acts, encourages recruits to join their cause. As in Pauline theology, we should not "give the devil a foothold" (Eph 4:27).

Partnership

Archbishop's Desmond Tutu engaged in a fruitful struggle in the political and societal reconstruction of post-apartheid South Africa.[27] In the United States, some probably would have started screaming about the "separation of church and state." Although I support the American Constitution's doctrine of the separation of church and state, I believe religious and political organizations can work together to achieve shared goals of justice and peace.

Dimensioning Dynamics of the Holy Spirit

Stanley S. Harakas argued for a sense of mystery and paradox in theology that carefully sustains opposite poles of truth. Applying this model enabled him to articulate a dynamic theology of multidimensional forgiveness and reconciliation extending to venues beyond his ecclesial boundaries.[28] I suggest Pentecostals may best engage his thought via pneumatology.

First, I appreciate Harakas for stressing that "the redemptive work of Jesus is realized, increases, and bears fruit in the Holy Spirit." He avoided the error of so many who view the Holy Spirit as some sort of extra or "add on," almost a divine afterthought, rather than an essential agent in Christian redemption (2 Thess 2:13–14). Second, I heartily agree that "the forgiving action of the Holy Spirit appears not to be limited to sacramental and pastoral practice." Harakas generously expanded pneumatology beyond the borders of a priestly caste into the worshiping community. The Holy Spirit works freely and fully in all willing saints because the Spirit is poured out on all people (Acts 2:17). Third, I affirm Harakas's insistence that the Holy Spirit makes the present dimension of forgiveness

---

27. See Tutu, *Forgiveness and Reconciliation*, ix–xiii.
28. Harakas, "Forgiveness and Reconciliation."

real, "concretely and specifically in the Sacrament of Holy Confession, and in a more diffused manner in the whole of life" (Rom 8:2).[29] I wish to affirm and expand on the last point in regard to "the present dimension" of the Holy Spirit's work "in a more diffused manner in the whole of life."

Harakas's model of the Spirit's work in the present age posits a dynamic approach to forgiveness. So also, Amos Yong proposes that the Pentecostal doctrine of baptism in the Spirit presupposes salvation in dynamic terms. The process and crisis experience work together in dynamic and multidimensional redemption.[30] Salvation, including forgiveness and reconciliation, has several levels of reality and verity. Therefore, Christians may without contradiction consider the church the divinely ordained and ordered community of God's saving-forgiving-reconciling activity along with religious others on a journey of joint participation. Pentecostal theologian Frank D. Macchia writes that the church remains the central locus of the Kingdom, but also exists as "a loving fellow traveler with the world's religions," even "while pointing them to the superiority of Christ."[31]

If forgiveness and reconciliation are dynamic and multidimensional, what does this mean for interreligious relations? First, note what it does *not* mean. It does not mean that we should lose respect for the radical differences of the religions. Competing religions hold vastly different worldviews that cannot and should not be minimized. They do not understand or experience spirituality in the same manner. Second, it *does* mean that

29. Ibid., 63, 64, and 67.

30. Yong, *The Spirit Poured Out*, 98–109. Yong suggested that Christian salvation includes personal, familial, ecclesial, material, social, cosmic, and eschatological dimensions, 91–98. Regarding interfaith forgiveness and reconciliation, I suggest highlighting several dimensions: *individual, familial, organizational, social,* and *political.* There may even be a progression of experiencing forgiveness and reconciliation. Possibly, as individuals of different faiths encounter each other in a forgiving environment and reconciling context then it may become more feasible for families affected by interreligious conflict to move forward. Certainly religious organizations should work cooperatively in partnership for mutual forgiveness and reconciliation among themselves, and may therefore be empowered to more effectively bring the same into the broader society where seeds of discord and mistrust also grow (oddly enough, even among those who may not even be committed devotees of either, i.e., as a kind of cultural prejudice). Further, when individuals, families, institutions, and societies are in better relationship, that is, in a relationship of forgiveness and reconciliation, they cooperate more effectively as partners for accomplishing common goals such as peace or poverty or by responding to conditions including inequality, loss of liberty, or various tragedies.

31. Macchia, *Baptized in the Spirit*, 188.

we should learn respect for the possibility that religious others experience divine encounter on some plane. If forgiveness and reconciliation are pneumatologically dynamic and multidimensional, we should not be surprised to discover that at least on some level the Holy Spirit is working to bring all people to the fullness of the humanity they are created to enjoy, all to the exhibition of God's glory. Nevertheless, the fullness of God's self-revelation in Jesus Christ doubtless tends to the conclusion that Christ is the eventual and eternal goal of all human faith and devotion (cf. John 1:14, 18; Eph 1:10).

If the above is accurate, then one very positive and practical result follows. Forgiveness and reconciliation between the religions is not something that one or the other of the religions grants to others out of arrogant superiority or benevolent humility, but out of a joint appreciation of a shared divine impulse. Forgiveness and reconciliation are always from, of, and for God. Relationally, religious others are lifted above diplomacy into intimacy. Notably, Jesus' profound statement on worship and worshipers "in spirit and in truth" so precious to the Pentecostal tradition occurred in a context of interreligious dialogue (John 4:23–24). Offering and receiving forgiveness and reconciliation with religious others is an exalted act of worship.

CONCLUSION

As a Wesleyan-Pentecostal Christian desirous of interreligious forgiveness and reconciliation, I am pleased that, at the most recent biennial International General Assembly of the Church of God (Cleveland, TN), my denomination, published a *Resolution* regarding war and violence in the Middle East. As a step in the right direction, I close with its inclusion. Before reading, please note that, in spite of a history of strong support for Israel, which is indeed undiminished, a move is also made to recognize others and offer humanitarian aid to all. I am hopeful that this indicates a broadening of the horizon of concern for all peoples. If so, this would suggest interfaith forgiveness and inter-religious reconciliation are in order. Perhaps most importantly, the entire document is set in the context of prayer for peace. Perhaps the most important act for peace may indeed be persevering prayer to "the God of peace" to be with us all (Rom 15:33).

RESOLUTION OF PRAYER FOR THE CURRENT CRISIS IN THE MIDDLE EAST

WHEREAS "Proclaiming the Power of Pentecost" is the theme chosen for the 71st Church of God International General Assembly; and

WHEREAS during this, the 71st International General Assembly, we are witnessing an escalation of conflict and acts of terrorism in the Middle East; and

WHEREAS the unfortunate nature of war involves the loss of innocent life; and

WHEREAS the call to pray for the peace of Jerusalem is explicitly stated in God's Word (Psalm 122:6); and

WHEREAS as prayer was timely and appropriate at the time of the Scriptural injunction, it is more necessary now as we observe the carnage and destruction of human life and property, and the suffering of women and children of both Jews and other peoples; now therefore,

BE IT RESOLVED that the international family of the Church of God reaffirms the previous resolutions on prayer for the peace of Jerusalem; and

BE IT FURTHER RESOLVED that the Church of God around the world pray that this conflict will end, and peace will come to Israel and the Middle East; and

BE IT FINALLY RESOLVED that humanitarian support be given to those suffering on all sides of the conflict, where possible.[32]

BIBLIOGRAPHY

Adams, J. Wesley, and Donald C. Stamps. "Ephesians." In *Full Life Bible Commentary to the New Testament: An International Commentary for Spirit-filled Christians*, edited by French L. Arrington and Roger Stronstad, 1019–86. Grand Rapids: Zondervan, 1999.

Aker, Benny C. "John." In *Full Life Bible Commentary to the New Testament: An International Commentary for Spirit-filled Christians*, edited by French L. Arrington and Roger Stronstad, 1–118. Grand Rapids: Zondervan, 1999.

32. Resolution of the 71st International General Assembly.

Arrington, French L. *Christian Doctrine: A Pentecostal Perspective.* Vol. 2. Cleveland, TN: Pathway, 1993.

Conn, Charles W. *Like a Mighty Army: A History of the Church of God 1886–1996.* Cleveland, TN: Pathway, 2008.

Cox, Harvey Gallagher. *Fire from Heaven: The Rise of Pentecostal Spirituality and the Reshaping of Religion in the Twenty-First Century.* New York: Addison-Wesley, 1995.

Evans, Craig A. *Luke.* New International Biblical Commentary 3. Peabody, MA: Hendrickson, 1990.

Gause, R. Hollis. *Living in the Spirit: The Way of Salvation.* Cleveland, TN: Pathway, 1980.

Harakas, Stanley S. "Forgiveness and Reconciliation: An Orthodox Perspective." In *Forgiveness and Reconciliation: Religion, Public Policy and Conflict Transformation,* edited by Raymond G. Helmick and Rodney L. Petersen, 51–80. Radnor, PA: Templeton Foundation Press, 2001.

Helmick, Raymond G., and Rodney L. Petersen, editors. *Forgiveness and Reconciliation: Religion, Public Policy and Conflict Transformation.* Radnor, PA: Templeton Foundation Press, 2001.

Johns, Cheryl Bridges. *Pentecostal Formation: A Pedagogy among the Oppressed.* Journal for Pentecostal Theology Series 2. Sheffield, UK: Sheffield Academic, 1993.

Lewis, C. S. *Letters to an American Lady.* Edited by Clyde S. Kilby. Grand Rapids: Eerdmans, 1967.

Macchia, Frank D. *Baptized in the Spirit: A Global Pentecostal Theology.* Grand Rapids: Zondervan, 2006.

O'Donnell, Patrick, editor. *Ku Klux Klan: America's First Terrorists Exposed: The Rebirth of the Strange Society of Blood and Death.* Shadow History of the United States 1. West Orange, NJ: Idea Men, 2006.

Petersen, Rodeny L. "A Theology of Forgiveness: Terminology, Rhetoric, and the Dialectic of Interfaith Relationships." In *Forgiveness and Reconciliation: Religion, Public Policy and Conflict Transformation,* edited by Raymond G. Helmick and Rodney L. Petersen, 3–26. Radnor, PA: Templeton Foundation Press, 2001.

"Report from Inter-Religious Consultation on 'Conversion—Assessing the Reality.'" Lariano, Italy, May 12–16, 2006.

Resolution of the 71st International General Assembly of the Church of God (Cleveland, TN). July 24–28, 2006.

Richie, Tony. "Healing Fire from Heaven: A Wesleyan-Pentecostal Approach to Interfaith Forgiveness and Reconciliation." *Wesleyan Theological Journal* 42:2 (2007) 136–54.

———. "John Wesley and Mohammed: A Contemporary Inquiry Concerning Islam." *The Asbury Theological Journal* 58:2 (2003) 79–99.

———. "'The Unity of the Spirit': Are Pentecostals Inherently Ecumenicists and Inclusivists?" *Journal of the European Pentecostal Theology Association* 26.1 (2006) 21–37.

Robeck, Cecil M. *The Azusa Street Mission and Revival: The Birth of the Global Pentecostal Movement.* Nashville: Nelson, 2006.

Sepúlveda, Juan. "Reflections on the Pentecostal Contribution to the Mission of the Church in Latin America." *Journal of Pentecostal Theology* 1 (1992) 93–108.

Sheridan, Mark, editor. *Genesis 12–50.* Ancient Christian Commentary on Scripture: Old Testament 2. Downers Grove: InterVarsity, 2002.

Thomas, John Christopher. *The Spirit of the New Testament.* Leiden: Deo, 2005.

Tutu, Desmond. "Foreword." In *Forgiveness and Reconciliation: Religion, Public Policy and Conflict Transformation*, edited by Raymond G. Helmick and Rodney L. Petersen, ix–xvi. Radnor, PA: Templeton Foundation Press, 2001.

Volf, Miroslav. "Forgiveness, Reconciliation, and Justice: A Christian Contribution to a More Peaceful Social Environment." In *Forgiveness and Reconciliation: Religion, Public Policy and Conflict Transformation*, edited by Raymond G. Helmick and Rodney L. Petersen, 27–50. Radnor, PA: Templeton Foundation Press, 2001.

Yong, Amos. *Discerning the Spirit(s): A Pentecostal-Charismatic Theology of Religions*. JPTS 20. Sheffield, UK: Sheffield Academic, 2000.

———. *The Spirit Poured Out on All Flesh: Pentecostalism and the Possibility of Global Theology*. Grand Rapids: Baker Academic, 2005.

Psychological Perspectives

7

The Psychology of Forgiveness, Reconciliation, and Restoration

Integrating Traditional and Pentecostal Theological Perspectives with Psychology

Geoffrey W. Sutton

In the last decade, a cornucopia of psychological research on interpersonal forgiveness has filled numerous journals including both mainstream scientific publications as well as those associated with Christian perspectives. Not surprisingly, theory and opinion papers of varying degrees of scholarship have appeared in a plethora of publications. Some focused on theological perspectives, some presented psychological models of forgiveness, and still others addressed the integration of Christian faith and psychology. Few studies addressed reconciliation and even fewer explored the restoration of people to society or previously held occupational or social roles following an offense. In this chapter, I review empirical research regarding forgiveness and reconciliation along with those few studies that deal with restoration. I conclude with an illustration suggesting how a psychological understanding of the processes of forgiveness, reconciliation, and restoration may interact with traditional Christian and Pentecostal perspectives in the case of a congregation faced with a revelation that their pastor has admitted to a sexual offense.

"What did you think of Pastor's apology? Can you believe it?" Unfortunately, Christians have witnessed a number of apologies from church leaders. Although pastors, like other Christians, sin in various ways, sexual sins garner the headlines and inflict psychological pain on family and friends of the pastor, the pastor's sexual partner, and those who regularly attend the church. Of course, the pastor and his or her sexual partner also experience considerable distress. Following the offense, the involved persons experience a myriad of negative emotional responses and take varied courses of action. At some point, the issues of forgiveness, reconciliation, and restoration arise for the victims. Because of the widespread ripple action of such an event, the pastor's sin and the sequellae allow for a consideration of how forgiveness, reconciliation, and restoration are different as well as an analysis of how these and related concepts might be viewed from a Pentecostal perspective.

OFFENSES: THE STARTING POINT

I recently returned from a trip to Kenya where I met survivors of the 2008 intertribal violence. Neighbors had turned on neighbors. Men wielded machetes and hacked to death those they lived with for years. A gang of men trapped a congregation in their church and set fire to them—ignoring their screams for help. Women and girls were raped in their homes and as they tried to escape. Their pain was palpable. Their emotional hurt was as visible as the scars on their bodies. I was aghast when I heard a pastor tell these distraught faces that they needed to forgive and forget!

Both a theological and psychological understanding of forgiveness begins with an appreciation of the offense or sin event. Although some people become exercised about what other people might consider *slights*, for most rational people, law and powerful social norms clarify the range of offensive events. Psychology is primarily concerned with those situations that link to observable effects on behavior.[1] Conceptually, the viola-

1. Animal research reveals analogues to human forgiveness and related concepts of reconciliation and restoration. Researchers have found evidence of reconciliation and consolation responses following aggression in gorillas and chimpanzees (e.g., Cordoni et al., "Reconciliation and Consolation"; and Palagi et al., "Possible Roles of Consolation"). Bekoff has written about the moral aspects of animal behavior including

tion of a rule produces a sense that justice must be served. As Worthington writes, victims perceive an *injustice gap* that needs to be reduced.[2]

Psychologists, like Huang and Enright as well as Worthington, have identified common emotional responses that people experience when they have been offended.[3] Those familiar with stress reactions will note the similarity. An offense is a stressor. We respond to stressors in predictable ways. In addition to the biological responses to stress (e.g., release of epinephrine, stimulation of the sympathetic nervous system), there are concomitant emotional reactions such as anger, anxiety, and hatred. Thoughts of revenge occur when we rehearse the offensive event.[4] Worthington has described this state as *unforgiveness*.[5] Many cope with the painful memories by avoiding places and objects that remind them of the offense. Of course, they avoid the offenders as well. A cold shoulder can cool down the simmering flames of anger. The relationship, or larger community, experiences an obvious rift.

THE PSYCHOLOGY OF FORGIVENESS

Forgiveness

Perhaps not surprisingly, psychologists disagree on the definition of forgiveness.[6] Most agree with a general notion that forgiveness is a process that takes time and involves letting go of the hurt, anger, and negative emotions associated with the offensive event.[7] In addition, most agree that forgiveness involves giving up on desires for revenge. Some believe forgiveness includes the cessation of avoidance responses and the development of prosocial responses toward the offender. Others view forgiveness as the accomplishment of a neutral state.

Given that offenses are emotionally stressful and produce biological effects, it is not surprising to find studies that show some benefit of

---

the forgiveness related emotion of empathy ("Animal Passions"). Dawkins's, classic, *The Selfish Gene* also contains a useful overview of analogue forgiveness in animals.

2. Worthington, *Forgiveness and Reconciliation*, 6–7.

3. Huang and Enright, "Forgiveness and Anger-Related Emotions in Taiwan," 71–79; and Worthington, *Forgiveness and Reconciliation*, 36–37

4. Worthington, *Forgiveness and Reconciliation*, 48.

5. Ibid., 49.

6. Sutton and Thomas, "Restoration, Reconciliation, and Forgiveness," 29–44.

7. McCullough et al., "Religion and Forgiveness," 394–411.

forgiveness on health.[8] Worthington has defined two types of forgiveness: emotional and decisional.[9] Worthington and Scherer reviewed the research on forgiveness and health and hypothesized ways in which an emotion-focused coping strategy would be effective in reducing the negative symptoms associated with the state of unforgiveness.[10] In a controlled lab study, Lawler- Row and her colleagues found positive associations between forgiveness and five measures of physical health, which were fewer self-reported symptoms, fewer medications used, improved quality of sleep, less fatigue, and fewer somatic complaints.[11] This line of research is still in the early stages and the models are examining the complex relationships involving types of forgiveness and variables such as religion and personality that may mediate or moderate health benefits. Even less surprising is the positive impact of forgiveness on mental health states such as depression and anxiety as well as reducing feelings of anger and hostility.

Forgiveness and Reconciliation

Only a few studies have examined the process of reconciliation. Worthington has developed a model for the reconciliation process, which includes exercises designed to enhance the process.[12] The process would appear to require trust and would likely be enhanced by forgiveness.[13] Regardless of psychologists' emphasis on separating the concepts of forgiveness and reconciliation, survey research indicates that most people view the concepts as intertwined. That is, forgiveness includes reconciliation.[14] To the extent that beliefs influence behavior, we would expect differences in progress toward forgiveness and reconciliation between those who separate the act of forgiveness from reconciliation and those who do not separate the concepts.

Following the replacement of the apartheid regime in South Africa, the government established a Truth and Reconciliation Commission

8. Worthington and Scherer. "Forgiveness Is an Emotion-Focused Coping Strategy," 385–405.

9. Worthington, *Forgiveness and Reconciliation*, 59.

10. Worthington and Scherer, "Forgiveness Is an Emotion-Focused Coping Strategy," 385–405.

11. Lawler-Row, et al., "The Role of Adult Attachment Style," 493–502.

12. Worthington, *Forgiveness and Reconciliation*, 18–19.

13. Sutton and Thomas, "Restoration, Reconciliation, and Forgiveness," 29–44.

14. Sutton and Allman, "Forgiveness, Reconciliation, and Spirituality."

(TRC). Some have praised the effort, while others offered criticisms from the perspective of justice as well as personal and community healing. For a discussion of the TRC, see the chapter by Mostert and van der Spuy in this volume. For a review of the efforts in Rwanda following the 1994 genocide, see Hittenberger and Mureithi in this volume.

Forgiveness and Community Restoration

It is easier to see how restoration differs from forgiveness than from reconciliation but writers have used the term restoration in different ways so I want to clarify the concept in this chapter. Theologically, we can speak of people being restored in their relationship with God. In Jesus' parable of the prodigal son (Luke 15:11–32), the wayward son requests a hired-hand status but his father *restores* him to sonship status. I recognize that restoration can be used as a term for the internal restorative action that people experience when they forgive someone. That inner healing can reasonably be called restoration (as in "restore my soul"). Similarly, it is meaningful to speak of restored relationships when people verbally express forgiveness and seek to reconcile. However, there is another sense of restoration that refers to the offender's status within a community. In this sense, a person's pre-offense status may be restored, not by the offended individual, but by others in the community. Likely, that new status will not be exactly the same as the one previously held; however, a person may regain a job, a professional license, a sense of respect and a feeling of being welcomed again. Sometimes the person is restored to the same position and/or the same community. At other times, the person experiences restoration to a new position and/or a new community. Because restoration is often not a literal return to things as they were before an offense, I suggest it may be better to speak of *symbolic restoration* when there is a variance from the former position.

CHRISTIAN THEOLOGY AND THE PSYCHOLOGY OF FORGIVENESS

Although forgiveness is a part of many world religions forgiveness holds a central position in Christian theology.[15] Many Christian theologians (e.g., N.T. Wright, Miroslav Volf) and Christian Psychologists (e.g.,

15. See McCullough et al., "Religion and Forgiveness," 394–411; Rye et al., "Religious Perspectives on Forgiveness," 17–40; and Exline, "Beliefs about God and Forgiveness," 131–39.

Worthington) have written about forgiveness.[16] In fact, the psychology literature on forgiveness has grown exponentially in the last two decades.[17]
Interestingly, Worthington found few empirical studies with a Christian
population when editing the *Handbook of Forgiveness* a few years ago. [18]
This discovery led to the 2008 publication of two special issues on forgiveness research in the *Journal of Psychology and Christianity* (*JPC*). *JPC*
along with the *Journal of Psychology and Theology* have provided leadership in the broader topic of the integration of psychology and Christian
theology. My focus here is on those areas where there is some evidence
for an integration of psychology and Christianity. In particular, I am
interested in the empirical findings of psychological research or at least
theoretical positions associated with research.

Forgiveness between God and Persons

Christian theologians and Christian psychologists agree that people are
in a basic sinful state before a holy God and require forgiveness of sins
through Jesus Christ, which leads to reconciliation with God and restoration of one's status from sinner to child of God. Exline identified several
a priori core beliefs that form a scriptural basis for forgiveness and examined those beliefs in a Baptist sample.[19] Based on several texts (e.g.,
Deut 4:31; 32:4; Luke 6:36) she phrased two items about God as a God
of mercy and justice and found very strong agreement with these beliefs.
Exline's respondents also strongly reported a personal need for God's forgiveness and a belief that God has forgiven all their sins. She reworded
other texts that suggest that God commands Christians to forgive (e.g.,
Matt 18:15–35; Luke 6:37). She found respondents strongly agreed with
the phrase, "God commands us to forgive others," but they less strongly
believed that, "If I do not forgive others, God will not forgive me."

In our lab, Jaimée Allman and I found that most respondents agreed
with the statement, "people must forgive others in order to obtain God's

---

16. Wright, *Surprised by Hope*, 247–48; Volf, *Free of Charge*, 127–224; and Worthington, *Forgiveness and Reconciliation*.

17. McCullough et al., "Religion and Forgiveness," 394–411.

18. Worthington, "Guest Editor's Page"; and *Handbook of Forgiveness*.

19. Wright, *Surprised by Hope*, 247–48; McMinn and Campbell, *Integrative Psychotherapy*, 37–51; and Exline, "Beliefs about God and Forgiveness," 131–39.

forgiveness."[20] Interestingly, most respondents did not see forgiveness as primarily a Christian idea.

Forgiveness between Persons

Research on interpersonal forgiveness dominates the psychological literature with a twist. The interpersonal aspect has to do with the fact that one person offends another person. Most psychologists view forgiveness as an *intrapersonal* event and view the expression of forgiveness toward another person as an aspect of reconciliation. As noted above, some recent work in our lab supports Kanz's finding that Christians view forgiveness and reconciliation as part of the same concept or at least tightly wedded concepts. [21] Exline found evidence for a belief in the mandate that Christians must forgive others. [22] She also found support for related beliefs that Christians should "turn the other cheek" and that revenge belongs to God.

Psychotherapy research indicates that people can learn to forgive others. There are several prominent models of forgiveness, which have been or could easily fit with general Christian beliefs about forgiveness. Enright and Fitzgibbons summarized research findings noting how Rodger Enright's model helps clients make changes in cognition, affect, and behavior to achieve forgiveness. [23] The model has been well publicized and was labeled the *gold standard* for therapy by Worthington, another well-known researcher.[24] DiBlasio developed a model of forgiveness based on helping clients reach a decision to forgive. Recently, DiBlasio and Benda demonstrated how the model was effective in treating Christian married couples who had hurt each other. [25] They measured change in forgiveness using the Enright Forgiveness Inventory. Worthington has intentionally shown how his model fits with Christian beliefs. Working through a five-stage process, clients learn to *REACH* (an acronym for the five stages) forgiveness. They begin by Recalling the hurt, Empathizing with the offender, giving an Altruistic gift of forgiveness, making a public

20. Sutton and Allman, "Forgiveness, Reconciliation, and Spirituality."

21. Sutton and Allman, "Forgiveness, Reconciliation, and Spirituality"; Kanz, "How do People Conceptualize and Use Forgiveness?" 174–86.

22. Exline, "Beliefs about God and Forgiveness," 131–39.

23. Enright and Fitzgibbons, *Helping Clients Forgive*; Enright, *Forgiveness Is a Choice*.

24. Worthington, *Forgiveness and Reconciliation*, 22.

25. DiBlasio and Benda, "Forgiveness Intervention with Married Couples," 150–58.

Commitment to forgive the offender, and finally working to Hold on to the act of forgiveness. His research finds support for a two-part model of decisional and emotional forgiveness, the effectiveness of the REACH model, and a scale to measure the two dimensions.[26]

Another dimension of forgiveness focuses attention on the offender. Studies have shown that Christian beliefs are associated with efforts by offenders to seek forgiveness from the persons they harmed. Bassett and his colleagues found some support for the notion that seeking forgiveness can lead to positive outcomes in a relationship.[27] At this point, few studies have examined the interaction of seeking forgiveness with other related variables.

Forgiveness of Oneself

Self-forgiveness is a controversial topic.[28] Exline found strong evidence in her sample that people believe they need God's forgiveness for themselves. Hall and Fincham reported evidence of a link between a belief in God's forgiveness of oneself and self-forgiveness.[29] In a large sample ($n = 1,423$), Toussaint and Williams found no differences among their groups of Christians (Conservative, Moderate, Liberal Protestant and Catholic) and non-Christians on the extent to which they had forgiven themselves regardless of beliefs that they had been forgiven by God.[30] They noted that their findings were similar to those of Tangney, Boone, and Dearing.[31]

Tangney, Boone, and their colleagues have studied shame and guilt, which may be relevant to understand forgiveness, especially in a Christian population. Briefly, they view shame as a general sense that one is unworthy as a person. Whereas guilt is a more narrow concept related to a moral failure associated with an identifiable wrongdoing. A pervasive sense of shame would make it harder to accept God's forgiveness but guilt related to a specific incident might make it easier to accept God's forgiveness. If this view is correct, self-forgiveness may depend on a person's sense of shame versus guilt. An alternative view suggested by Bassett et al. is that Christians, like Isaiah (Isaiah 6:5) experience a shame-like condition

26. Worthington, *Forgiveness and Reconciliation*, 55–60.
27. Bassett et al., "Seeking Forgiveness," 132–49.
28. Toussaint and Williams, "National Survey Results," 120–30.
29. Hall and Fincham, "Self-forgiveness," 621–37.
30. Toussaint and Williams, "National Survey Results," 120–30.
31. Tangney et al., "Forgiving the Self," 143–58.

in the presence of the holiness of God.[32] Given the Christian belief that God transforms the entire individual in the salvation experience, there is a Christian basis for belief that Christians might more easily achieve forgiveness regardless of the felt-experience of shame or guilt.

Although we did not ask about self-forgiveness, we did find that guilt was an important component of forgiveness.[33] Most of our respondents agreed with the statement, "I feel guilty if I do not forgive someone." Of course, it is not clear if the *someone* would include *oneself.*

Forgiveness as a Characteristic of Personality

Some studies have examined forgiveness as a personality trait or disposition. When Jesus asserted that his disciples should forgive seventy times seven, he established a long-term pattern. Today we might call this a personality trait or disposition to forgive. Psychologists have developed a few scales to measure forgiveness as a trait. In our lab, we have used the Willingness to Forgive scale, which has good psychometric properties in our samples.[34] We have found that the scores are positively correlated with a willingness to restore fallen pastors to the ministry. In addition, people with a high willingness to forgive were more likely (a) not to require an apology before granting forgiveness, (b) not to need an admission of wrongdoing and change before granting forgiveness, and (c) less likely to believe that being too free with forgiveness will encourage people to continue hurting others.

In summary, psychologists recognize several dimensions of forgiveness. From the perspective of individuals as offenders, researchers can examine the concept of seeking forgiveness from God and from others. From the perspective of victims, researchers have looked at both the emotional and decisional aspects of forgiving offenders. Researchers have also considered forgiveness as a disposition or personality trait sometimes referred to as a *willingness to forgive.* Finally, psychologists have considered the notion of self-forgiveness but this construct remains an ill-defined conundrum given the splitting of the self into roles as offender and victim.

---

32. Bassett et al., "Seeking Forgiveness," 140–49.

33. Sutton and Allman, "Forgiveness, Reconciliation, and Spirituality."

34. Sutton et al., "Does Gender Matter?" 645–63; Deshea, "A Scenario-Based Scale of Willingness to Forgive," 201–17.

Forgiveness and Reconciliation

As noted above, few studies have focused on reconciliation. Scripture does not make a clear distinction between the concepts of forgiveness and reconciliation. Clearly, in relation to God, a forgiven believer is also one who has been reconciled with God. Jesus expects his followers to love each other. In fact, Christians are expected to love their neighbors as broadly defined in the Good Samaritan parable (Luke 10:25–37) and even to love those who are enemies (Matthew 5:44).

Researchers have noted the barriers to reconciliation when people have functioned as perpetrators and victims of violence as in South Africa and Northern Ireland.[35] On a less extreme scale, forgiveness and reconciliation appear to function as twin pillars for successful outcomes in marriage and family work. It is easy to imagine how forgiving an offender might help a victim and offender attempt to work together on a project. In this scenario, forgiveness serves as a catalyst for reconciliation. Trust is a key ingredient in reconciliation. Working together can build or destroy trust. Alternatively, it is easy to see how the process could work the other way. That is, working with an offender and learning to build some degree of trust can invoke some cognitive reframing of the offender as well as afford an opportunity for the reduction of negative emotions thus promoting forgiveness.

Beliefs about forgiveness and reconciliation can vary with the sample. In our research, relatively few Christian students required an apology before they would forgive (15.8%) in contrast to the community college student sample (70.9%).[36] Both groups were similar in their belief that "true forgiveness means you also reconcile with the person who offended you" (Christian college 70.9%, community college 81.9%). Curiously, both groups of students were similarly less willing to agree that if you forgive you must start trusting the offender again. Although we did not clarify the trust and reconciliation matter further, there seems to be some room for a variation in trust. A sensible explanation would be that trust has the potential to grow if other aspects of the reconciliation process are successful. Two important factors affecting relationships are anger and avoidance. We found that most agree that anger decreases when you forgive and that

---

35. For example, see Castillejo-Cuéllar, "Knowledge, Experience, and South Africa's Scenarios of Forgiveness," 11–42; de Vries and de Paor, "Healing and Reconciliation in the LIVE Program in Ireland," 329–58.

36. Sutton and Allman, "Forgiveness, Reconciliation, and Spirituality."

you stop avoiding the offender when you see him or her. These latter two responses support the positions taken by the leading theorists.

From a psychological perspective, what is missing in traditional theological teaching about forgiveness and reconciliation is the time dimension. It is easy to view God as *miraculously* forgiving, reconciling, and restoring a repentant sinner. I know of no teaching that suggests sinners must give God time to forgive them and learn to trust them before reconciliation is achieved. The research suggests that some people can reach a decision to forgive their offenders in a matter of hours. What is not as obvious is the time it takes to experience emotional forgiveness and to build a level of trust that allows people to work together in a marriage, friendship, or organizational relationship. For more research on the time dimension of human forgiveness, see the work by McCullough and his colleagues.[37]

Forgiveness and Restoration in the Christian Community

Again, there have been few studies on restoration of people to the Christian Community following an offense. It is no surprise that religious bodies have restored errant clergy to pulpits at significant personal and financial costs to their adherents, pastors, and treasury when many pastors re-offended. In a series of studies, several graduate students have led or joined with me in conducting studies that found several factors affecting how church members might respond to derailed clergy. We found a cross-gender effect in that women were more forgiving of a male pastor and men were more forgiving of a female pastor for the same offense. Dispositional (trait) forgiveness was positively associated with the willingness to restore a pastor to ministry following a moral offense. Women appeared more restorative following an act of embezzlement but less restorative following an act of child abuse.[38] When clergy considered various adultery scenarios, a younger pastor obtained more favorable restoration ratings than did an older pastor.[39] More recently, we examined the role of apology in forgiveness and restoration.[40] Overall, regardless of apology condition, men were more apt to restore than were women. We also found a cross gender effect related to an apology. Men and women

37. McCullough et al. "Forgiveness, Forbearance, and Time," 540–57.
38. Sutton et al., "Does Gender Matter?" 645–63.
39. Sutton and Thomas, "Can Derailed Pastors be Restored?" 583–89.
40. Thomas et al., "Religious Leadership Failure," 16–29.

were more forgiving of the opposite sex pastor who did not apologize. In this context, we speculated that the apology functioned to highlight the awareness of wrongdoing, which made it more difficult to forgive than a mere formal statement of wrongdoing. How can we explain the cross-gender effect? One possibility is that it may represent a generalization of normal experiences in which heterosexual couples learn to forgive each other in the course of maintaining their marriages, which are relationships that require a considerable investment (e.g., emotional, social, financial, parental) compared to the investment in same-sex friendship relationships.

When we looked at the specific features of the apology in our scenarios, men were more forgiving of a male pastor who did not take responsibility but women were more forgiving of a male pastor who took responsibility. This latter finding suggests a nuance to be further explored in the way men and women view responsibility for sin.

TOWARD A PENTECOSTAL PERSPECTIVE

Jesus' forgiveness of a woman (Luke 7:36–50) illustrates changes that prefigure a Pentecostal worldview. I am drawing from an article by Van Til.[41] The sinful woman in the story seeks Jesus outside the mainstream religious practice. Jesus discerns that she is in need of forgiveness for sin. He recognizes the sincerity of her act and further violates religious tradition by granting forgiveness. From a psychological perspective, Jesus' use of the debt metaphor in the pericope (7:40–42) illustrates a justice gap-love-forgiveness dose-dependent relationship. Let me clarify my terms. Victims feel that offenders owe them an apology, if not restitution. Offenders need to "make things right." Although difficult to quantify, people seem to have a sense that some offenses are more costly than are others. Until justice is served, there is a gap or an unpaid debt. When victims, forgive debts, it is natural to feel warmth and appreciation for such an expression of love. In the story, the debts are quantified thus; it appears Jesus is noting an observation about relationships that people respond with greater amounts of love when they experience forgiveness for greater quantities (higher doses) of debt.

I wish to show how the story fits with the 1906 Pentecostal movement of the outpouring of the Spirit commonly associated with Azusa

41. Van Til, "Three Anointings and One Offering," 73–82.

Street in Los Angeles, California, although there were other revivals of Pentecost preceding the Azusa event.[42] These early Pentecostals, filled with the Holy Spirit, believed in miracles, and were overwhelmed by the love of Jesus.

The Pentecostal tradition has focused much on empowerment for service and has been quick to embrace the dramatic supernatural acts of healing and deliverance. In contrast, they have been criticized for neglecting the fruit of the Spirit (Galatians 5) and the love context of empowerment (1 Corinthians 13). I propose three aspects to a Pentecostal perspective on the psychology of forgiveness that should be observable. These hypotheses, drawn from Pentecostal theological tradition, can serve as scientific hypotheses.

First, observers should expect to see evidence of a sense of empowerment for victims to forgive their offenders if the Pentecostal victims avow that they have received the baptism in the Holy Spirit. In addition, observers ought to see evidence that Spirit-filled offenders would feel convicted by the presence of the Spirit in their lives and empowered to seek forgiveness from God and others. As a corollary, observers should find less grudge-holding and a shorter latency (time between offense and forgiveness) of offense-forgiveness in any representative sample of Pentecostals compared to a sample of other Christians or nonbelievers.

A second aspect of the Pentecostal experience is the commonly observed phenomenon of an emotional experience during worship. Once aroused, emotions serve a motivational purpose. The woman in Luke 7 was clearly distressed. She obviously took action, which may have brought a different sense of relief than she expected. When she encountered Jesus, she received forgiveness. Given Jesus' teaching and my own observations of salvation experiences, I would expect her to have left the encounter motivated by the love experience to forgive others. Again, the love context of Spirit empowerment in 1 Corinthians 13 suggests that an enhanced experience of God's love comes with the Pentecostal experience and because of the love-forgiveness link, observers can expect a high level of motivation toward forgiveness within a Pentecostal community. Empathy has been found to be highly correlated with forgiveness. One aspect of the development of empathy is the ability to take the perspective of others.[43]

42. McGee, *People of the Spirit.*

43. See Konstam et al., "Toward Forgiveness," 26–39; and Welton et al., "Forgiveness in the Trenches," 168–77.

Therefore, it seems reasonable to expect that Spirit-filled believers would be attuned to sin in their own lives and the felt experience of God's love despite their sinful state. Thus equipped with Jesus' perspective, they might be more willing to forgive others. Because emotions often lead to actions, observers might also expect a propensity toward acts of reconciliation and restoration to be higher among Pentecostals than among other groups as noted previously.

A third concomitant of the Pentecostal experience is a sense of immediacy. By immediacy, I mean a focus on miraculous, instantaneous change, sometimes referred to as "deliverance." There is no sense that Jesus expected the woman to process her life events in therapy or carry out some series of actions before receiving forgiveness. Jesus' miracles suggest a fairly immediate change from impairment to health. In the case of forgiveness, reconciliation, and restoration, a Pentecostal worldview often includes an expectation for immediate results and frowns upon the slower process of natural healing (including traditional psychotherapy).

PASTORAL RESTORATION: AN EXAMPLE OF FORGIVENESS, RECONCILIATION, AND RESTORATION

Pentecostal pastors are not alone in garnering glaring headlines for egregious offenses that hurt their families and their parishioners as well as their supporters (e.g., former U.S. President, Bill Clinton, as well as other political figures). Unfortunately, prominent television ministries (e.g., Jim Bakker, Jimmy Swaggart) spotlighted their sins to create a dramatic spectacle disproportionate to the equally tragic experiences of those who witness similar sins *off-stage*. We know that pastors face temptations common to other humans. However, nothing gains national media attention like sexual sin and even more so in people who preach purity and come from a holiness tradition. The sin of pastoral sexual infidelity provides a useful focus for consideration of the forgiveness process. Because most Pentecostal clergy are men and most clergy who have adulterous relationships are also men, I will analyze the typical case of a married male pastor who has a sexual relationship with a female congregant.[44]

The ripple of impact begins with his wife and children, the *other* woman and her family, relatives and friends, and spreads to the faith community. Predictably, some will support their pastor no matter what.

44. Thomas et al., "Religious Leadership Failure," 16–29.

Others will experience the desire for justice, the wish for revenge, and the negative emotions previously mentioned. Although empirical research noting the impact on clergy and their families is only beginning, similar research on client victims of psychotherapist- client sex is available. These studies revealed that clients experience the expected negative emotions and behavioral responses reflecting a stress syndrome and in some cases full-blown posttraumatic stress disorder.[45] There is an important difference between pastors and congregants vs. psychotherapists and clients. No cultural norm dictates that the therapy client *stand by* her therapist following a sexual liaison. Anecdotally, it seems Christians expect their pastor's wife to be the faithful stoic supporting her husband during the efflorescent apology and request for forgiveness of all those who have been harmed by the senseless sensual sin. The Pentecostal color to this stage-drama is emotion-focused, lachrymose lamentation similar to that displayed by the woman of Luke 7. Classic Pentecostal theology focuses on the powerful, the emotional, and the immediate. Thus, following a courageous act of contrition, an errant pastor can walk away with an expectation that he is forgiven, reconciled with Jesus, and restored to the community (Luke 7:50). Within this worldview, he can expect the members of the faith community to act toward him as Jesus acted toward the tearful woman.

In classical Pentecostal theology, the emphasis is on powerful, Spirit-induced regeneration. Time is compressed. God acts in the now. A miracle connotes immediate and powerful healing, not a process brought about by slow-moving human interventions. Acting by faith often means denying the influence of negative feedback (i.e., bad feelings) to lay hold on a promise of recovery. Considering this lens, if God can instantaneously forgive the pastor, some may ask how the wife and children can be so arrogant as to deny forgiveness to this repentant son of God. The congregation and fellow church leaders should acknowledge the divine dispensation and quickly restore the pastor to fellowship. Those congregants who share this worldview may not experience significant dissonance.

When a pastor, standing in a pulpit, seeks forgiveness from a congregation, he occupies the same place he stood when previously leading people into a deeper relationship with God. As before, the service may be very emotional, though for different reasons. For those who pay attention to their feelings, they can feel caught in a maelstrom of confusion. Nevertheless, the emotional experience can enhance the motivation to

45. Sutton and Thomas, "Restoration, Reconciliation, and Forgiveness," 29–44.

act. In the case of an emotional apology in the context of expectations to forgive and a belief that God forgives and reconciles, the stage is set for simultaneous decisional and emotional forgiveness.

Finally, the classical Pentecostal view on miracles allows for an expectation that forgiveness and reconciliation will be instantaneous because the pastor will be immediately healed or delivered from sexual sin. The congregation expects immediate deliverance from sin and its effects. As crutches are tossed aside, blind people instantly cured, and addicts delivered from the clutches of alcohol and tobacco, so too can sinners be delivered from sexual sin. To these believers, sin is something foreign to the believer. It came from an external source: if not the woman, surely the devil. Given variations on this belief system, most congregants are ready to restore the pastor. Any dissidents within the congregation or external church authority would not be viewed as believers in the power of the full gospel.

What I have presented is my sense of what errant pastors seem to expect. Some Pentecostal scholars, however, express a more nuanced, albeit conservative approach to forgiveness and restoration. For example, in its commentary on 1 Tim 3:2, 7, the *Full Life Study Bible* asserts that "an overseer who throws aside his loyalty to God and his Word and his fidelity to his wife and family must be removed from the office of an overseer. He cannot thereafter be regarded as 'above reproach.'"[46] The writers further quote Prov 6:33 to note, "his shame will never be wiped away."[47] They clarify their position that forgiveness may follow the expression of godly sorrow and repentance, but the shame remains after forgiveness for the rest of their lives.

Pentecostal theology may be changing in other subtle ways. As reported in a study by Paloma, pastors in the Assemblies of God (AG), one of the largest Pentecostal groups, appear to be increasingly identifying with mainstream Evangelicals.[48] Some will appreciate a broader meaning of *miracle*. God can work over time and in partnership with human agents. Although psychology remains taboo in some Pentecostal outposts, others are open to approaches that integrate scripture with psychological principles. Here, a recent formulation of types of forgiveness might prove beneficial. My colleague, Eloise Thomas, and I wrote an article for an AG

46. Stamps and Adams, *The Full Life Study Bible*, 1882–83.

47. Ibid.

48. Paloma, "The Future of American Pentecostal Identity," 147–65.

publication (*Enrichment*) that suggested a difference between dutiful and emotional forgiveness.[49] We received favorable comments from persons in the AG leadership. At about the same time, Worthington published a book, *Forgiveness and Reconciliation*, that argues the empirical case for a distinction between decisional (similar to our notion of dutiful) and emotional forgiveness and includes a new questionnaire that has strong psychometric properties.[50] These nuances may hold some promise for those who wish to reconcile the more immediate change, qua classical Pentecostal theology, that can occur in a person's thinking (i.e., decision motivated by duty to forgive) compared to the slower change at the emotional level as documented by psychological research.

CONCLUSION

Forgiveness is a central tenet of Christian theology. Christians experience God's forgiveness, and they are expected to forgive others as they have been forgiven. Psychological research has documented important links between forgiveness of interpersonal offenses and physical and mental health. In addition, interpersonal forgiveness appears to serve as a catalyst in reconciliation and restoration. I wrote this chapter to suggest what might constitute a Pentecostal perspective on forgiveness, reconciliation, and restoration. I suggested three major ways that a Pentecostal perspective might make a difference. First, I proposed that the Pentecostal belief in empowerment by the Holy Spirit could enable Pentecostals to be more forgiving. Second, I suggested that the emotional-experiential component typical of Pentecostal worship might be a reflection of God's love and thereby motivate Pentecostals toward forgiveness as an expression of God's love. I suggested this motivation to forgive might occur by means of a heightened awareness of personal sin that enhances perspective-taking, a key ingredient of empathy, which is linked to forgiveness. Finally, I suggested that the Pentecostal emphasis on immediacy might fit with recent psychological findings that some people can quickly achieve decisional forgiveness while taking longer to attain emotional forgiveness.

---

49. Sutton and Thomas, "Following Derailed Clergy."
50. Worthington, *Forgiveness and Reconciliation*, 55–60.

BIBLIOGRAPHY

Bassett, Rodney, et al., "Seeking Forgiveness: The View From An Experimental Paradigm." *Journal of Psychology and Christianity* 27 (2008) 132–49.

Bekoff, Mark, "Animal Passions and Beastly Virtues: Cognitive Ethology As The Unifying Science For Understanding The Subjective, Emotional, Empathic, And Moral Lives Of Animals." *Zygon: Journal of Religion and Science* 41 (2006) 71–104.

Castillejo-Cuéllar, Alegandro. "Knowledge, Experience, and South Africa's Scenarios of Forgiveness." *Radical History Review* 97 (2007) 11–42.

Cordoni, Giada, et al. "Reconciliation and Consolation in Captive Western Gorillas." *International Journal of Primatology* 27 (2006) 1365–82.

Dawkins, Richard. *The Selfish Gene*. New Edition. New York: Oxford University Press, 1999.

Deshea, Lise. "A Scenario-Based Scale of Willingness to Forgive". *Individual Differences Research* 1 (2003) 201–217.

DiBlasio, Frederick A., and Brent B. Benda. "Forgiveness Intervention with Married Couples: Two Empirical Analyses." *Journal of Psychology and Christianity* 27 (2008) 150–58.

de Vries, Jan M.A. and Jacinta de Paor, "Healing and Reconciliation in the LIVE Program in Ireland." *Peace and Change* 30 (2005) 329–58.

Enright, Robert D. *Forgiveness is a Choice: A Step-by-Step Process for Resolving Anger and Restoring Hope*. APA Life Tools. Washington, DC: American Psychological Association, 2001.

Enright, Robert D., and Richard P. Fitzgibbons. *Helping Clients Forgive: An Empirical Guide for Resolving Anger and Restoring Hope*. Washington, DC: American Psychological Association, 2000.

Exline, Julie J. "Beliefs about God and Forgiveness in a Baptist Church Sample." *Journal of Psychology and Christianity* 27 (2008) 131–39.

Hall, Julie H., and Frank D. Fincham. "Self-forgiveness: The Stepchild of Forgiveness Research." *Journal of Social and Clinical Psychology* 24 (2005) 621–37.

Huang, Shih-Tseng, and Robert D. Enright. "Forgiveness and Anger-Related Emotions in Taiwan: Implications for Therapy." *Psychotherapy* 37 (2000) 71–79.

Kanz, Jason E. "How do People Conceptualize and Use Forgiveness? The Forgiveness Attitudes Questionnaire." *Counseling and Values* 44 (2000) 174–86.

Konstam, Varda, et al. "Toward Forgiveness: The Role of Shame, Guilt, Anger, and Empathy." *Counseling and Values* 46 (2001) 26–39.

Lawler-Row, Kathleen et al., "The Role of Adult Attachment Style in Forgiveness Following an Interpersonal Offense." *Journal of Counseling and Development* (2006) 493–502.

McCullough, Michael E., et al. "Forgiveness, Forbearance, and Time: The Temporal Unfolding of Transgression-Related Interpersonal Motivations." *Journal of Personality and Social Psychology* 84 (2003) 540–57.

———. "Religion and Forgiveness." In *Handbook of the Psychology of Religion*, 394–411. New York: Guilford, 2005.

McGee, Gary B. *People of the Spirit: The Assemblies of God*. Springfield, MO: Gospel, 2004.

McMinn, Mark R., and Clark D. Campbell. *Integrative Psychotherapy: Toward A Comprehensive Christian Approach*. Downers Grove, IL: InterVarsity, 2007.

Palagi, Elisabetta, et al. "Possible Roles of Consolation in Captive Chimpanzees." *American Journal of Physical Anthropology* 129 (2006) 105–11.

Paloma, Margaret "The Future of American Pentecostal Identity." In *The Work of the Spirit: Pneumatology and Pentecostalism*, edited by Michael Welker,147–65. Grand Rapids, MI: Eerdmans, 2006.

Pop, Jennifer, et al. "Restoring Pastors Following a Moral Failure: The Effects of Self-Interest and Group Influence." *Pastoral Psychology* 57 (2008) 275–84.

Rye, Mark S., Kenneth I. Pargament, M. Amir Ali, Guy L. Beck, Elliot N. Dorff, Charles Hallisey, Vasudha Narayanan, and James G. Williams. "Religious Perspectives on Forgiveness." In *Forgiveness: Theory, Research, and Practice*, edited by Michael E. McCullough, Kenneth I. Pargament, and Carl E. Thoresen, 17–40. New York: Guilford, 2000.

Smedes, Lewis B. *Forgive and Forget: Healing the Hurts We Don't Deserve*. New York: Harper & Row, 1984.

Stamps, Dennis C., and J. Wesley Adams. *The Full Life Study Bible: New International Version*. Grand Rapids, MI: Zondervan, 1992.

Sutton, Geoffrey W. "Forgiveness: Psychological Theory, Research, and Practice." *Journal of Psychology and Theology* 35 (2007) 347–48.

Sutton, Geoffrey W., and Jaimée Allman. "Forgiveness, Reconciliation, and Spirituality: Empirical Findings Regarding Conceptual Differences." Paper presented at the annual meeting of the Christian Association for Psychological Studies, Orlando, Florida, 2009.

Sutton, Geoffrey W. and Eloise Thomas. "Can Derailed Pastors be Restored? Effects of Offense and Age on Restoration." *Pastoral Psychology* 53 (2005) 583—89.

————. "Following Derailed Clergy: A Message of Healing for a Shocked Congregation." *Enrichment Journal* (Spring 2009). Http://enrichmentjournal.ag.org/200902/200902_000_Following_Derailed_Clergy.cfm

————. "Restoration, Reconciliation, and Forgiveness: State and Process Conceptualizations." *American Journal of Pastoral Counseling* 8 (2005) 29–44.

Sutton, Geoffrey W., et al., "Does Gender Matter? An Exploration of Gender, Spirituality, Forgiveness and Restoration Following Pastor Transgressions." *Pastoral Psychology* 55 (2007) 645–63.

————. "Professional Ethics' Violations, Gender, Forgiveness, and the Attitudes of Social Work Students." *Journal of College and Character* 7 (2006) 1–7.

Tangney, J., et al., "Forgiving the Self: Conceptual Issues and Empirical Findings." In *Handbook of Forgiveness*, edited by Everett L. Worthington Jr., 143–58. New York: Routledge, 2005.

Thomas, Eloise, and Geoffrey W. Sutton, "Religious Leadership Failure: Forgiveness, Apology, and Restitution. *Journal of Spirituality in Mental Health* 10 (2008) 308–27.

Thomas, Eloise, et al. "Religious Leadership Failure: Apology, Responsibility-Taking, Gender, Forgiveness, and Restoration." *Journal of Psychology and Christianity* 27 (2008) 16–29.

Toussaint, Loren L., and David R. Williams. "National Survey Results for Protestant, Catholic, and Nonreligious Experiences of Seeking Forgiveness and of Forgiveness of Self, or Others, and by God." *Journal of Psychology and Christianity* 27 (2008) 120–30.

Van Til, Kent A. "Three Anointings and One Offering: The Sinful Woman in Luke 7.36–50." *Journal of Pentecostal Theology* 15 (2006) 73–82.

Volf, Miroslav. *Free of Charge: Giving and Forgiving in a Culture Stripped of Grace*. Grand Rapids, MI: Zondervan, 2005.

Welton, Gary L., et al. "Forgiveness in the Trenches: Empathy, Perspective Taking, and Anger." *Journal of Psychology and Christianity* 27 (2008) 168–77.

Worthington, Everett. L. Jr. *Forgiveness and Reconciliation: Theory and Application*. New York: Routledge, 2006.

———. *Forgiving and Reconciling: Bridges to Wholeness and Hope*. Downers Grove, IL: InterVarsity, 2003.

———. "Guest Editor's Page." *Journal of Psychology and Christianity* 27 (2008) 99.

Worthington, Everett L. Jr., editor. *Handbook of Forgiveness*. New York: Routledge, 2005.

Worthington, Everett L. Jr., and Michael Scherer. "Forgiveness is an Emotion-Focused Coping Strategy That Can Reduce Health Risks and Promote Health Resilience: Theory, Review, and Hypotheses." *Psychology and Health* 19 (2004) 385–405.

Wright, N. T. *Surprised by Hope: Rethinking Heaven, the Resurrection, and the Mission of the Church*. New York: HarperOne, 2008.

8

Truth and Reconciliation in South Africa

A Pentecostal Perspective

Johan Mostert and Mervin van der Spuy

It was 1997 and I (Mostert) was excited to attend the official government release of the long-awaited Poverty and Inequality Report that had been funded by the Carnegie Foundation. We were three years into our fragile democracy and things were going a whole lot better than what we Afrikaners had ever expected. I was also excited because the chairperson of this function was Frank Chikane, the Director General of the Presidency, the highest civil service office in the government of Thabo Mbeki.[1] Frank had been a pastor in the Apostolic Faith Mission (AFM) that also ordained both of us (Mostert and van der Spuy).[2] I was aware that he had been imprisoned by our government for his "subversive" activities of opposing apartheid and excommunicated by our church in

1. President Thabo Mbeki succeeded Nelson Mandela as South Africa's second democratically elected President and served in that office from 1999 to 2009.
2. The AFM is the largest Pentecostal church in South Africa.

1981 for his activism in helping the poor.[3] I had been glad when he was finally reinstated as our colleague in 1990 even though "everyone" knew he was a "liberation theologian" because he was the General Secretary of the South African Council of Churches (SACC), stepping into the shoes of such legendary anti-apartheid activists such as Anglican Archbishop Desmond Tutu and Dr. Beyers Naude. But all of that had now been swept under the proverbial rug and we were now all brothers again in our new democracy!

I saw the newspaper posters declaring that testimony before the Truth and Reconciliation Commission (TRC) had uncovered the secrets behind an attempt to assassinate Chikane while he was General Secretary of the SACC. I bought a newspaper on the way to the function and read in horror of how Frank had been tortured while in prison. I read that his torturer was a lay leader of one of our white AFM churches! I read about the approval our Minister of Police had given for the poisoning of Chikane and how he suffered in a hospital in the United States and had not been expected to live.

The TRC revelations brought the injustices and human rights violations of the government that I had supported into the light. Although I was always in favor of the moves that the National Party had made toward reform, in many respects I was a collaborator with the apartheid regime. But here I was in a meeting where Frank was introducing cabinet ministers to the press, smiling to the cameras, reveling in the significant recommendations of the report, and completely ignoring the shocking revelations of the TRC. When we broke for morning tea, I pushed my way through the crowds to greet Frank. With a lump in my throat I confessed to him my ignorance and my guilt. Frank smiled and shook his head and said, "You were a child of your time. It's not your fault." The TRC had uncovered atrocities against my friend. On behalf of my people, the Afrikaners, I was able to say "I'm sorry," and Frank was graciously able to forgive me! More than anything else, this experience brought the healing power of the TRC process into my life!

The South African TRC was set up to deal with the human rights violations of apartheid during the years 1960–1994. Apartheid generated

---

3. "Apartheid," an Afrikaan's word meaning "separateness," was a system of legal racial segregation enforced by the National Party government in South Africa between 1948 and early 1994. It was a political and social policy of racial segregation involving political, economic, and legal discrimination against people who were not Whites.

gross violations of human rights and the transgression of humanitarian principles. South Africa's deeply divided society was characterized by violent conflict, strife, untold suffering, injustices, and a legacy of hatred, fear, guilt, and revenge. The adoption of a new Constitution (1994) laid the foundation for the people of South Africa to transcend the divisions of the past and move towards a future where human rights are recognized, democratic principles upheld, and peaceful co-existence made possible. The TRC played a major role in helping the transition take place in an atmosphere of understanding instead of vengeance, reparation instead of retaliation, and reconciliation instead of victimization.

The TRC's final report asserted the claim that the process of giving testimony (speaking truth), served a therapeutic function and that the truth-telling process contributed to victims' ability to forgive their perpetrators.[4] In this chapter, we want to evaluate this claim of the TRC in South Africa. This was the first time that a therapeutic technique commonly used in pastoral and psychological settings, was being used on such a large scale in the context of national reconciliation. What does the literature say about truth leading to reconciliation? Did the TRC process promote and facilitate psychological wellbeing? Were there spiritual benefits to victims and perpetrators that participated in the TRC process? Can the TRC be seen as a successful sociopolitical model for dealing with institutionalized human rights abuses in other countries? What are the implications for a Pentecostal understanding of forgiveness in the reconciliation process?

It needs to be said that we are writing this from the perspective of two white Afrikaner men who lived through the apartheid years and the dawning of democracy in our nation. We could be said to have benefitted significantly from the apartheid regime and in some respects the critique could be made that we collaborated with the regime. It also needs to be said that we were significantly disillusioned by the system and have subsequently spent years in prayerful retrospection about what we could have done to facilitate the transition to democracy. Our evaluation of the TRC must be seen against this backdrop.

From an integrated psychological/theological perspective we describe some of the lessons learned and some of the misconceptions and we draw some conclusions to inform a Pentecostal understanding of forgiveness in the process of truth and reconciliation.

4. *Truth and Reconciliation Commission of South Africa.*

THE TRC AS A SOCIOPOLITICAL MODEL

Apartheid embodied a sociopolitical system that blatantly codified racism into the legal and social structures of South African society. There have been many other nations where racism was tolerated as a cultural manifestation (e.g., the "old South" of the United States), or where cultural status ordered societal relations (e.g., the caste system in India). But there have been none that so painstakingly used racial origin as the determining factor for inclusion, privilege, and power. Eventually, the system not only determined where you could live, it physically (and sometimes violently) removed you from your ancestral community when the land you occupied was deemed necessary for white resettlement (similar to the Israeli occupations of Palestinian territories on the West Bank). It also determined where you received your education, the occupations you were allowed to pursue, the beaches you were allowed to visit and even the park bench on which you were allowed to rest.

It is therefore understandable that Kadar Asmal wrote that "Apartheid was evil . . . It was a crime against humanity."[5] He, like so many other human rights activists, favored the "punishment-model" of tribunals and the punishment of human rights violators as a way to deal with these crimes justly. However, negotiators of the South African transition rejected the "Nuremburg trial option" and the "blanket amnesty" (or "national amnesia option" as Archbishop Desmond Tutu referred to it)[6] and chose a middle way in which individuals would be granted amnesty in exchange for full allocution.[7] Later Asmal, who had campaigned for years for a South African equivalent of the Nuremberg trials, changed his mind during the negotiated transition, and became a proponent for the TRC.

Even with a significant volume of criticisms against it, it is generally accepted that, as a sociopolitical process, the TRC was successful in reconciling the oppressors and the oppressed within the South African

---

5. Kadar Asmal was an African National Congress (ANC) activist, human rights lawyer, and later cabinet minister in Presidents Mandela's government. See Asmal, Asmal, and Roberts, *Reconciliation through Truth.*

6. Tutu (*No Future without Forgiveness,* 30) was the former head of the Anglican Church in South Africa and was appointed to serve as the Chairperson of the Truth and Reconciliation Commission.

7. The Nuremburg Trials were instituted to deal with German war criminals after World War II and culminated in a death sentence being imposed on 12 Nazi leaders.

context.[8] The political transition took place in a relatively free and stable environment without harsh revenge.

In 1976, resistance to apartheid spilled over into the streets. Young people in Soweto, a large black township outside Johannesburg, protested against the mandatory use of Afrikaans (the language of the majority of whites and perceived as the language of the oppressors) as the official medium of instruction in their schools. The civil disobedience of thousands of unarmed youth, dancing, singing, and putting old tires on fire in the streets was countered by a show of force by heavily armed security forces. The troops who represented the white minority of the nation reacted with deadly force and a period of bloodshed erupted that pushed South Africa to the brink of civil war. For more than a decade, the security of our nation deteriorated as "freedom fighters" fled the country and obtained funding from former communist nations who helped them to engage in a "terrorist onslaught" against the regime. Against the backdrop of Western international sanctions, the South African government responded with emergency legislation that severely curtailed the due process of law and limited civil liberties. The security forces responded with brutal force, both during hot-pursuit into neighboring states as well as against the protesting disenfranchised black majority in the townships. On both sides of the struggle human rights were abused, inhumane torture was used to extract information, and thousands of innocent bystanders were killed in the crossfire.

As a chaplain I (van der Spuy) had the privilege to minister to the Brigadiers and Generals during their Combined Staff Training courses. They were often unsure what to do about my outspoken opposition to apartheid and the war, but often responded positively to my preaching on grace, peace, forgiveness, and reconciliation. Long before any public mention of Mandela's release, these top echelon officers had already been given the task to plan for his release and a future peaceful transition to democracy.

---

8. The arguments of Wilson, a leading critic of the TRC process and others are addressed later in this chapter. Tutu, *No Future without Forgiveness*; Coletti, "Reconciliation"; Eisikovits, "Rethinking the Legitimacy of Truth Commissions"; Foster, "Evaluating the Truth and Reconciliation Commission of South Africa"; Gibson, "The Contributions of Truth to Reconciliation"; Gobodo-Madikezela, "Trauma, Forgiveness, and the Witnessing Dance"; Schaffer and Smith, "Human Rights, Storytelling, and the Position of the Beneficiary."

For those of us who lived our adult lives through these years, how the process eventually led to a relatively peaceful transition and the establishment of a functional democracy remains a total mystery. That our situation did not degenerate into the political quagmire that other nations in a similar situation, remains a source of great thankfulness to God. What made this possible in the end was a perfect storm—the coming together of three disparate factors in the period of just a few months.

The first factor was that the more moderate F. W. de Klerk took over the Presidency of South Africa from the harsh and uncompromising P. W. Botha in 1989. Tutu wrote, "Nothing will ever take away from F. W. de Klerk the enormous credit that belongs to him for what he said and did then."[9] Second, in Nelson Mandela, F. W. De Klerk found not a vindictive bitter angry opponent but a forgiving and peace-seeking statesman and ally. This laid the foundation for the release of Mandela from prison in 1990. "Nelson Mandela emerged from prison not spewing words of hatred and revenge. He amazed us all by his heroic embodiment of reconciliation and forgiveness."[10] The third element was the collapse of Communism in 1989.[11] The Berlin Wall came down, Russia withdrew its support from Cuba and the Cuban troops withdrew from Angola leaving the liberation forces without military and financial support. These three elements, taking place within a few months of each other, enabled these two statesmen, de Klerk and Mandela to change history and set the tone for the TRC to work towards forgiveness and reconciliation—a bloodbath was averted!

By the mid-1980s it had already become clear that no military solution would be found and behind-the-scenes negotiations began between military, business, and political leaders to try to resolve the impasse. The resultant Peace Accord put our nation onto a path of recognizing the democratic rights of all the people. Political prisoners were released (including Nelson Mandela after 37 years of imprisonment), liberation movements were unbanned, a constitution-generating body for the new democracy was convened, and provisions were made for the establishment of the TRC as the mechanism to deal with the human rights abuses during "the struggle".

One of the leading critics of the TRC, Richard Wilson, argued that the establishment of the TRC was in direct contrast to the philosophy that was

9. Tutu, *No Future without Forgiveness*, 37.

10. Ibid., 39.

11. Wilson, "Reconciliation and Revenge in Post-Apartheid Africa."

operative in the township courts at that time. Township courts (referred to as *lekgotla*) were a grass-roots conception of legal order that sought to influence social change by emphasizing punishment and retribution.[12] They often meted out severe punishments to those who were found to be guilty of collaboration with the security forces and instituted the dreaded "necklacing" method of execution where the guilty party was executed by binding a tire around his neck with thick wire, dousing with petrol, and set alight. These courts were very active even as the goals of nation-building were being sought by the political negotiation process. Willa Boesak reflected this anger when he suggested that the reconstruction process in South Africa needed to be "undergirded by a comprehensive 'ethic of vengeance' as a basis of giving constructive direction to the anger and determination that lives in the souls of the black oppressed people."[13]

We reflect back with a sense of awe at the grace of God, which kept our nation from degenerating into complete chaos. Instead of seeking vengeance, the previously oppressed and new regime sought reconciliation. Without retaliation and punitive revenge, the political transition took place in a surprisingly stable and free environment.

Some authors remain highly critical of the TRC process. Some suggested that the TRC process defended the architects of apartheid.[14] Others criticized the delays in the provision of reparation, reawakening the trauma that testimonies left behind.[15] Still others were skeptical of a process that expected South Africans, brutalized by the legacy of apartheid, to reconcile themselves with partial truths as perpetrators gave their edited versions of the "truth."[16]

It has to be admitted that the question whether the TRC granted amnesty to perpetrators at the cost of justice being done, is a relevant question.[17] Writing about the TRC before it began its task, ANC activist Kader Asmal suggested that 'speaking truth' meant that the 'illegitimacy of apartheid' had to be acknowledged.[18] But he was adamant that "sinning

---

12. Ibid.

13. Boesak, *God's Wrathful Children*, xvi.

14. Hamber, "'Ere Their Story Die.'"

15. Skinner, "An Evaluation of a Set of TRC Public Hearings in Worcester."

16. Walaza, "Reconciling with Partial Truths."

17. Wilson, "Reconciliation and Revenge in Post-Apartheid Africa."

18. The ANC led the liberation struggle under apartheid and became the first democratic government after the general election under Nelson Mandela in 1994. Asmal, Asmal, and Roberts, *Reconciliation through Truth*.

against apartheid" (the atrocities committed by the ANC and others) was a "blessed thing to do". For him "genuine reconciliation" had to involve "moral and political restitution"—not to "restore friendship" between rivals, but to "make good again". He called for "corrective action" to be taken. In the "Afterword," written a year later and included in the second edition of his book, it seems clear that he did not believe that the action was sufficient, and still maintained that the TRC placed reconciliation above justice.

Many on both sides of the political spectrum, for different reasons, would agree with Asmal that justice was not adequately served. Soon after the termination of the TRC, the new South African government released all African National Congress (ANC) prisoners from jail whose applications for amnesty were turned down by the TRC. The argument can also be made that the ANC policy of affirmative action has created an increasing number of impoverished whites and some could feel that these actions did not serve the aims of justice. But we have to agree with Gibson that the TRC's procedural justice (giving voice to the victims and their families) and its restorative justice (the apologies) contributed significantly toward political reconciliation and compensated for the inherent unfairness of granting amnesty to human rights violators.[19]

Today, with the benefit of hindsight, it is the criticism of a group of researchers, which we would have dismissed as "left-wing radicals" in those days that haunts us. Clint Van der Walt, Vije Franchi and Garth Stevens suggest that the unity and reconciliation process was pursued at the expense of substantial reparations to the majority of South Africans.[20] When Jacob Zuma assumed the presidency in 2008 he was touted as "the people's choice," the one who would stand up for the workers to ensure that the prosperity of South Africa began to trickle down to his comrades from the struggle. Since democracy in 1994, the policies undergirding Black Economic Empowerment (BEE) had successfully wiped away the discriminatory legislation, and through affirmative action had created many opportunities for the advancement of formerly disadvantaged individuals. But it has not succeeded in redressing significant economic disparities of the past. Even today, the majority of black people are still poor, and the gap between the rich and the poor has widened. They suggest

19. Gibson, "Does Truth Lead to Reconciliation?"

20. Van der Walt, Franchi, and Stevens, "The South African Truth and Reconciliation Commission."

that by ignoring the issues of land reform and socio-economic issues, the process "has resulted in the maintenance of an economic system promoting a de-racialised insider and a persistently black outsider."

In a particularly scathing attack on the TRC process Shane Moran suggests that the entire democratization process did not contribute to the birth of the promised political miracle.[21] He suggests provocatively that it could actually have buried its promise. His anger is vented against the fact that the central issue of wealth distribution and land re-distribution was completely overlooked throughout the entire process. He even accuses icons like Nelson Mandela to have sold out the people to colonial powers because they clearly agreed beforehand that "the pillars of the house must be left standing" at the conclusion of the democratization process.[22] Moran's most biting criticisms of the TRC are those that focus on its refusal to leave the legal door open to claims for state compensation because such a move would have threatened the resources of the state necessary to rebuild the economy. The new system is simply a perpetuation of the colonial legacy where the elite were acting behind the scenes to gently pass control of the levers of power from white masters to a new black elite.

THE TRC AS A CHRISTIAN MODEL FOR OTHER NATIONS WITH HUMAN RIGHTS ABUSES

Reconciliation was not clearly defined as a concept by the TRC and "no one seems to know what 'reconciliation'" means.[23] Gibson suggests that "reconciliation was not given a great deal of specific content, although the framers of the process clearly sought to shape the views of individual South Africans—for instance, by getting them to accept the collective memory about the country's past and to endorse an expansive definition of human rights."[24] In the South African context, it seems clear that it referred to the reconciliation of the four main racial groups in the country: Whites, Africans, Coloreds (mixed race), and Asians. The TRC's final report suggests that reconciliation requires a better and more respectful understanding of each other's culture; that reconciliation is based on

21. Moran, "South Africa and the Colonial Intellectual."

22. Ibid., 120.

23. Gibson, "Does Truth Lead to Reconciliation?"

24. Ibid.

respect for "our common humanity". More importantly, it had the intention of reconciling perpetrators and victims to ensure a stable environment for political transition and the birth of a new unified *Rainbow Nation*. This was symbolized by the adoption of the new rainbow flag in 1994. It therefore went beyond racial reconciliation.

Brandon Hamber and Richard Wilson questioned whether the claims made in Christian theology about the possibility of reconciliation between people would apply to relationships between nations.[25] Nations, they argued, do not have collective psyches, and truth commissions often have to subordinate individual needs to attain nation-building goals. They suggest that retribution may be just as effective as reconciliation at creating symbolic closure for a nation that has been divided by conflict.

On the other side of the spectrum, Brian Stanley saw the TRC as an example of how a Christian approach to reconciliation can work politically in a nation divided by atrocities.[26] In fact, he suggested that the TRC experience is credited with the acceptance of the term *reconciliation* by social scientists as more than a religious concept. In religious and political contexts, reconciliation requires that conflicting groups mutually accept the other's identity and humanity, which paves the way to an alternative to conflict.[27] Holness and Wüstenberg also saw a rich potential for reconstructing the theological dimensions of reconciliation in politics.[28]

Jonathan Tepperman was already able to count more than 21 truth commissions that had been established since 1972.[29] Prestigious American universities offered academic courses on reconciliation but the entire process remains a source of intense debate, mostly within the human rights community. Administering justice, achieving accountability, and reaching a point of national reconciliation remain difficult tasks.

The TRC's process stands in stark contrast to the work of the International Criminal Court of Justice (ICC), which was established to deal with human rights abuses in the world.[30] The ICC was established in 2002 to prosecute individuals for genocide, crimes against humanity, and war crimes. On its July, 2009 cover the influential pan-African news magazine,

25. Hamber and Wilson, "Symbolic Closure."
26. Stanley, "Mission and Human Dignity."
27. See also Kelman, "Reconciliation from a Social-Psychological Perspective."
28. Holness and Wüstenberg, *Theology in Dialogue.*
29. Tepperman, "Truth and Consequences."
30. Griffiths, "Comments."

New African led with a story on the ICC which raised serious questions about its legitimacy. In the editorial which precedes a 14-page debate for and against the ICC, the author suggested that although the court had received 2,887 communications about alleged war crimes and crimes against humanity in at least 139 countries, by March 2009 the prosecutor had opened investigations into just four cases, which were all African nations: Uganda, Democratic Republic of the Congo, Central African Republic and Sudan/Darfur.[31] In addition, all of the 13 public warrants of arrest that the ICC had issued were against Africans. The author suggests that, "this creates the impression that the ICC is deliberately targeting Africa or that the continent has a monopoly over crimes against humanity."[32] The situation had become so contentious that the African Union held a closed-door meeting in Addis Ababa in June, "on the work of the ICC in relation to Africa, in particular in the light of the processes initiated against African personalities."[33]

Debate in some Third-World countries now centers on whether the ICC has become a symbol of Western legal colonialism. This will unnecessarily cloud the debate about the relative validity of dealing with human rights abuses with one or the other approach. We suspect that we will continue to see some authors appeal to retributive justice, such as Abdul Lamin's call for Charles Taylor to be held accountable for war crimes and not be given immunity.[34] Recently, I (Mostert) was asked to review the book, *"Girl Soldier"* in which the authors document the unspeakable atrocities committed by members of the Lord's Resistance Army in northern Uganda.[35] I was surprised by my own aggressive feelings of retributive justice as I worked through the pages of Grace Akallo's story of personal abuse and ultimate triumph.

On the other hand, I understand when opposition leader Morgan Tsvangirai from Zimbabwe chooses to engage his former political enemy, Robert Mugabe, and agrees to serve in a government of national unity, even though Mugabe humiliated him, jailed him, and almost had him killed. In an interview with *New African* magazine, Tsvangirai explained that he drew inspiration from Nelson Mandela who though unjustly jailed

31. Ankomah, "Justice in Africa."

32. Ibid., 11.

33. Ibid.

34. Lamin, "Building Peace through Accountability."

35. McDonnell and Akallo, *Girl Soldier.*

for 27 years, decided to forgive and work towards a negotiated future. Referring to the transformation process that Zimbabwe is experiencing, he said that this approach "is better than the experience everywhere else in Africa where conflicts are resolved by armed conflict, and then you move from violence to violence, from conflict to conflict, endlessly."[36]

We find ourselves in agreement with researchers like Alan Torrance who argued that there are theological grounds for advocating forgiveness and reconciliation in the sociopolitical realm.[37] Truth commissions should be regarded as a defensible moral compromise between the demands of justice and the need for social unity.[38] However, we also agree with Wilson who suggested that justice can be sought through punishment as well as through reconciliation.[39] Truth commissions "are not magic elixirs, either for individuals or societies", but one of a variety of interventions that a nation may employ when dealing with intranational violence; the outcomes of such commissions may not generalize to other transitional processes.[40]

The passage of time now affords researchers the opportunity to more objectively evaluate the case studies where nations must deal with mass violence and repression. For example, Laurel Fletcher, Harvey Weinstein, and Jamie Rowen studied seven nations with a recent history of mass violence and repression and concluded that neither trials nor truth commissions should necessarily be introduced early in the process to initiate transitional justice processes.[41]

As those who have lived through the South African process, there is a sense of immense relief that we did not pursue the ICC route. We wholeheartedly side with Pumla Gobodo-Madikizela who suggested that forgiveness is the only option for postconflict societies where victims and perpetrators have to live together in the same country after cessation of the conflict.[42]

---

36. Sasa, "Tsvangirai," 47.

37. Torrance, "The Theological Grounds for Advocating Forgiveness."

38. Allen, "Between Retribution and Restoration," 22.

39. Wilson, "Reconciliation and Revenge."

40. Quinn and Freeman, "Lessons Learned."

41. Fletcher, Weinstein, and Rowen, "Context, Timing and the Dynamics of Transitional Justice."

42. Gobodo-Madikizela, "Trauma, Forgiveness, and the Witnessing Dance."

THE TRC AND PSYCHOLOGICAL HEALING

On May 20, 1983, the ANC bombed the headquarters of the South African Air Force in Church Street Pretoria. Although their intended target was a military installation, most of the people killed were civilians. As a military chaplain I (van der Spuy) was summoned to assist in the aftermath of the bombing. I remember climbing up the dark stairs to the operations room on the top floor of the headquarters building. Blood and water were pouring down the stairs and there was devastation everywhere. Many years later when the New York twin-towers came down on September 11, I re-experienced the devastation of the Church Street bombing and wept in empathy for all those thousands involved.

In the Church Street bombing, twenty-one people died and over 200 were injured. When confirmation of the first victim's identity was established, I was given the task to drive to his home and notify his wife. I remember praying for strength as I drove to the suburb to announce that her husband was not coming home that afternoon. Throughout that night, I had the task to inform countless families that their loved ones had died. I screamed at God about this senseless war. My spirit longed for peace and reconciliation, and I prayed with each family that God would give them the courage and strength to forgive those who perpetrated these acts of violence against them. Some of them did. When the perpetrators of the Church Street bombing applied to the TRC for Amnesty, Neville Clarence, a victim blinded by the bomb, attended the TRC session and expressed forgiveness to the bombers.[43] He found the strength to shake the hand of the spokesman of the operational team in a symbolic expression of reconciliation.

Undoubtedly, the TRC process, which emphasized the expression of truth, helped achieve forgiveness and reconciliation, and thereby helped achieve psychological healing as well. But *truth* has many faces. Tutu used Judge Mohamed's concept of *truth of wounded memories* to describe personal truth and refers to it as the *healing truth*.[44] The TRC did all it could to corroborate the stories of perpetrators but decided to allow victims to *tell their stories* in their own words. This therapeutic narrative provided the context for a psychological healing that would never have been possible in a court of law or judicial tribunal.

43. Tutu, *No Future without Forgiveness.*
44. Ibid., 26.

"We want to forgive, but we don't know whom to forgive."[45] These words of one of the daughters of a victim brutally killed by the police, underlines the importance that the allocution of truth played in the healing process of victims. Although the TRC only required that an applicant make a full disclosure of all the relevant facts relating to the offence— asking for forgiveness was not a prerequisite—most applicants at least expressed remorse and asked for forgiveness from their victims and/or their families.[46] Forgiveness is cancelling a debt too big to pay.[47] In releasing wrongdoers from their moral debt, victims and societies experience forgiveness.

Colonel Horst Schobesberger was the officer who gave the order to open fire during the September, 1992 Bisho massacre when 30 unarmed demonstrators were killed. At one of the TRC hearings, he spoke on behalf of the police officers involved in the shootings: "I say we are sorry. I say the burden of the Bisho massacre will be on our shoulders for the rest of our lives . . . But please, I ask specifically the victims not to forget, I cannot ask this, but to forgive us."[48]

Miroslav Volf in sharing his own story of interrogation, torture and suffering in communist Yugoslavia wrote that "psychological wounds caused by suffering can be healed only if a person passes through the narrow door of painful memories."[49] Remembering "Rightly in a Violent World" requires speaking truth and practicing grace. Realizing that memories are always an approximation of the truth and a reconstruction of the past, Volf concluded that healing is only possible when a person recalls a "wounding event with the emotional reaction that accompanied it."[50] In allowing victims and their families access to the *truth*, the TRC contributed to psychological healing. But reconciliation "requires more than truth, more even than full disclosure. It also requires moral judgment, and along with moral judgment the wrongdoer's acceptance of moral responsibility—as well as the victim's willingness to release the wrongdoer from genuine moral debt."[51]

45. Ibid., 149.

46. Tutu, *No Future without Forgiveness.*

47. Stoop and Masteller, *Forgiving Our Parents.*

48. Tutu, *No Future without Forgiveness,* 151.

49. Volf, *The End of Memory,* 27.

50. Ibid.

51. Ibid., 219.

Several researchers have examined the therapeutic value of survivors taking part in a public truth commission. Whether survivors participated in telling the world about their loss, there appeared to be little difference in their relative levels of distress and traumatization.[52] Bearing testimony was not necessarily helpful to them, nor did it appear to have a beneficial effect on their psychiatric status or current forgiveness attitude.[53]

Researchers were also able to isolate certain factors in the TRC process that were beneficial to the participants. Debra Kaminer found that the act of forgiveness was associated with better psychiatric health.[54] Gibson's research on more than 3700 subjects suggests that truth telling did in fact contribute to racial reconciliation.[55] When subjects accepted the "truth" about the past, they were more likely to hold reconciled attitudes. Gibson also found that reconciliation was influenced by the *contact hypothesis*, that is that reconciliation was positively associated with higher levels of interracial contact.[56] Alfred Allan and fellow associates found that when the victim perceived that wrongdoers were truly sorry about their actions, their capacity to forgive was positively influenced.[57] Providing details of the violation against them also helped TRC participants forgive. In contrast, when commissioners unintentionally universalized their experience of suffering, participants were more likely to remain unforgiving.[58]

Leonia Kurgan (2001) studied human rights abuses in South Africa, United States, and the Holocaust. He concluded that some atrocities are so evil that it is perhaps unreasonable to expect first and second generations to move to a point of reconciliation.[59] He suggested a more reasonable goal for victims and perpetrators would be reaching a point where the painful past no longer has the power to control and poison their souls.

52. Kagee, "The Relationship between Statement Giving."

53. Stein et al., "The Impact of the Truth and Reconciliation Commission"; and Kaminer et al. "The Truth and Reconciliation Commission in South Africa."

54. Kaminer et al., "The Truth and Reconciliation Commission in South Africa."

55. Gibson, "The Contributions of Truth to Reconciliation"; Gibson, "Does Truth Lead to Reconciliation?"; and Gibson, "'Truth' and 'Reconciliation' as Social Indicators."

56. Gibson, "Does Truth Lead to Reconciliation?"

57. Allan, Allan, Kaminer, and Stein, "Exploration of the Association between Apology and Forgiveness."

58. Kaminer, "Forgiveness Attitudes of Truth Commission Opponents."

59. Kurgan, "Memories, Healing, Reconciliation, and Forgiveness."

REPARATIONS AND REHABILITATION

Amnesty was granted by the TRC to any person who applied, met the criteria, and fully allocuted to their actions. But this meant that victims could not subsequently claim compensation in civil court actions for these atrocities. We have already mentioned the criticism of some who suggested that the unity and reconciliation process was pursued at the expense of substantial reparations to the majority of South Africans.[60] In addition to the amnesty hearings, it was also a part of the TRC's mandate to pursue reparation and rehabilitation. The TRC committee focused on Human Rights Violations and speedily dealt with the amnesty applications that were submitted. But the Committee for Reparation and Rehabilitation (CRR) was not as successful. One of Wilson's harshest criticisms of the TRC process was his criticism of the work of the CRR.[61] Although some individualized reparations took place (the TRC consciously avoided the term compensation), the budget was simply inadequate to cover reparation much less rehabilitation. In their final report, the TRC warned that healing and reconciliation, either at an individual or a community level, might not take place if the reparation and rehabilitation measures were not adequate.

Tutu pointed out that a major weakness of the TRC was that although perpetrators were granted amnesty as soon as their applications were approved, victims were not granted reparations by application.[62] The TRC could only make recommendations to the President concerning reparation for the victims. Three years after the TRC had started its hearings, no final reparations had been approved. Urgent interim relief was paid to about 20,000 victims, usually no more than the equivalent of about US$330 per victim. There was also very little money available to provide ongoing psychosocial-spiritual care and support to those who participated in the TRC process. Tutu admitted that they were "unable to provide long-term counseling and support" and that it is possible that individuals, "because they reopened their wounds . . . and did not receive sufficient professional help to deal with the anguish, went away more traumatized than before."[63]

60. Van der Walt, Franchi, and Stevens, "The South African Truth and Reconciliation Commission."

61. Wilson, "Reconciliation and Revenge in Post-Apartheid Africa."

62. Tutu, *No Future without Forgiveness.*

63. Ibid., 233.

It is clear that the TRC did not adequately plan for those retraumatized by telling their story. The vicarious traumatization experienced by the staff of the TRC also did not get needed attention. I (van der Spuy) arranged for Everett Worthington, a prominent Christian psychologist and forgiveness researcher, to visit the TRC in Johannesburg. We addressed the TRC committee on the difference between forgiveness and reconciliation. As Worthington shared his personal story about forgiving the person who murdered his mother, one of the TRC staff members became overwhelmed with emotions and ran out of the room.[64] I followed her and listened to her story. Her son had been abducted by the police and subsequently murdered. The policeman who killed her son applied for and received amnesty. Although he did not express remorse, he did reveal the location where her son was buried in an unmarked grave and she could find solace in the fact that she could rebury her son and grieve his death. As a TRC staff member she felt compelled to reconcile with her son's murderer. But her emotional turmoil was compounded because after the hearings she heard that he had arrogantly boasted, 'I got away with it'. She wanted to forgive, but did not feel that she could reconcile. Our visit was the first time she felt that the pressure to reconcile was lifted and that she could forgive even if no reconciliation was possible.

To a large extent the TRC was able to facilitate reconciliation on a national level, and in some instances on an interpersonal level, but it clearly did not give enough support to victims and perpetrators to work through the challenges of reconciliation. Minimal aftercare diminished the impact that the TRC could have had on individual psychological healing.

THE TRC AND THE SPIRITUAL CONNECTION

> O God of justice, mercy and peace. We long to put behind us all the pain and division of apartheid together with all the violence which ravaged our communities in its name. And we ask You to bless this Truth and Reconciliation Commission with your wisdom and guidance as it commences its important work of redressing the many wrongs done . . . We pray that all those people who have been injured in either body or spirit may receive healing . . . for those who may be found to have committed these

64. Worthington shares this story in McCullough, Sandage, and Worthington, *To Forgive is Human.*

162 FORGIVENESS, RECONCILIATION, AND RESTORATION

> crimes against their fellow human beings, that they may come
> to repentance and confess their guilt . . . that they too might be-
> come the recipients of Your divine mercy and forgiveness . . . We
> ask that the Holy Spirit may pour out its gifts of justice, mercy,
> and compassion . . . that truth may be recognized . . . and that the
> end may bring reconciliation and love . . .[65]
>
> —*Opening prayer at the first public hearing of the TRC,*
> *April 1996*

Our Christian understanding of reconciliation is rooted in the restoration of our relationship with God through Jesus Christ. Russell Botman
in his chapter on "Truth and Reconciliation: the South African Case"
wrote, "restorative justice relates directly to the biblical understanding of
reconciliation."[66] In addition, he wrote "Christianity has always been concerned about memory, confession, guilt, and forgiveness in the interest of
reconciliation."[67] Breytenbach argued that Paul transferred the concept
of reconciliation as a political-diplomatic process, to the theological field
in order to express the relationship between God and human beings and
that it therefore lost its social political dimensions.[68]

Reflecting on his appointment as chairperson of the TRC Tutu wrote,
"The President must have believed that our work would be profoundly
spiritual. After all, forgiveness, reconciliation, and reparation were not
normal currency in political discourse . . . Forgiveness, confession, and
reconciliation was far more at home in the religious sphere."[69] When victims and perpetrators came to testify at hearings there would often be a
solemn atmosphere with prayers, hymns, and ritual candle lightings to
commemorate those who had died. At the insistence of his Hindu and other
colleagues, Tutu presided over the proceedings, in his formal Archbishop's
cassock. "Very few people objected to the heavy spiritual and indeed
Christian religious emphasis of the commission," he said.[70] No matter how
diabolical the deeds of some perpetrators, Tutu constantly challenged the

---

65. Tutu, *No Future without Forgiveness*, 113.

66. H. Russel Botman, "Truth and Reconciliation: The South Africa Case," in
Coward and Smith (eds.), *Religion and Peacebuilding*, 243–60 (250).

67. Ibid.

68. Cilliers Breytenbach, "Using Exegesis: On 'Reconciliation' and 'Forgiveness' in
the Aftermath of the TRC," in Hollness and Wüstenberg (eds.), *Theology in Dialogue*,
245–56.

69. Tutu, *No Future without Forgiveness*, 80.

70. Ibid., 83.

TRC not to demonize them. He wrote, "as I listened to the stories of victims I marveled at their magnanimity, that after so much suffering, instead of lusting for revenge, they had this extraordinary willingness to forgive. Then I would thank God that all of us, even I, had this remarkable capacity for good . . . theology undergirded my work in the TRC."[71]

Some researchers have speculated that the influence of Tutu may have been underestimated as the negotiators turned away from the retributive justice of the township courts and rather decided to establish this commission with the power to forgive.[72] Tutu consistently articulated the philosophy that forgiveness is better than retributive justice. Antjie Krog, the Afrikaner reporter for the *South African* state broadcasting services argued that Tutu's articulation of the worldview of *ubuntu* contributed more than what is generally recognized.[73] She suggested that people need to understand *ubuntu* before they can understand the seemingly contradictory demands of reconciliation with someone who was accused of abusing your loved ones. *Ubuntu* helps to explain the impetus to granting of amnesty, the rehabilitation of perpetrators, and the interdependence of forgiveness and reconciliation in the process of healing a nation.

The concept of *ubuntu* implies that people are connected. What one person tends to affect his whole world. When you do well, it spreads out; it is for the whole of humanity. The concept of *ubuntu* is exemplified in the letter that President Mandela wrote as an introduction to Kader Asmal's work on reconciliation.[74] He wrote that people marvel and complement him on emerging from prison without bitterness, but he stated that millions of South Africa's people spent a longer time in the "prison of apartheid" or the *racism of the mind*. In identifying with people and their pain, he stated that "personal bitterness" is an unaffordable luxury that becomes irrelevant.

With the appointment of Tutu and his promotion of the values of *ubuntu* over retribution, the spiritual underpinnings of the TRC are irrefutable. But it is also necessary to assess the role of church structures

71. Ibid., 86.

72. Battle. "A Theology of Community."

73.. Xhosa word meaning "I am because you are." It speaks about our interconnectedness, that you can't exist as a human being in isolation and you can't be human all by yourself. It is regarded as fundamental to the way Africans approach life it epitomizing kindness, humanity, compassion, and goodness (Krog, "This Thing Called Reconciliation").

74. Asmal, Asmal, and Roberts, *Reconciliation through Truth*.

in the process of reconciliation. Megan Shore concluded that religion, specifically Christianity, played a central, but ambiguous role in the TRC process.[75] The Dutch Reformed Church functioned as the *state church* and provided the theological rationale for apartheid. Apartheid laws were sanctioned by the white institutional church because of a mistaken understanding of the *election* of the white race by God to be *His people* and the channel of His blessings to the rest of humanity. In its purest form, this theology promoted the idea that white people were the modern day equivalent of Old Testament Israel and therefore the separation that God ordered for the children of Abraham needed to be reflected in the socio-political realities of South African society. Worship was segregated and any form of social or sexual contact across the race bar was metaphorically elevated to *mortal sin*. Sexual relations across racial lines became not only a moral ethical issue but also a punishable crime as determined by the Immorality Act.

It would have been wonderful to report at this point that the racially divided Pentecostal churches in South Africa had retained the nonracial character of the Azusa street revival. As at Azusa Street, the Pentecostal movement in South Africa started as a nonracial experience, but as in Azusa Street, soon lost its nonracialism. John G. Lake (the founder of the AFM in 1908) started his ministry in a black Zionist church in Doornfontein, Johannesburg.[76] Only six months after the mighty outpouring of the Holy Spirit in this first Pentecostal church plant, the AFM executive decided to separate the baptism of white and black congregants. From then on the AFM quickly moved from separate congregations to full support of the Apartheid regime.[77]

Lake has the dubious honor to be associated with those who are considered the fathers of the segregation policy in South Africa.[78] Later when the National Party needed to expand the Senate in their successful strategy to disenfranchise the Coloured population in South Africa, G. R. Wessels, the vice-president of the segregated, white AFM was accorded the "honor" to become a senator in the apartheid government in 1955. It was abundantly clear that the AFM had become an active partner in the process of segregation and apartheid. Nico Horn stated that

75. Shore, "Christianity and Justice."

76. Van der Spuy, "Die Spanning Tussen Vryheid."

77. Horn, "After Apartheid."

78. De Wet, "The Apostolic Faith Mission in Africa."

"Throughout the years of Verwoerdian apartheid, the AFM never raised its voice against the crude oppression of the vast majority of the people" and actively supported the system right up to the end. Instead of being God's prophetic voice to an oppressive regime, the AFM was just a mirror reflection of the system.[79]

Horn pointed out that even in their eventual pursuit to structurally unite the four racially divided sections of the church they were only following the reform process initiated by the government.[80] While other majority white denominations (e.g., the Dutch Reformed Church) were severely reprimanded and condemned by their international counterparts for their support of apartheid, the international Pentecostal community maintained good relationships with the AFM. For the most part, the international Pentecostal churches remained silent about the apartheid atrocities and should therefore accept co-responsibility with their South African Pentecostal brothers and sisters for this silence. Although there have always been sympathizers of the oppressed in South Africa and in the AFM, they were never *visible* enough to be heard in the international Pentecostal conferences and church councils. Horn concluded that the majority of black Pentecostals "felt no less oppressed amongst the white middle class Pentecostal movement of America, Europe and Britain" than what they felt amongst the Pentecostals of South Africa.[81] There are probably many reasons why South African, European and American Pentecostals turned a blind eye to apartheid - we all stand guilty before God and can only pray with Horn that the Holy Spirit may "guide the Pentecostal movement through repentance and confession to cross the racial borders once again! May the Spirit of Azusa Street be revived amongst us!"[82]

But there were also white religious leaders who spoke out fearlessly against the atrocity of human rights violations. These included people like Peter Storey (former head of the Methodist Church), Beyers Naude (prominent Afrikaner dissident and also General Secretary of the SACC), and Denis Hurley (formerly Roman Catholic Archbishop of Durban).

---

79. Hendrik Verwoerd, Prime Minister of South Africa from 1958 to his assassination in 1966, is often referred to as the architect of apartheid.

80. Horn, "After Apartheid."

81. Ibid., para. 94.

82. Ibid., para. 115.

They were joined by black clerics like Allan Boesak the former leader of the Dutch Reformed Mission Church.

I (van der Spuy) was part of a young group of Pentecostals who often spoke out at general church council meetings and condemned the divisions in the church. As a young pastor and chaplain I met with members of the "spiritual committee" of the banned United Democratic Party and ANC members to talk about reconciliation and unity in the Pentecostal Church. While some of my white colleagues at times referred to me as a traitor and a communist, and some of my black colleagues referred to me as a comrade, it was my fervent wish that unity could be attained and reconciliation achieved. On the other hand, I (Mostert) was not as fortunate as my colleague to grow up in an environment where speaking out against the status quo was encouraged or condoned. My disillusionment with the system only grew over time. By the time I became the director for the AFM's all white Welfare Department in 1989, I too was being accused of being a "card carrying member of the ANC."[83] Nevertheless, we did achieve the goal of fully integrating our institutions and our social work services and submitting the 450 employee organization to a fully integrated management board in the same year as the country's general election in 1994. It remains a source of great shame that social justice goals were dictated by politicians, and not Pentecostals who claim to be led by the Spirit of God!

We opened this chapter with the story of our colleague, Frank Chikane. We now return to his story because two components of the narrative provide powerful illustrations of reconciliation. First, he was chosen by the black AFM church to lead them into unity with the white church. In 1996, he was elected as Vice President of our re-united, racially integrated church. In this position, he became part of a delegation of four AFM leaders to testify to the TRC about the miraculous reconciliation brought about in our church as it achieved structural unity for the first time since the 1960s.

The second illustration was an incident that demonstrated the power of reconciliation. In August 2006, Adrian Vlok, the former Minister of Police who was responsible for the order to assassinate Chikane while he was General Secretary of the SACC, made an appointment to see Frank at his offices in the Presidency in Pretoria. Upon his arrival he removed a

---

83. Within Afrikaner culture at that time this would be akin to accusing someone of being a communist in the cold war McCarthian era.

small plastic basin from the bag he was carrying and in an act of humble submission and reconciliation, pleaded with Chikane to wash his feet!

SOME CONCLUSIONS ABOUT TRUTH, FORGIVENESS, AND RECONCILIATION FROM A PENTECOSTAL PERSPECTIVE

It would be appropriate to conclude by first suggesting that we need to approach the concepts of truth, forgiveness, and reconciliation, with a reasonable measure of hermeneutical suspicion.[84] Some regard the concepts as synonyms and some consider reconciliation as a tolerance for abuse. Then, in religious circles reconciliation is used interchangeably with forgiveness. We need to appropriately differentiate between these concepts.

Truth

Telling the truth (or a personal perspective of the truth) does not necessarily lead to forgiveness and/or reconciliation. In fact, the re-telling of the story may retraumatize the victim and prevent psychological wellbeing. For healing to take place, we need to hear the truth, which is an aid in the process of remembering rightly.[85] It is gratifying to see the results of Gibson's research, which indicates that in the South African experience, truth contributed to the process of reconciliation.[86]

Forgiveness

Forgiveness is not the same thing as reconciliation.[87] In fact forgiveness does not always lead to reconciliation and neither should it. Our understanding of child and spousal abuse has suggested that there are times when reconciliation is neither possible nor wise. Botman suggested that in the TRC process there was unbearable pressure on victims to forgive and that this could actually militate against ultimate reconciliation. As the TRC process indicated, there were those who were able to extend the gift of forgiveness to their perpetrators even though the gift was not received by all. Sometimes forgiveness needs to be left to another generation.[88]

84. Botman, "Truth and Reconciliation."

85. Volf, *The End of Memory.*

86. Gibson, "'Truth' and 'Reconciliation.'"

87. Enright and the Human Development Study Group, "Piaget on the Moral Development of Forgiveness."

88. Kurgan, "Memories, Healing, Reconciliation, and Forgiveness."

Forgiveness should also not be confused with pardoning, condoning, excusing, forgetting, or denying.[89] Most of what the TRC did was grant *amnesty* to perpetrators, which could be confused with forgiveness. For the Christian, the question of *rightly remembering wrongs* suffered is part of the larger issue of redemption, and especially the redemption of the past.[90] We cannot forget. We should remember. But people should never be coerced into forgiving. Genuine forgiveness is always voluntary and unconditional. Genuine forgiveness requires three facets: the injured party must be able to recognize the actual injustice done, he/she must willingly choose (without coercion) to respond with mercy rather than *justifiable retribution*, and the process must be concerned with the good of all.[91]

Reconciliation

Worthington concluded that forgiveness happens inside the individual while reconciliation happens within a relationship.[92] Understanding reconciliation as a *restoration of violated trust* earned through *mutually trustworthy behavior* seems to indicate that the TRC's expectations of *truth speaking* leading to reconciliation was unrealistic.[93] To forgive is imperative and a free gift (especially for Spirit filled Christians), but reconciliation has preconditions.[94] Forgiveness is based on the perpetrator's acceptance of moral responsibility, a rebuilding of trust and is eventually deserved as the victim is willing to release the harm done. There are times, because of our brokenness, when reconciliation is not possible or even wise. The *demand-characteristic* of the TRC that there *must* be reconciliation when the truth has been revealed, could therefore actually have prevented the process of forgiveness. The TRC research has added another caveat to our understanding of reconciliation. Even the achievement of political rec-

89. Robert D. Enright and Catherine T. Coyle, "Researching the Process Model of Forgiveness Within Psychological Interventions," in Worthington (ed.), *Dimensions of Forgiveness*, 139–162.

90. Volf, *The End of Memory*.

91. Enright and Coyle, "Researching the Process Model of Forgiveness."

92. Worthington, *Dimensions of Forgiveness*.

93. Everett L. Worthington Jr., "The Pyramid Model of Forgiveness: Some Interdisciplinary Speculations about Unforgiveness and the Promotion of Forgiveness," in Worthington (ed.), *Dimensions of Forgiveness*, 107–38 (129).

94. Volf, *The End of Memory*.

onciliation was insufficient to deal with the victimization caused by the poverty and economic imbalances perpetrated under apartheid.[95]

Finally, a comment on the proclivity of Western Pentecostals to seemingly disengage from social issues. "Pentecostals are not known for their social involvement, at least not in the first world. If one speaks of the Pentecostal movement, one thinks of their zeal for evangelism, their enthusiasm and their emphasis on the baptism in the Spirit with the initial evidence of speaking in tongues."[96] But the South African TRC process reminds us that Pentecostals were so focused on the vertical dimension of reconciliation that they neglected the horizontal dimension.

Our South African colleague, Mathew Clarke argues similarly in his chapter on *Pentecost and Socio-political Concerns*.[97] Although Clarke acknowledged that the general move of the AFM in the 1960's was "support of the governing National Party", he argued that Pentecostals should not get involved in sociopolitical actions. "The Pentecostal world-view sees a far more serious challenge to human well-being in oppressive forces of personal evil than in temporary social structures."[98] According to Clarke, Pentecostal understanding of oppression is that it is "a real spiritual slavery to demon forces" and the "hope of the world" is to escape from the coming destruction.

Clarke was writing at a time when the political tensions of the "White and Black political debate" in South Africa were at a fever pitch and he warned his readers against the propaganda and media images and incorrect international understanding of the "real situation". He suggested that to "become engaged in this sort of understanding would be a contradiction of the Pentecostal experience and perception."[99] He seemed to imply that the apartheid atrocities were "distorted versions of the true situation" and concluded that the Truth (Holy Spirit) makes Pentecostal involvement in these "media-publicized issues" problematic.

By now it should be abundantly clear that we would lovingly, but firmly reject such a hermeneutic of a Pentecostal world-view. The atrocities committed by fellow citizens in the name of Christianity reminds all Pentecostals that we have a sociopolitical responsibility to speak out

95. Moran, "South Africa and the Colonial Intellectual," 109–124.

96. Horn, "After Apartheid," para. 84.

97. Clark and Lederle, *What is Distinctive about Pentecostal Theology?* 85.

98. Ibid., 93.

99. Ibid., 94–95.

against atrocities and human rights violations, especially if the perpetrators are claiming biblical or theological support for their actions.

Finally, we are acutely aware that human rights abuses and atrocities are being committed on a global scale even today. Although we acknowledge that justice could be sought through retributive processes such as the ICC we want to submit that the TRC has provided sufficient evidence that a truth commission remains a defensible moral compromise between the demands of justice and the need for social unity.[100] God has blessed us richly so that our experiences might become a beacon of hope to others locked in deadly and senseless conflict. If it can happen in South Africa, it can certainly happen anywhere.

Structures like the TRC can create a space where truth about human rights abuses can be heard and where gracious people can extend forgiveness. We implore the Holy Spirit to guide us individually and collectively into such a space; a place where we can learn to wash one another's feet in national reconciliation. May the spirit of Azusa be revived in us again!

BIBLIOGRAPHY

Allan, Alfred, Maria Allan, Debra Kaminer, and Dan Stein. "Exploration of the Association between Apology and Forgiveness amongst Victims of Human Rights Violations." *Behavioral Sciences & the Law* 24 (2006) 87–102.

Allen, Jonathan. "Between Retribution and Restoration: Justice and the TRC." *South African Journal of Philosophy* 20 (2001) 22.

Ankomak, Baffour. "Justice in Africa . . . The Great Debate Continues." *New African* 486 (2009) 10–11.

Asmal, Kader, Louise Asmal, and Ronald Suresh Roberts. *Reconciliation through Truth: A Reckoning of Apartheid's Criminal Governance.* 2nd ed. Mayibuye History and Literature Series 74. Cape Town: David Philip, in association with Mayibue Books, University of the Western Cape, 1996.

Battle, Michael. "A Theology of Community." *Interpretation: A Journal of Bible & Theology* 54 (2000) 173.

Boesak, Willa. *God's Wrathful Children: Political Oppression and Christian Ethics.* Grand Rapids: Eerdmans, 1995.

Clark, Matthew S., and Henry L. Lederle. *What is Distinctive about Pentecostal Theology?* Miscellanea Specialia 1. Pretoria: University of South Africa Press, 1989.

Coletti, Elisabetta Anna. "Reconciliation: South Africa's Greatest Export?" *Christian Science Monitor* (August 24, 2000). http://www.csmonitor.com/2000/0824/p1s3.html.

---

100. Allen, "Between Retribution and Restoration," 22.

Coward, Harold G., and Gordon S. Smith, editors. *Religion and Peacebuilding*. SUNY Series in Religious Studies. Albany: State University of New York Press, 2004.

De Wet, Chriso. "The Apostolic Faith Mission in Africa: 1908–1980: A Case Study in Church Growth in a Segregated Society." PhD diss., University of Cape Town, South Africa, 1989.

Eisikovits, Nir. "Rethinking the Legitimacy of Truth Commissions: 'I Am the Enemy You Killed, My Friend.'" *Metaphilosophy* 37 (2006) 489–514.

Enright, R. D., and the Human Development Study Group. "Piaget on the Moral Development of Forgiveness: Identity or Reciprocity?" *Human Development* 37 (1994) 63–80.

Fletcher, Laurel E., Harvey Weinstein, and Jamie Rowen. "Contest, Timing and the Dynamics of Transitional Justice: A Historical Perspective." *Human Rights Quarterly* 31 (2009) 163–220.

Foster, Don. "Evaluating the Truth and Reconciliation Commission of South Africa." *Social Justice Research* 19 (2006) 527–40.

Gibson, James L. "The Contributions of Truth to Reconciliation." *Journal of Conflict Resolution* 50 (2006) 409–32.

———. "Does Truth Lead to Reconciliation? Testing the Causal Assumptions of the South African Truth and Reconciliation Process." *American Journal of Political Science* 48 (2004) 201–17.

———. "'Truth' and 'Reconciliation' as Social Indicators." *Social Indicators Research* 81 (2007) 257–81.

Gobodo-Madikizela, Pumla. "Trauma, Forgiveness, and the Witnessing Dance: Making Public Spaces Intimate." *Journal of Analytical Psychology* 53 (2008) 129–88.

Griffiths, Anne. "Comments." *Current Anthropology* 41 (2000) 89.

Hamber, Brandon. "'Ere Their Story Die': Truth, Justice, and Reconciliation in South Africa." *Race & Class* 44 (2002) 61.

Hamber, Brandon, and Richard Wilson. "Symbolic Closure through Memory, Reparation and Revenge in Post-Conflict Societies." *Journal of Human Rights* 1 (2002) 35–53.

Holness, Lynn, and Ralf K. Wüstenberg, editors. *Theology in Dialogue: The Impact of the Arts, Humanities, and Science on Contemporary Religious Thought: Essays in Honour of John W. de Gruchy*. Grand Rapids: Eerdmans, 2002.

Horn, Nico J. "After Apartheid: Reflections on Church Mission in the Changing Social and Political Context of South Africa." *Transformation* 11 (1994) 25–28.

———. "Crossing Racial Borders in Southern Africa: A Lesson from History." *Cyberjournal for Pentecostal-Charismatic Research*. Pentecostal-Charismatic Theological Inquiry International (June 1991). http://www.pctii.org/cyberj/cyberj3/nico.html (accessed April 26, 2010).

Kagee, Ashraf. "The Relationship between Statement Giving at the South African Truth and Reconciliation Commission and Psychological Distress among Former Political Detainees." *South African Journal of Psychology* 36 (2006), 10–24.

Kaminer, Debra. "Forgiveness Attitudes of Truth Commission Deponents: Relation to Commission Response during Testimony." *Peace and Conflict: Journal of Peace Psychology* 12 (2006) 175.

Kaminer, Debra, et al., "The Truth and Reconciliation Commission in South Africa: Relation to Psychiatric Status and Forgiveness among Survivors of Human Rights Abuses." *British Journal of Psychiatry* 178 (2001) 373–77.

Kelman, Herbert C. "Reconciliation from a Social-Psychological Perspective." In *The Social Psychology of Intergroup Reconciliation*, edited by Arie Nadler, Thomas E. Malloy, and Jeffrey D. Fisher, 15–36. New York: Oxford University Press, 2008.

Krog, Antjie. "'This Thing Called Reconciliation . . . ' Forgiveness as Part of an Inter-connectedness-towards-Wholeness." *South African Journal of Philosophy* 27 (2008) 353–66.

Kurgan, Leonia. "Memories, Healing, Reconciliation, and Forgiveness." *Psycho-Analytic Psychotherapy in South Africa* 9 (2001) 1–10.

Lamin, Abdul Rahrnan (2003). "Building Peace through Accountability in Sierra Leone: The Truth and Reconciliation Commission and the Special Court." *Journal of Asian & African Studies* 38 (2003) 295–320.

Lindsay, Gordon. *John G Lake: Apostle to Africa.* Dallas: Christ for the Nations, 1981.

McCullough, Michael E., Steven J. Sandage, and Everett L. Worthington. *To Forgive Is Human: How to Put Your Past in the Past.* Downers Grove, IL: InterVarsity, 1997.

McDonnell, Faith J. H., and Grace Akallo. *Girl Soldier: A Story of Hope for Northern Uganda's Children.* Grand Rapids: Chosen, 2007.

Moran, Shane. "South Africa and the Colonial Intellectual." *Research in African Literatures* 40 (2009) 109–24.

Sasa, Mabasa. "Tsvangirai 'Those Who Accept Me Have to Accept Mugabe'" *New African,* (2009) 46–49.

Quinn, Joanna R., and Mark Freeman. "Lessons Learned: Practical Lessons Gleaned from inside the Truth Commissions of Guatemala and South Africa." *Human Rights Quarterly* 25 (2003) 1117–49.

Schaffer, Kay, and Sidonie Smith. "Human Rights, Storytelling, and the Position of the Beneficiary: Antjie Krog's Country of My Skull." *PMLA: Publications of the Modern Language Association of America* 121 (2006) 1577–84.

Shore, Megan. "Christianity and Justice in the South African Truth and Reconciliation Commission: A Case Study in Religious Conflict Resolution." *Political Theology* 9 (2008) 161–178.

Skinner, D. "An Evaluation of a Set of TRC Public Hearings in Worcester: A Small Rural Community in South Africa." *Psychology, Health, & Medicine* 5 (2000) 97.

Stanley, Brian. "Mission and Human Dignity in the Light of Edinburgh 1910." *Mission Studies: Journal of the International Association for Mission Studies* 26 (2009) 80–97.

Statman, James M. "Performing the Truth: The Social-Psychological Context of TRC Narratives." *South African Journal of Psychology* 30 (2000) 23.

Stein, Dan J., et al., "The Impact of the Truth and Reconciliation Commission on Psychological Distress and Forgiveness in South Africa." *Social Psychiatry & Psychiatric Epidemiology* 43 (2008) 462–68.

Stoop, David A., and James Masteller. *Forgiving our Parents, Forgiving Ourselves: Healing Adult Children of Dysfunctional Families.* Ann Arbor, MI: Vine, 1991.

Tepperman, Jonathan D. "Truth and Consequences." *Foreign Affairs* 81 (2002) 128–45.

Torrance, Alan J. "The Theological Grounds for Advocating Forgiveness and Reconciliation in the Sociopolitical Realm." In *The Politics of Past Evil: Religion, Reconciliation, and the Dilemmas of Transitional Justice,* edited by Daniel Philpott, 45–86. Kroc Institute Series on Religion, Conflict, and Peace Building. Notre Dame, IN: University of Notre Dame Press, 2006.

Truth and Reconciliation Commission of South Africa. Distributed for the Truth and Reconciliation Commision by Juta. Kenwyn, Cape Town, 1998.

Tutu, Desmond. *No Future without Forgiveness.* An Image Book. Doubleday: New York, 1999.

Van der Spuy, Mervin. "Die Spanning Tussen Vryheid en Formalisering tov die liturgiese Verskuiwinge Binne die Apostoliese Geloof Sending van Suid-Afrika." MA thesis, Pretoria, South Africa: University of South Africa, 1985.

van der Walt, Clint, Vijè Franchi, and Garth Stevens, "The South African Truth and Reconciliation Commission: 'Race', Historical Compromise, and Transitional Democracy." *International Journal of Intercultural Relations* 27 (2003) 251–67.

Volf, Miroslav. *The End of Memory: Remembering Rightly in a Violent World*. Grand Rapids: Eerdmans, 2006.

Walaza, Nomfundo. "Reconciling with Partial Truths: An Assessment of the Dilemmas Posed by the Reconciliation Process in South Africa." *Smith College Studies in Social Work* 73 (2003) 189–204.

Wilson, Richard A. "Reconciliation and Revenge in Post-Apartheid South Africa." *Current Anthropology* 41 (2000) 75–87.

Worthington, Everett L., editor. *Dimensions of Forgiveness: Psychological Research and Theological Perspectives*. Laws of Life Symposia Series 1. Philadelphia: Templeton Foundation Press, 1998.

A Sociological Perspective

9

Public Acts of Forgiveness

What Happens When Canadian Churches
and Governments Seek Forgiveness
for Social Sins of the Past?

Michael Wilkinson

INTRODUCTION

Since the end of World War II the number of public acts of forgiveness has increased exponentially. There is a globalization of forgiveness spreading throughout the world. Public confessions of every type have emerged across all continents, cultures, religions, and states. These intergroup apologies suggest a form of collective guilt requiring some sort of public act of forgiveness following the Abrahamic faith traditions of Judaism, Christianity, and Islam. Germany apologized to the Jews for the genocide and atrocities of war. The Pope apologized for Catholic prejudice towards Jews and Muslims, the Crusades and slavery. The Australian government apologized to the aborigines. The Mormon Church apologized to black Mormons for refusing them the priesthood. George H. W. Bush apologized to Japanese-Americans for loss of rights and property when put into internment camps. Southern Baptists apologized for the evil of slavery. United Methodists apologized for the 1864 massacre of Cheyenne and Arapaho Indians, led by Methodist preacher Chin Chivington. The Dutch Reformed Churched apologized to black South Africans for religious justification of apartheid. The US government apologized for the overthrow of the Kingdom of Hawaii in the nineteenth century. Truth and Reconciliation Commissions were established not only in South Africa but also in Canada to deal with the ill treatment of First Nations peoples.[1] White Pentecostals in North America also offered an apology to black Pentecostals for their racist attitudes and actions.[2]

These examples represent just a few of the many acts of public apology, forgiveness and reconciliation the world has witnessed in the past fifty years. How do we understand public acts of forgiveness? What role does religion play? What role does government play? How do we understand collective guilt and intergroup relations? The purpose of this chapter is to explore sociologically the role of public forgiveness, make comparisons between church and government apologies, and include a response by those in the Pentecostal communities. More specifically, I will examine the recent public apologies by church and state toward First Nations peoples in Canada. To proceed I offer a theoretical orientation from sociology, a case study of aboriginal and European contact in North America, the residential school system, and an assessment of the types of public acts of forgiveness.

RELIGION AND THE SOCIOLOGY OF FORGIVENESS: A THEORETICAL ORIENTATION

Sociology has not dealt with the topic of forgiveness as extensively as some other social sciences like psychology. Most of the social scientific literature deals with forgiveness as an intrapersonal issue as opposed to an intergroup dynamic. Furthermore, the relationship between religion, forgiveness, and global society is an underdeveloped area. In this section,

1. For a list of public acts of forgiveness see Oliner, *Altruism, Intergroup Apology, Forgiveness, and Reconciliation*, 245–49.

2. See Rosenior, "The Rhetoric of Racial Reconciliation."

I work through some theoretical ideas from Robert Wuthnow, Samuel Oliner, Pitirim Sorokin, Jacque Derrida, and Peter Beyer for understanding the relationship between religion and forgiveness as a social act in our contemporary global world. Each of these authors contributes ideas that frame my analysis.

Robert Wuthnow conducted a national study on forgiveness as a cultural construct mobilized by religious organizations, especially small groups, to bring about healing and reconciliation to social relationships.[3] Forgiveness, according to Wuthnow, is generated by much social capital. However, religious groups provide more than social means in the production of forgiveness. Religious groups also offer other resources which are cultural, emotional, and spiritual. For Wuthnow, forgiveness is a social process; "a culturally available category that people associate with a loosely defined set of attitudes and behavior that often includes making sense of or giving a new interpretation to a past action, overcoming anger or guilt, gaining a feeling of cleansing or wholeness, and being able to think about or interact with an offending or aggrieved person in a new way."[4] This conceptualization rightly points to the cultural component of forgiveness which is particularized in North America. I do not assume that non-Western cultures or other religious traditions will necessarily conceive of forgiveness as an act related to the past that also assumes a future orientation or ability to move forward in a new way. I will return to this point later when discussing aboriginal views of time, forgiveness and the past.

The production of forgiveness, according to Wuthnow, is related to the process of socialization or the lifelong process of learning one's culture and in this instance forgiveness. Religions play important roles in socializing members to understand the social script of forgiveness. Scripts are learned and religious organizations facilitate this learning especially in childhood (but not limited to childhood) about the importance of apologizing, confessing, forgiving, and reconciling especially through sacred texts like the Bible. Forgiveness is also reinforced by religious organizations and for adults through interaction in small groups.

Wuthnow hypothesized that participation in small religious groups would be positively related to forgiveness. He examined the effects of certain kinds of activities in generating forgiveness for example, how closely connected people felt to each other, the role of studying and singing, the

3. Wuthnow, "How Religious Groups Promote Forgiving."
4. Ibid., 127.

level of emotional support, sharing needs, reading the Bible, discussing forgiveness, and prayer. He discovered that these group characteristics were related to prosocial behavior like love or altruism, helping others, and forgiveness especially in the area of broken relationships. In eleven of fifteen items measured, prosocial behavior was significantly associated with forgiveness.[5] This study shows that members of religious groups who participate in small groups experienced healing and forgiveness and worked on improving broken relationships. In other words, participation in small religious groups is positively related to forgiveness.

Samual Oliner also contributes to our understanding of forgiveness and the role religion plays. Oliner sees an important relationship between apology, forgiveness and reconciliation with altruism. He wrote: "By altruism, we mean helping another person or group of people who are in need of help and welcome it, where help is voluntary and the helper expects no external reward. Altruism is associated with both apology and forgiveness—they are really the two sides of the same coin."[6] Forgiveness is a manifestation of love associated with empathy, efficacy, reciprocity, personal morality, caring, courage, and faith.[7] Oliner's view is that a process of reconciliation includes altruistic behavior (putting the welfare of others on a level with your own), true apology (taking responsibility and telling the truth), true forgiveness (renouncing vengeance and rehumanizing the enemy), restorative justice (making amends), empathy (finding common humanity) and reconciliation (reestablishing positive relations between victim and offender).[8]

Oliner argues that these points are especially important for understanding intergroup forgiveness: "Intergroup forgiveness does not take place rapidly. It takes time, especially between unequal groups; the weaker group must not be pressured into a quick accommodation. Healing has to take place slowly. This is especially true when harm has been done to the weaker group. Asking for forgiveness, in this social/political sense, must be performed by some prestigious authority, such as a president or important leader. While the consequences of private and interpersonal

---

5. Ibid., 136.

6. Oliner, *Altruism, Intergroup Apology, Forgiveness, and Reconciliation*, 8. See also Wuthnow, *Acts of Compassion*, especially chapter seven on the role of love, voluntary institutions, and caring for others.

7. Oliner, *Altruism, Intergroup Apology, Forgiveness, and Reconciliation*, 11–27.

8. Ibid., 197.

apology are much better known, social/political forgiveness, or *collective forgiveness*, is understudied."[9] Oliner raises some important questions that need to be addressed. For example, how can we understand how nations can forgive when mass murder or genocide has occurred? What role does group identity play in the process of forgiveness and the ability to take action? How does the tendency to divide according to ingroup and outgroup negatively affect forgiveness? What is the social nature of evil and how can societies respond? Conflict resolution is one way in which forgiveness and reconciliation may begin but there are still important factors to consider. Building trust may be a long process depending on how atrociously people were violated. Reconciliation also includes the establishment of restorative justice; tribunals and commissions all serve to rehumanize social relationships.

Pitirim Sorokin argued that love has a number of aspects including religious, ethical, ontological, physical, biological, psychological, and social.[10] On the social level, he wrote love is a meaningful interaction—or relationship—between two or more persons where the aspirations and aims of one person are shared and helped in their realization by other persons."[11] The power of love is its ability to stop aggression by bringing enemies together. Love is a life giving force for individuals and social movements.[12] The relationship between love and forgiveness must be understood as an important dimension for reconciliation. Love for Sorokin is a kind of energy produced by groups, institutions, and cultures. In this classic sociological treatment of love, Sorokin wrote: "A greatly increased knowledge of love is essential if there is to be a greater production, accumulation, and circulation of love energy in the human world. Both a better knowledge and a greater production of love are desperately needed for the very survival of mankind and for the continuation of its creative mission."[13] For Sorokin, an inflow of love from a higher source of love leads to acts of love, which according to Oliner, includes forgiveness.

The role of nation states in the production of forgiveness is quite complicated. Jacques Derrida argues that one of the problems with states offering forgiveness is that they are also the perpetrators. He questions

9. Ibid., 162.
10. Sorokin, *The Ways and Power of Love*, 3–14.
11. Ibid., 13.
12. Ibid., ch. 4.
13. Ibid., 46.

whether states can forgive the sins of the past if they are also implicated and need forgiveness. Furthermore, when it comes to crimes against humanity, no one is innocent. Yet, argues Derrida, if we are all guilty as heirs to some past social sin, are these public acts of forgiveness offered by heads of states hypocritical? Derrida thinks so and says forgiveness ought to "remain exceptional and extraordinary."[14]

The madness of forgiveness, according to Derrida, is a forgiveness not imposed by a state where states are products of violence and colonialism, which makes it difficult for them to exercise authority to forgive. Public acts of forgiveness are nearly impossible, although they do occur, and increasingly so throughout the world. Forgiveness is globalized as the memory of all crimes against humanity. Oliner believes the state needs to play a role in these public acts. Derrida, however, is skeptical. Forgiveness, says Derrida, is a matter of reason and the heart requiring religion and individuals to play a role. This sounds odd in many ways considering the secular nature of Western societies. What happens when states use religious language to seek and offer forgiveness, traditionally a domain of religion in the West for so many centuries? Who forgives? What is forgiven? Are these public acts a form of civil religion? Do states have the authority to forgive? Are these acts of forgiveness efficacious and if so in what way? Further, when churches become involved in these public acts, are they simply supporting the state's role or are they functioning in a substantially different way?

Peter Beyer offers an important idea which helps to understand the role of church and state in global society.[15] Beyer recognizes that secularization and privatization have come to dominate the cultures of many societies, especially in the West. However, these ideas while limiting the role of religion, do not exclude religion from playing a public role, which is differentiated from the state's role. While globalization favors secularization, argues Beyer, globalization "also provides fertile ground for the renewed public influence of religion."[16] However, for religion to have public influence it is not enough that large numbers of people practice the religion. Individual religiosity does not translate into publically influential religion. According to Beyer, three things need to be understood. First, religious organizations, leaders, and movements must demonstrate some clear leadership in an area the society deems important. Second, the

14. Derrida, *On Cosmopolitanism and Forgiveness*, 32.

15. Beyer, *Religion and Globalization*.

16. Ibid., 71.

traditional way in which religions have exerted influence in society has weakened requiring a rethinking of the role of religion. Third, if religion is to have public influence it must, therefore, find some way to influence other subsystems of society, like politics, through a new role as cultural resource for these other spheres of society.[17]

This implies that religions find a way to serve or assist the political process of forgiveness with its cultural values, beliefs, and narratives that address sins of the past. This does not mean the return to a traditional society whereby the separation of church and state is void. Nor, in my view does it mean a new kind of civil religion, a point I will return to later. It does mean that global society and contemporary states are characterized by differentiation with the specialization of subsystems like politics and education that are secularized. Religion, however, does not disappear from our global world. It changes and adapts offering important cultural, social, emotional, and spiritual capital to address a variety of issues, including sins of the past. And, I would argue when a church offers public forgiveness the meaning is similar but different from the state's apology. Further, the state borrows from the church its cultural and spiritual resources to offer forgiveness. In this way, the public influence of the church is directed toward the state, the offender, and the offended. Ultimately, from the perspective of the church, forgiveness is efficacious if people are truly loved and valued, the apology is sincere, reconciliation is sought, justice is served, and God is honored.

PUBLIC APOLOGY IN COLONIAL CONTEXT: A CASE STUDY

The past five hundred years witnessed the global expansion of European societies to the extent that they have come to dominate the world. Trans-Atlantic travels brought Europeans to the shores of North America, which began a troubling relationship between Europeans and Native Americans.[18] The Norse were the first to establish a colony about 1,000 years ago in Newfoundland and Labrador, albeit their stay was short. About five hundred years later Europeans from Portugal and Spain began to explore the

17. Ibid., 71–72.

18. The terms for the inhabitants of the North American continent are in flux, especially in Canada. Indian, native, aboriginal, and First Nations all have specific meanings, depending on context. Readers must pay attention to who uses these terms and how they are used.

East coast looking for resources and passage further east. By 1600, the French had founded permanent settlements developing important economic ties with Native Americans through fur trading, fishing, and other seasonal activities. The English too were part of the new economy between Europeans and the inhabitants of North America. The encounters between these groups, however, quickly demonstrated radically different worldviews. The Europeans, says Choquette, "were bent on acquiring goods and on imposing their cultural values, which included religious values. Such an agenda clashed with that of Amerindian people for whom most goods were intended to be shared, and for whom religious values, being fundamental to one's cultural heritage, were also to be shared."[19]

The main areas of conflict had to do with different views of hierarchy, authority, technology, religion, and culture. For example, the French in the seventeenth century "were not inclined to distinguish readily between their religion and French-European culture. What was considered good for France was understood to be good for Christianity and vice versa."[20] The implications included a view of the Catholic Church as the one true faith and for those outside of the church, no salvation. The practices of Native Americans were considered inferior, false, superstitious, and demonic. According to Choquette, Native spiritualities "were so far removed from Christianity that they could hardly be included on the Christian scale of truth. These native religions were condemned outright as mere savagery and witchcraft. This conviction of having a monopoly on the truth grounded the belief of the French in their superiority. It prevented them from developing any meaningful understanding of Amerindian spiritualities because the latter were categorized as false from the outset. It was the same conviction that underlay the arrogance of all Europeans of the period, an arrogance that was both enthocultural and religious."[21]

Missionaries played a critical role in North America. However, there was much variation among missionaries about cultural issues. Choquette says "the primary objective of all missionaries was evangelization; all other considerations whether national, cultural, economic, or political were secondary. However, Christian evangelization of Amerindians immediately

---

19. Choquette, *Canada's Religions*, 54. See Miller, *Skyscrapers Hide the Heavens*; and Frideres and Krosenbrink-Gelissen, *Aboriginal Peoples in Canada* for extensive historical and sociological accounts of aboriginal and European relations in Canada.

20. Choquette, *Canada's Religions*, 56.

21. Ibid., 56.

raised the question of the degree of European civilization that should accompany it. Whereas all missionaries, including the *Récollects*, the Québec Seminary priests, the Sulpicians, and the Jesuits were intent upon evangelization, they frequently differed on the degree of civilization that they felt was desirable in order to achieve that objective."[22]

How did missionaries understand their role as they interacted with Native Americans? Among the French in the seventeenth century the primary goal was evangelization. However, it soon came to include some level of acculturation which included the development of villages for Native American Christians where they could learn French culture. These villages developed schools where they learned the French language, culture, and behavior, which furthered the goals of New France.[23] When the French were defeated in war with the British in the eighteenth century, the missionary pattern continued in the colonies. Missionaries have a number of motivations for doing their work. There is the mandate of the faith itself to love God, love others, and go into the world and preach the gospel. There is also the belief among Western missionaries that they are to do good works, which often includes notions of development and education. Second, missionaries are motivated by a sense of calling or vocation, which is central for understanding what they do. A high priority is placed upon one's vocation, which is supported through prayer, devotion, conviction, and commitment.[24]

The classical pattern of mission work in North America revolved around the missionary working alongside the governing bodies as people settled, moving further into the North and the West of the continent.[25] Missionaries would travel and establish a settled mission post, which became the model by the end of the nineteenth century. Native Americans were also settled through a series of treaties and reservations. The classical mission, with some variation, would include a church building. For example, in Catholic contexts village life revolved around the church with daily calls to prayer, the celebration of mass, catechism classes in the after-

22. Ibid., 60–61. For a detailed analysis of the Oblate missionaries work in Canada's Northwest during the nineteenth century, see Choquette, *The Oblate Assault on Canada's Northwest*.

23. Choquette, *Canada's Religions*, 86–89.

24. Burridge, *In the Way*.

25. For an excellent historical treatment of missionaries in Canada see Grant, *Moon of Wintertime*. For details on the classical missionary pattern see especially ch. 8.

noon, evening prayers, teaching, and choirs for children. The Methodists followed a similar pattern with daily prayer, afternoon classes, and evening prayer meetings supervised by the missionaries. The Methodist class system was also incorporated into the life of Native Americans. Anglicans followed a similar pattern as the Methodists with a variation on the class meeting; small groups met in the home of the missionary. Services were supplemented with a variety of other church activities for youth, children, and among Protestants, temperance societies. Special evangelistic events or revival meetings were also conducted with some frequency. Missionaries ran a tightly scheduled community. The missionary was thought to be a person with much authority in the community and spoke on many matters outside of religious duties. Churches provided for leadership among Native Americans. However, moving into the hierarchy of the church proved to be another challenge.[26]

Missionaries also worked alongside governments to establish hospitals, schools, and social services, which introduced new people into the community including doctors, nurses, and teachers. There were three kinds of schools that developed which included day schools on the reserves, boarding schools, also on reserves, and industrial schools, focusing on trades, which were sponsored by the Canadian Federal government off the reserve. Schools received financial support from the Federal government. By 1902, there were 221 day schools, 40 boarding schools, and 22 industrial schools. Most of the schools were Roman Catholic (100), Anglican (87), Methodist (41), and Presbyterian (14).[27] It was not long, however, that complaints began to be made over such things as inadequate funding, poor quality of education, lack of food, abuse, high mortality rates, exploitation, discrimination, and condemnation of Native American culture.[28]

The history of the Native residential school system is the basis for the public apologies offered by the state and the churches. The residential school system came into being in 1883 as an official state program and then terminated in 1969, although its roots are in the early work of both French and English missionaries.[29] The context for the development of

26. Grant, *Moon of Wintertime*, 173–74.

27. Ibid., 177.

28. Ibid., 179–83.

29. Probably the most extensive treatment of the residential school system in Canada is Miller, *Shingwauk's Vision*.

the residential school system is the establishment of a series of treaties between 1871 and 1877 in northwestern Ontario and the Prairies. Each of these seven treaties included an obligation by the government to provide schooling for aboriginal peoples. Although the missionaries shaped the day schools and boarding schools, the industrial school has as its inspiration an institution in Pennsylvania developed by Richard Pratt.[30] While Americans had an influence on the residential school system in Canada there are some important differences including the role of the churches. In the United States the relationship between church and state for the provision of aboriginal education did not last long while in Canada it existed until the end of the program in 1969. In Canada the residential schools were also operated by the churches. There was also the idea that religious education was far more important for aboriginals than for Euro-Canadians. Missionaries would therefore, play a central role. Still, American and Canadian residential schools were patterned after similar ideas about practical education, and the assimilation of native peoples.[31]

Throughout the twentieth century the residential school system in Canada came under greater scrutiny. Questions were raised about what people do after they graduate. Most were not prepared for the work world as they faced ongoing racism, discrimination, and the awareness that the education they received was not adequate. The churches increasingly felt the pressure of running schools without adequate funding from the government as they tried to find ways to get out of their treaty responsibilities for providing education. These economic issues were exacerbated during the war years and the depression. The cost of education was further put onto the students and the churches and soon the churches were questioning their role. After 1945 the enthusiasm for operating the schools declined especially among those in the United and Anglican churches. Ambivalence increased among the churches as they were more valued by the government for their ability to be teachers and social workers than evangelists. This created some tension for the missionaries who not only worked for very little, but saw their primary task as evangelization.[32]

For aboriginal communities, the problems came from other expectations not consistent with the motivation of churches and governments. Poor education, abuse, discrimination, and racism all contributed to the

30. Miller, "The State, the Church, and Indian Residential Schools," 110.
31. Ibid., 110–12.
32. Ibid., 114–17.

frustration experienced through inadequate schooling and the denigration of their people. According to Miller, the "frictions, tensions, and open criticisms that became audible over this aspect of the pedagogical program in the post-1945 period constitute but one of many indicators that the supposed partnership of crown and altar in residential schooling was an uneasy one."[33] When the residential school program ended in 1969, rumors of abuse persisted even though denial and attempts to cover-up sexual exploitation continued until the 1990s. Soon the horrors of sexual abuse were revealed at Mount Cashel Orphanage in Newfoundland. Reports of mistreatment began to pour in from former residents at schools across Canada perpetrated by church representatives of every denomination. The 1990s was a period of great sorrow and disbelief among Canadians as ongoing investigations into the residential schooling system revealed horrors unimaginable emotional, sexual, and physical abuse.[34]

PUBLIC APOLOGIES FROM CHURCH AND STATE

The United Church of Canada first issued an apology to Native peoples in 1986 and then in 1998. The first apology was related to the churches' role of imposing European culture upon native peoples generally while the second focused on the particular problems associated with the residential school system. The first apology was acknowledged by native communities but not accepted. In 1988 a response was offered by Edith Memnook of the All Native Circle Conference: "The Apology made to the Native People of Canada by The United Church of Canada in Sudbury in August 1986 has been a very important step forward. It is heartening to see that The United Church of Canada is a forerunner in making this Apology to Native People. The All Native Circle Conference has now acknowledged your Apology. Our people have continued to affirm the teachings of the Native way of life. Our spiritual teachings and values have taught us to uphold the Sacred Fire; to be guardians of Mother Earth, and strive to maintain harmony and peaceful coexistence with all peoples."[35] The second apology focused upon the churches' role in the residential school

33. Ibid., 120.

34. See Miller, *Shingwauk's Vision*, chapter 11 for details on the abuse of aboriginal peoples.

35. Memnook, "Response to the 1986 Apology."

and offered a formal apology for the role they played. Included is a confession for pain and suffering, physical, sexual, and mental abuse. The apology also indicated that aboriginal peoples were victims and for that the church sincerely acknowledges its role: "We pray that you will hear the sincerity of our words today and that you will witness the living out of this apology in our actions in the future."[36] The United Church also developed a number of resources for healing, restoration, justice, and the celebration of native culture.[37]

The Missionary Oblates of Mary Immaculate, Roman Catholic Church Canada, offered an apology in 1991 and likewise expressed regret for the role it played in the suffering and pain of aboriginal students in residential schools.[38] The document referred to the historical reasons for making such an apology including the five hundredth anniversary of the arrival of Europeans to North America, the recent criticisms of the residential schools, and the abuse many students experienced. The Oblates apologized for the role they played "in the cultural, ethnic, linguistic, and religious imperialism that was part of the mentality with which the peoples of Europe first met the aboriginal peoples and which consistently has lurked behind the way the Native peoples of Canada have been treated by civil governments and by the churches."[39] They go on to apologize for the role they played in establishing and running the schools and the abuse native peoples experienced. The Oblates offer one significant qualification; they locate missionary activity in cultural context to account for the heroic role missionaries played and that we must understand they were also products of the time.[40] The Oblate apology is one example of a number of apologies coming from the Roman Catholic Church.[41]

36. Phipps, "Apology to Former Students of United Church Indian Residential Schools."

37. See "United Church Apologies."

38. Crosby, "An Apology to the First Nations of Canada."

39. Ibid.

40. I have not read any criticism of this qualification. However, in reading the apology I found this paragraph to distract from the sincerity of the apology and perhaps could have been left out.

41. The Roman Catholic Church in Canada states it is a decentralized community and each Diocesan Bishop is autonomous and although related to the Canadian Conference of Catholic Bishops, is not responsible to it. This is why, it says, the Canadian Conference of Catholic Bishops has not made an apology for the residential schools. A number of documents and initiatives were established to deal with the abuse at residential schools. See http://www.cccb.ca/site/content/view/2630/1019/lang,eng/ for details,

In 1993, the Anglican Church of Canada offered an apology to the National Native Convocation.[42] The apology included statements acknowledging the humiliation of native peoples, the suffering inflicted upon them, the shame, pain, and hurt. It stated the church was sorry for its role and confessed before God and the community its failures recognizing that healing must be part of the process between the church and native communities. It also acknowledged the value of the native communities including its people, stories, language, and culture. Included with the statement is a response to the Archbishop and Primate of the church that the National Native Convocation acknowledged and accepted the apology and that it was offered with sincerity, sensitivity, compassion, and humility. "We offer praise and thanks to our Creator for his Courage."[43]

In 1994 the Presbyterian Church of Canada also offered an apology.[44] It too included a statement about its role. They confessed their sin and shortcomings calling the church to speak out in love. The church confessed wrongdoing, the attempt to assimilate native communities, colonial attitudes and practices, and its participation with the Canadian government in the operation of residential schools. The church confessed the sin of their ethno-centric attitudes and actions toward aboriginal communities and apologized for the deep pain and sorrow brought upon aboriginal children and their homes. It regretted the deep scars upon the lives of its students and sought forgiveness with hope for reconciliation.[45]

Finally, in 2008, the first public apology made in the Canadian Parliament was offered by Prime Minster Stephen Harper.[46] The Prime Minster stood before the members of Parliament as well as aboriginal guests, and offered an apology which acknowledged the historical role played by the government in establishing residential schools which removed children from their homes. It admits aboriginal children were deprived of care, parents, communities, and lost cultural practices like language. It acknowledged that many children were abused emotionally,

---

including "Let Justice flow like a Mighty River" and "Statement by the National Meeting on Indian Residential Schools" (accessed October 16, 2009).

42. Peer, "Anglican Church of Canada's Apology to Native People."

43. Ibid.

44. Presbyterian Church in Canada, "Apology to Aboriginals."

45. I found all the apologies to be moving. This one was especially so with its confession, regret, and attempt at reconciliation.

46. Harper, "Prime Minister Stephen Harper's Statement of Apology."

physically, and sexually. Further, it states that the residential school system contributed to current social problems in aboriginal communities. The Prime Minister states: "The government recognizes that the absence of an apology has been an impediment to healing and reconciliation. Therefore, on behalf of the government of Canada and all Canadians, I stand before you, in this chamber so central to our life as a country, to apologize to aboriginal peoples for Canada's role in the Indian residential schools system."[47] Harper goes on to recognize wrongs committed and states "we are sorry." Further, the Canadian government implemented the "Indian Residential Schools Settlement" to move towards healing and reconciliation. Aboriginal leaders were allowed to respond to the public apology including Phil Fontaine, National Grand Chief saying it was a turning point in the history of native/nonnative relations.[48]

Responses from the evangelical community in Canada include an official letter from the President of the Evangelical Fellowship of Canada. In a letter addressed to Prime Minister Harper, Bruce Clemenger thanked the Prime Minister for taking leadership and courage. The apology, says Clemenger, "is a significant initiative which I believe will contribute substantially to the process of reconciliation between Canada and its First Nations people."[49] Ray Aldred, chair of the Aboriginal Ministries Council for the Evangelical Fellowship of Canada, also wrote a response to the Prime Minister's apology.[50] Aldred was pleased to hear the apology, admitting there was some concern among those in the Council that the apology would not be sincere. "The residential school experience has shaped the relationship between Aboriginal and non-Aboriginal in Canada. The hurt was particularly felt by those who were in the residential school system." He goes on to say that good can come out of the apology if we continue to address the issues raised in the apology which will lead to reconciliation and healing. Aldred also points to three steps that Canadian evangelicals need to take to be agents of reconciliation. These include: acknowledging the sin of the residential school system by telling the truth; developing a theology of suffering that begins with listening to those who were violated; and developing a shared plan for reconciliation

47. Ibid.

48. See video clip at http://archives.cbc.ca/societe/religion_spiritualite/clips/15394/ (accessed April 29, 2010).

49. Clemenger, "Re: Apology for Residential Schools."

50. Aldred. "Response to the Prime Minister's Apology to Aboriginal Peoples."

and restoration. Aldred concludes by saying: "I think that the Church has been a part of the problem in the past, but now it is going to continue to be a vital part of the solution."

Pentecostalism among Canada's aboriginal peoples has a shorter history than the historical mainline churches. Pentecostalism was well received in many communities and continued to grow among aboriginal peoples at a higher rate than the rest of the population. John Webster Grant credits the expansion of Pentecostalism to "affinities with Indian concepts of communion with the spirits . . . and in developing native leadership."[51] Robert Burkinshaw has made a similar argument showing how native leadership was crucial for the development of Pentecostalism in British Columbia.[52] Pentecostalism spread through the evangelistic efforts of the native leaders prior to the establishment of denominations like the Pentecostal Assemblies of Canada in many of these remote areas. While residential schools were never operated by Pentecostals, a message of spirit empowerment, healing, and restoration was well received among those in the aboriginal communities.[53]

In the 1980s the Pentecostal Assemblies of Canada supported the development of a National Native Leadership Council (NNLC) to wrestle with issues of interest to aboriginal communities. The Council was sponsored by the National Home Missions Department. In 1986, the NNLC brought together key native leaders for a "free exchange of concerns between native people and leaders" on church leadership, education, evangelism, healing, spiritual gifts, native spirituality and pastoral issues.[54]

Gordon Upton, former Executive Director of Home Mission and Bible Colleges for the PAOC, wrote about aboriginals as "Canada's forgotten People" in a 1987 article in *The Pentecostal Testimony* to highlight the poverty and despair in native communities.[55] Upton highlighted social problems like alcoholism, unemployment, violence and suicide in native communities as comparable to third world countries. However, Upton also pointed to a resurging hope as God was "reaching down and granting new life and liberty to increasing numbers of native Canadians."[56] In

---

51. Grant, *Moon of Wintertime*, 202.

52. Burkinshaw, "Native Pentecostalism in British Columbia," 142–70.

53. Laugrand and Oosten, "Reconnecting People and Healing the Land."

54. Upton, "Native Leadership in Canada," 35.

55. Upton, "Canada's Forgotten People," 4–5.

56. Ibid., 5.

the 1990s the NNLC was addressing not only church leadership issues but also social and political issues like native self-government, religious freedom, AIDs and family dysfunction, although there is no direct discussion of the residential school system.[57] However, Pentecostals did participate in a "Sacred Assembly" in Ottawa in 1995 where Christians across Canada gathered to discuss and pray about how aboriginal people were treated in residential schools.[58]

Matthew Coon Come is the most well known and controversial Pentecostal aboriginal leader in Canada. Coon Come, the former national chief of the Assembly of First Nations and former grand chief of the Grand Council of the Crees of Quebec, responded to the apology by the Prime Minster.[59] He spoke of how he was taken from his parents and forced to attend a residential school where he was physically and sexually abused. He says: "As a former residential school survivor, I have waited a long time for this day. And I accept the apology. Each survivor must make his or her own decision. I decided a long time ago that I would move forward. I want broad change, but that change must start with me." He also says he will continue to fight for the rights of aboriginal peoples. "It is time for me to move on. And to continue being Cree, in defiance of everything the federal government intended for me and my people. And to continue asserting our peoples' human rights to self-determination, to our cultures and to our resources and lands."

Terry LeBlanc, Pentecostal and Executive Director of "My People International" and the "North American Institute for Indigenous Theological Studies" also offered a response to the apology.[60] LeBlanc pointed out that a sincere apology must be accompanied by acts that demonstrate contrition if restoration is to occur. The problem, according to LeBlanc, however, is that aboriginal people view time differently than those with a Western worldview. The idea of forgetting the past is foreign to aboriginal peoples. Looking back and reconciling with the past is necessary. Further, reconciliation is not an event. It must be understood as a reality that includes the past, present and future. LeBlanc talked about a relational understanding of reconciliation whereby relationships are restored. The appropriate place to begin, said LeBlanc, is in Genesis 1

57. Sonnenberg, "Native Church Leaders Confront the Issues of the 90s," 16–17.

58. Kennedy, "Ottawa Sacred Assembly '95," 24.

59. Coon Come, "I Choose to Forgive."

60. Personal interview with Michael Wilkinson, September 30, 2009.

where the intent of God is relationship with Creation. We look back to the beginning to move forward, says LeBlanc. Reconciliation involves people acting like God in relationship with Creation.

CONCLUSION

In conclusion, public acts of forgiveness raise a number of issues. First, the role of churches in Canadian society has changed. The traditional view that placed the churches at the center with much authority is no more. However, this does not mean the end of religion. The churches still play an important role as a cultural resource for the society including the state as it models in this case forgiveness and reconciliation. The state too plays an important role offering forgiveness for sins of the past. However, to say it is an example of civil religion is not accurate. While it borrows from religious language the ideas of forgiveness and reconciliation it does not tie them with a strong sense of nationalism. Nor do the churches play a secondary role which simply supports the state. Both contribute as separate spheres of society to its healing. The tragic case of residential schools ought to be a reminder of the precarious relationship between church and state, the power of love, the healing power of forgiveness and reconciliation.

BIBLIOGRAPHY

Aldred, Ray. "Response to the Prime Minister's Apology to Aboriginal Peoples." The Evangelical Fellowship of Canada. www.evangelicalfellowship.ca/NetCommunity/Page.aspx?pid=5885.

Beyer, Peter. *Religion and Globalization*. Theory, Culture & Society. London: Sage, 1994.

Burkinshaw, Robert K. "Native Pentecostalism in British Columbia." In *Canadian Pentecostalism: Transition and Transformation*, edited by Michael Wilkinson, 142–70. McGill-Queen's Studies in the History of Religion, series two, 49. Montreal: McGill-Queen's University Press, 2009.

Burridge, Kenelm. *In the Way: A Study of Christian Missionary Endeavours*. Vancouver: University of British Columbia Press, 1991.

Choquette, Robert. *Canada's Religions: An Historical Introduction*. Religions and Beliefs Series 12. Ottawa: University of Ottawa Press, 2004.

———. *The Oblate Assault on Canada's Northwest*. Religions and Beliefs Series 3. Ottawa: University of Ottawa Press, 1995.

Clemenger, Bruce J. "Re: Apology for Residential Schools: Letter to the Prime Minister." The Evangelical Fellowship of Canada. www.evangelicalfellowship.ca/NetCommunity/Page.aspx?pid=5349 (June 13, 2008).

Coon Come, Matthew. "I Choose to Forgive." http://www.canada.com/vancouversun/news/story.html?id=c9d5dff5-4432-4b18-ad61-075f599f6b0c.

Crosby, Doug. "An Apology to the First Nations of Canada by the Oblate Conference of Canada." Open letter by President of the Oblate Conference of Canada on behalf of the 1200 Missionary Oblates of Mary Immaculate living and ministering in Canada, 1991. http://www.cccb.ca/site/images/stories/pdf/oblate_apology_english.pdf.

Derrida, Jacques. *On Cosmopolitanism and Forgiveness*. Thinking in Action. New York: Routledge, 2001.

Frideres, James S., and Lilianne Ernestine Krosenbrink-Gelissen. *Aboriginal Peoples in Canada: Contemporary Conflicts*. Fifth ed. Scarborough, ON: Prentice Hall, 1998.

Grant, John Webster. *Moon of Wintertime: Missionaries and the Indians of Canada in Encounter Since 1534*. Toronto: University of Toronto Press, 1984.

Harper, Stephen. "Prime Minister Stephen Harper's Statement of Apology." Excerpts on CBC News, June 11, 2008. http://www.cbc.ca/canada/story/2008/06/11/pm-statement.html.

Kennedy, Peggy. "Ottawa Sacred Assembly '95." *The Pentecostal Testimony* March (1996) 24.

Laugrand, Frédéric, and Jarich Oosten. "Reconnecting People and Healing the Land: Inuit Pentecostal and Evangelical Movements in the Canadian Eastern Arctic." *Numen* 54 (2007) 229–69.

Leblanc, Terry. "Let Justice Flow like a Mighty River." Interview with Michael Wilkinson, September 30, 2009. CCCB Brief.

Memnook, Edith, and the All Native Circle Conference. "Response to the 1986 Apology." In the Record of the Proceedings from the 32nd General Council, Victoria. http://www.united-church.ca/aboriginal/relationships/response.

Miller, J. R. "The Church, the State, and Indian Residential Schools." In *Religion and Public Life in Canada: Historical and Comparative Perspectives*, edited by Marguerite Van Die, 109–29. Toronto: University of Toronto Press, 2001.

———. *Shingwauk's Vision: A History of Native Residential Schools*. Toronto: University of Toronto Press, 1996.

———. *Skyscrapers Hide the Heavens: A History of Indian-White Relations in Canada*. Third ed. Toronto: University of Toronto Press, 2000.

Oliner, Samuel P., assisted by Piotr Olaf Zylicz. *Altruism, Intergroup Apology, Forgiveness, and Reconciliation*. St. Paul, MN: Paragon House, 2008.

Peers, Michael. "Anglican Church of Canada's Apology to Native People." A Message from the Primate, Archbishop Michael Peers, to the National Native Convocation Minaki, Ontario, Friday, August 6, 1993. http://www.anglican.ca/rs/apology/apology.htm.

Phipps, Bill. "Apology to Former Students of United Church Indian Residential Schools, and to Their Families and Communities (1998)." United Church Social Policy Positions. United Church of Canada. http://www.unitedchurch.ca/beliefs/policies/1998/a623 (accessed October 16, 2009).

Presbyterian Church in Canada. "Apology to Aboriginals." http://www.presbyterian.ca/ministry/canada/nativeministries/confessions.

Rosenior, Derrick. "The Rhetoric of Racial Reconciliation: Looking Back to Move Forward." In *A Liberating Spirit: Pentecostals and Social Action in North America*, edited by Michael Wilkinson and Steven M. Studebaker. Eugene, OR: Pickwick, forthcoming.

Sonnenberg, Klaus. "Native Church Leaders Confront the Issues of the 90s." *The Pentecostal Testimony* (November 1992) 16–17.

Sorokin, Pitirim Aleksandrovich. *The Ways and Power of Love: Types, Factors, and Techniques of Moral Transformation*. Philadelphia, PA: Templeton Foundation Press, 1954. Reprint with introduction by Stephen Post, 2002. All references are to the 2002 printing.

"Statement by the National Meeting on Indian Residential Schools." Saskatoon, Saskatchewan, March 13–15, 1991. http://www.cccb.ca/site/images/stories/pdf/apology _saskatoon.pdf.

"United Church Apologies to First Nations Peoples." The United Church of Canada. http://www.united-church.ca/aboriginal/relationships/apologies.

Upton, Gordon R. "Canada's Forgotten People." *The Pentecostal Testimony* (November 1987) 4–5.

———. "Native Leadership in Canada." *The Pentecostal Testimony* (December 1986) 35.

Wuthnow, Robert. *Acts of Compassion: Caring for Others and Helping Ourselves*. Princeton, NJ: Princeton University Press, 1991.

———. "How Religious Groups Promote Forgiving: A National Study." *Journal for the Scientific Study of Religion* (2000) 125–39.

An Educational Perspective

10

Learning Forgiveness and Reconciliation

A Model of Education for Peace in Rwanda

Jeff Hittenberger and Patrick Mureithi

In 1994, from April 6th through mid-July (approximately one hundred days), close to a million ethnic Tutsis and moderate Hutus were massacred in the Central African nation of Rwanda. The world watched as neighbor killed neighbor, and families and communities were systematically destroyed. This genocide, which was premeditated and promoted through radio and print propaganda, was brought to a halt when the Rwandan Patriotic Front, a rebel army comprised mostly of Tutsi refugees from previous conflicts, captured the capital city and overthrew the government. For those that survived, even a decade and a half later, the pain is as real as ever. A country of eight million people was reduced to seven million. Even today there are suppressed emotions that, if left unacknowledged, might lead to retaliatory killings of the "other." How can Rwanda avoid another genocide? This chapter explores the possibility that education for forgiveness and reconciliation might be a key to breaking this historic cycle of violence.

Recognizing the need for reconciliation, the Tutsi-led government of Paul Kagame has outlawed the use of ethnic identity terms, routed out the remnants of Hutu power, and established a political regime that has successfully restored order to Rwanda, though some say it has done so at the expense of political freedom. In spite of these approaches, ethnic conflict simmers beneath the surface and the challenge of building a sustainable peace is substantial. While the government has legislated coexistence, it is impossible to legislate forgiveness.

In an effort to contribute to peacebuilding and reconciliation efforts in Rwanda, the African Great Lakes Initiative (AGLI), a nonprofit organization based in St. Louis, MO, has been hosting three-day workshops called Healing and Rebuilding our Communities (HROC, pronounced "he-rock"). The workshops bring ten Tutsis and ten Hutus together for three days, providing learning experiences designed to heal wounds caused by decades of violence.[1]

This chapter examines the strategies and effects of these workshops and suggests possible applications of these strategies in other settings, addressing the following questions:

1) What is the nature of the Hutu-Tutsi conflict in Rwanda?

2) What have previous studies found about the effects of forgiveness and reconciliation efforts in Rwanda?

3) What are the underlying principles and strategies of the HROC model?

4) What are the effects of the HROC workshops on participants?

5) What lessons might be derived from the HROC experience for reconciliation efforts elsewhere?

6) What can Pentecostals learn from and contribute to education for forgiveness and reconciliation?

The study includes a review of literature to answer questions 1–3, ethnographic filmmaking to address question 4, an analysis based on the REACH and Bridge to Reconciliation models to address question 5 and the authors' synthesizing reflections to address question 6.[2]

1. See African Great Lakes Initiative, "Healing and Rebuilding."
2. Worthington, *Forgiving and Reconciling*.

WHAT IS THE NATURE OF THE HUTU-TUTSI CONFLICT IN RWANDA?

The precise origins of the Hutu-Tutsi conflict in Rwanda are still uncertain, leaving contemporary cultural historians to attempt to piece together explanations. Zorbas suggests three "histories" of Rwanda, three versions of history that seek to explain the Hutu-Tutsi division.[3]

The first version (referred to as the "essentialist" position) suggests that the Tutsi and Hutu peoples came from separate parts of Africa in separate immigrations many generations ago and settled in a land where the Twa people (now constituting around 1% of the Rwandan population) were already settled. Advocates of this view point to differences in physical features that distinguish Hutus from Tutsis, though with intermarriage those distinctions have diminished. This view of history was embraced by the Hutu advocates of the genocide, who claimed that the Tutsi emigrated from the Horn of Africa and imposed their rule on the Hutu and the Twa.

A second version of history (known as the "social constructivist" view) suggests that the Hutu and Tutsi were distinguished not by ethnic or geographic origin, but by cultural and economic distinctions, with Hutus primarily engaged in cultivation and Tutsi primarily engaged in cattle-herding. Distinct cultures arose from these different economic activities, with greater wealth and political power accumulated by the Tutsis. In this version, however, these distinct cultural groups lived mostly in peace prior to the arrival of the Europeans during the colonial era.

Zorbas citing Uvin suggests a third version of history in which Tutsi and Hutu came from different parts of Africa (like the essentialist view), but co-existed mostly in peace until the Europeans arrived and heightened ethnic tensions for colonial ends (as in the social constructivist view).

What is clear is that under German and then Belgian colonial rule, Tutsis (who constitute only 15% of the population) were given superior political and social status, often justified in European racialist and eugenicist terms, and Hutus were limited to subservient roles. All Rwandans were required to carry identification cards, which specified their ethnicity. Toward the end of Belgian rule, the colonial government reversed this order, siding with a Hutu government and encouraging the subjugation of the Tutsis. This led to the first wave of mass killings of Tutsis in 1959. Following independence under a Hutu government in 1962, waves of violence continued for several decades, with hundreds of thousands of Tutsis

3. Zorbas, "Reconciliation in Post-Genocide Rwanda."

fleeing to neighboring countries. A civil war raged in the early 1990s. Following the plane crash that killed the long-time Hutu President in 1994, Hutus blamed Tutsis for the assassination, and the genocide of 1994 was unleashed, encouraged by Hutu media that fed the frenzy with slogans like "Kill the cockroaches." A Tutsi army finally defeated Hutu forces in July and put an end to the genocide, but not before as many as 1 million Rwandans, both Tutsis and moderate Hutus, had been slaughtered.

WHAT HAVE PREVIOUS STUDIES FOUND ABOUT THE EFFECTS OF FORGIVENESS AND RECONCILIATION EFFORTS IN RWANDA?

The most notable studies of the effects of reconciliation education in Rwanda, apart from those done by HROC (discussed below), have been carried out by Staub, Pearlman, and Gubin.[4] Staub and Pearlman wrote, "When one group has victimized another, or when there has been mutual victimization by two groups, if the groups continue to live near each other, reconciliation is essential both to stop a potentially continuing cycle of violence and to facilitate healing."[5] Reconciliation is defined as follows:

> Reconciliation is more than the coexistence of formerly hostile groups living near each other. It is more even than formerly hostile groups interacting and working together, although working together for shared goals is one important avenue to overcoming hostility and negative views of the other and working toward reconciliation. Reconciliation means coming to accept one another and developing mutual trust. This requires forgiving. Reconciliation requires that victims and perpetrators come to accept the past and not see it so much as defining the future as simply a continuation of the past, that they come to see the humanity of one another, accept each other, and see the possibility of a constructive relationship.[6]

Staub and his colleagues created and implemented a two-week seminar to train Rwandese staff members in strategies to promote healing, forgiveness, and reconciliation. These staff represented a variety of community organizations from around Rwanda. The training included

---

4. Staub, Pearlman, and Gubin, "Healing, Reconciliation, Forgiving and the Prevention of Violence."

5. Ibid., 206.

6. Ibid., 206–7.

brief lectures and discussions of various topics, including the origins of genocide, the impact of trauma on individuals and communities, avenues toward healing, and basic human needs. The goal of the workshop was to provide Rwanda community leaders with tools to help bring about healing in their communities.[7]

The challenges of carrying out a controlled study in this setting were substantial, but the findings are still worth noting. In their study, Staub and colleagues found that Rwandan participants reported a significantly higher number of traumatic experiences than had Cambodian survivors of the Khmer Rouge or Bosnian survivors. The results also suggested that participation in the workshops "had beneficial effects both in reducing trauma symptoms and creating a more positive orientation in members of each group toward the other."[8]

WHAT ARE THE UNDERLYING PRINCIPLES AND STRATEGIES OF THE HROC MODEL?

The HROC project is supported by the Friends Peace Teams (FPT) movement. According to its mission statement, the FPT "is a Spirit-led organization working around the world to develop long-term relationships with communities in conflict to create programs for peacebuilding, healing and reconciliation. FPT's programs build on extensive Quaker experience combining practical and spiritual aspects of conflict resolution."[9] AGLI was launched by FPT to help bring peace and reconciliation to the war torn great lakes region of Africa, a region that includes Rwanda and Burundi as well as Kenya, Tanzania, Uganda, and Congo. AGLI began its work in these nations in 1999. Members of the Friends Churches in Rwanda and Burundi gathered to jointly develop a program to address the deep conflicts within their nations and the program they created was named HROC, which is now one of AGLI's key initiatives in both Rwanda and Burundi.

HROC is based on an underlying philosophy and the following set of key principles:

Principle #1: In every person, there is something that is good.

---

7. Ibid., 216.
8. Ibid., 324.
9. See Friends Peace Teams, "About FPT."

Principle #2: Each person and society has the inner capacity to heal, and an inherent intuition of how to recover from trauma. Sometimes the wounds are so profound that people or communities need support to reencounter that inner capacity.

Principle #3: Both victims and perpetrators of violence can experience trauma and its after-effects.

Principle #4: Healing from trauma requires that a person's inner good and wisdom is sought and shared with others. It is through this effort that trust can begin to be restored.

Principle #5: When violence has been experienced at both a personal level, and at a community level, efforts to heal and rebuild the country must also happen at both the individual and communal level.

Principle #6: Healing from trauma and building peace between groups are deeply connected. It is not possible to do one without the other. Therefore, trauma recovery and peace building efforts must happen simultaneously.[10]

AGLI produced a detailed curriculum manual to guide the training of Rwandan and Burundian facilitators of the workshops and another manual to guide the implementation of the workshops. The HROC Training Manual includes a chapter entitled Designing and Implementing a Successful Program, which includes guidelines for carrying out a needs assessment and a checklist for planning a workshop. The chapter also includes sample agendas and notes for facilitators. HROC takes a strengths-based perspective, seeking to tap into the wisdom of participants. Subsequent chapters include guidance for building the group, creating safety, how to open the workshops, how to give people a sense of connection through "gatherings," and how to enliven the group with "energizers." The manual also includes guidance for helping participants understand violence, trauma, and the consequences and how to facilitate "the journey of healing." The manual concludes with a chapter entitled "Helping Others." In short, HROC provides a comprehensive guide for organizing and facilitating a workshop for victims and perpetrators of violence or trauma, drawing on the traditions of Quakerism, but with generic content that can be used with people of any faith.

---

10. Chico and Bizimana, *Healing and Rebuilding Our Communities*, 5–6.

WHAT ARE THE EFFECTS OF THE HROC WORKSHOPS ON PARTICIPANTS?

The research method employed for this study was documentary film-making, drawing on the strategies of ethnography. Co-author Patrick Mureithi spent multiple weeks in Rwanda and Burundi filming reconciliation workshops and interviewing the participants, with an initial visit in 2007 and follow-up rounds of filming and interviews in 2008 and 2009. During the 2008 visit, Mureithi interviewed participants six months after their participation in the HROC workshops. Mureithi collected more than 90 hours of film, documenting the process and effects of the reconciliation workshops. Insights about the effects of the workshops were derived from the processes and interviews documented in the film. The authors also read and analyzed other studies of reconciliation efforts in the region, including other studies of the effects of HROC workshops to compare their findings with the findings of others.

Filmed workshops and interviews were analyzed and a small number of participants became the focus of the in-depth study on the effects of participation in the workshops. To corroborate the initial findings, Mureithi shared them with participants when he interviewed them again six months later and made adjustments accordingly.

The findings were also corroborated when Mureithi showed the first draft of the documentary in Rwanda in 2008, as described below.

Evidence collected from workshops and interviews strongly indicates that the HROC workshops are having a profound and enduring effect on the lives of participants. Victims of violence frequently extend forgiveness to perpetrators. Perpetrators are frequently able both to ask for and receive forgiveness from the victims. This giving and receiving of forgiveness makes possible a reconciliation between victims and perpetrators that sometimes results in genuine friendship. A case study of one particular Tutsi victim and one particular Hutu perpetrator illustrates this finding.

Mama Aline is a Tutsi survivor whose husband was killed during the genocide. A mother of three children, she is the only member of her generation to survive. She lives in Gisenyi, Rwanda, in a neighborhood that was built by the Rwandan government to house survivor widows and orphans. She was interviewed the day before the workshop when she spoke of the trauma of survivors being "like a disease," and said that what she expected from the workshop was "to try to learn how to get a second chance to live a simple life" and to learn how to "be able to live a normal life like anybody else who has not yet experienced the genocide, a life free from trauma . . . Sometimes I get invaded by this whole anger from what has happened to me, and sometimes I tend to put it on everyone, especially the people I know who committed the crime, and they're still my neighbors . . . They killed a part of me."

Jean-Baptiste, a Hutu farmer, was 24 years old at the time of the genocide. During the genocide, he was told that either he would kill or be killed. He was forced to murder a Tutsi woman he was dating. After the act, he said that he felt that he had "a fear that I can't run away from. I lost all peace . . . I couldn't even eat anything."

After his crime, Jean-Baptiste fled to neighboring Congo, where he lived in a refugee camp for two years. Deciding that life in the camp was too hard, he then returned to Rwanda, where he was arrested and imprisoned for seven years (from 1996 to 2003) at the Gisenyi Central Prison.

In 2003, President Kagame issued a decree releasing up to 40,000 inmates. This move, the government said, was to "ease overcrowding in prisons and to foster reconciliation." The judicial system in Rwanda was overwhelmed by the enormous backlog of cases, and it would have taken 100 years to address all of them. Instead, prisoners who confessed to taking part in the genocide were released from prison to go through the country's traditional justice system, a form of arbitration known as "Gacaca." It was at this time that Jean-Baptiste was freed.

During the course of the 2007 workshop, which Mama Aline and Jean-Baptiste attended together, one could see their transformation as they moved from a stance of fear and wariness to one of mutual acceptance. "Before this workshop came," said Jean Baptiste, "I never saw myself as a traumatized person. But it was during the workshop that I saw what trauma really was, and I saw myself in that situation."

Mama Aline chose to sit next to Jean-Baptiste during lunch on the second day of the workshop, after a very emotional session of remembering past hurts. "I speak as someone who has no brothers or sisters," she said, "someone who has seen her father get stoned in front of her. It's hard . . . yet when I got the tears out of myself, I felt peace . . . I didn't know it could be possible to eat with him at the same table. I didn't know. But we ate together." Forgiveness was given and received. Reconciliation began and a friendship was born.

Six months later when Mureithi returned to Rwanda to explore the longer term effects of the workshops on the lives of Mama Aline and

Jean-Baptiste, he found that they were now friends, frequently eating meals together. In extensive interviews they spoke of the change that had occurred in their lives as a result of the workshops, making it possible for them to now be friends.

Another of the workshop participants was John, an 18 year old who spoke of having to be his own mother and father. He said that the workshop was the first time in his entire life that he had ever spoken about his pain. During the genocide, when John was four, he lost both his parents and his seven other siblings and subsequently lived on the streets for three years. Eventually, his aunt found him and took him in for the past eleven years. Never once, before the workshop, had he expressed his torment. His story now gives voice to the many genocide orphans in Rwanda who themselves have not had the opportunity to express their feelings, and he demonstrates what can happen when people are given an opportunity for forgiveness and reconciliation.

Testimonials of this kind are replicated in the follow-up interviews with HROC participants conducted by AGLI. The story of Bizimana Theoneste, a Burundian whose story is included in an AGLI compilation of testimonials by HROC participants, entitled *After the Guns Have Stopped*, said:

> Before attending the HROC workshop I was too sad. I could not trust any person because I had heard that my father died of poison and from that time I hated people. When I remembered my difficult childhood, I felt angry! I was asking myself how I could just find the person who killed my father or his relatives for revenge! I had many bad thoughts and no person could know that! But after attending the workshop, it was like the key of healing and hope to me!! During the workshop we shared our histories and for me it was hard just to open up and talk! I remember one day we were in the gathering time and Adrien Niyongabo was the facilitator. He asked us to share a good thing we remember that our mother had done for us. I remembered that we had been separated from her when I was a very young baby!! I started to cry and after 10 minutes I spoke out. From that day I felt rested and happy. By hearing others' stories I saw that others suffered more than me, and I felt my pain decrease! After that, I decided to become a facilitator to help others during the workshops and even after.[11]

11. Bizimana and Sandidge, "After the Guns Have Stopped," 14.

Upon his return to Rwanda in 2008, co-author Mureithi showed the first draft of the documentary, entitled *Icyizere*, meaning "Hope" in the Kinyarwanda language at the 2008 Rwanda Film Festival, traveling to seven different towns in seven days.[12] After each screening, Mureithi interviewed many people who expressed their appreciation for seeing not only the perspective of a survivor, but of a perpetrator as well. They said that the film showed them how people could live together after conflict, and that it taught them a lot about trauma. After the festival, *Icyizere* aired on Rwanda Television three times, and was shown at Gisenyi Central Prison, where Jean-Baptiste had been imprisoned for his crimes against humanity in 1994, and even there viewers reaffirmed the effectiveness of the HROC workshops in bringing about reconciliation.

In summary, evidence is strong that the reconciliation workshops had a profound impact on the lives of the participants, made it possible for them to give and receive forgiveness, and brought about reconciliation in their lives. Studies of participants in other HROC workshops confirmed that this phenomenon was not an isolated incident. Responses to screenings of the film in Rwanda also confirmed the finding that these workshops do in fact promote reconciliation.

WHAT LESSONS MIGHT BE DERIVED FROM THE HROC EXPERIENCE FOR FORGIVENESS AND RECONCILIATION EFFORTS ELSEWHERE?

Co-author Mureithi visited Kenya for two weeks in 2008, where interest in the documentary and the HROC model were especially strong because of the urgent need for reconciliation after the post-election violence in Kenya that had manifested along tribal lines. Mureithi showed the film to medical staff and students, civil servants, the Kenya National Commission on Human Rights, the Nairobi Peace Initiative, and the Great Lakes Parliamentary Forum on Peace. All of the viewers of the film felt that this was a process that could be applied in Kenya as well as to different situations of conflict, be they personal or global.

"This approach," the HROC manual explains, "builds a strong sense of community among group members, instills a new confidence in a wounded self, and ensures that the lessons learned are steeped in the context of the particular conflict and the post-conflict recovery process.

---

12. Mureithi, *Icyizere*.

Thus, the elicitive nature of the program enhances the program's adaptability to new contexts and cultures."[13]

What makes HROC effective? An examination of the REACH forgiveness model and the Bridge to reconciliation model articulated by Everett L. Worthington Jr. provides a theoretical framework in which to analyze HROC.[14]

Worthington defined forgiveness as "the emotional juxtaposition of positive emotions (such as empathy, sympathy, compassion, agape love or even romantic love) against 1) the hot emotions of anger or fear that follow a perceived hurt or offense or 2) the unforgiveness that follows ruminating about the transgression, which also changes our motives from negative to neutral or even positive."[15] Note that the strong emphasis on emotion here, in contrast to what Worthington calls "decisional forgiveness," which does not necessarily involve the emotions. HROC likewise strongly emphasizes the importance of the emotions in forgiveness, providing many opportunities for participants to express their emotions about what they experienced. Often, participants are expressing emotion about their experiences for the first time, even though the events may have happened thirteen or fourteen years ago, or more. This expression of negative emotions associated with their pain often makes room for the possibility of positive emotions and those positive emotions then make possible steps toward reconciliation.

Worthington defined reconciliation as "reestablishing trust in a relationship after trust has been violated."[16] All the activities in the workshops, including blindfolded walks and active listening, are meant to reestablish trust among Tutsis and Hutus.

Worthington suggests a five-step approach called REACH for Forgiveness that he and his colleagues at Virginia Commonwealth University have used with thousands of clients in a variety of settings.

> Recall the hurt—HROC participants are invited to share what they experienced, to reflect on a personal loss, to tell their story.
>
> Empathize—By genuinely listening to each others' stories, HROC participants are able to begin to empathize with the victims and

13. Chico and Bizimana, *Healing and Rebuilding Our Communities*.

14. Worthington, *Forgiving and Reconciling*.

15. Ibid., 41–42.

16. Ibid., 42.

even with the perpetrators who, like Jean-Baptiste were caught up in the hysteria and forced to participate in killings.

Give the Altruistic gift of forgiveness—HROC's manual includes a graphic entitled Breaking the Cycle of Violence and Revenge which shows "Choosing to Forgive" as key to breaking free from acts of aggression.[17]

Commit to publicly forgive—HROC does not require participants to publicly forgive, but this outcome is common.

Hold on to forgiveness—Where possible, regular reconnections with participants in the months following the workshops, such as the continuing relationship between Mama Aline and Jean-Baptiste, allow for the continuation of the healing.

Worthington's REACH model does not require the presence of the offending other and forgiveness can be given whether or not the perpetrator asks forgiveness or admits guilt. Reconciliation goes beyond forgiveness by including the perpetrator and seeking to reestablish a foundation for relationship. Reconciliation is the objective of HROC.

Worthington writes,

Using the principles I described in the Pyramid Model to REACH Forgiveness, the Bridge to Reconciliation adds principles about how to reconcile that I discovered through research and my practical experience as a marital and family counselor. The Bridge to Reconciliation involves four planks. We *decide* whether, how and when to reconcile (plank one). Then we *discuss* the transgression with 'soft attitudes' (plank two). We *detoxify* our relationship of past poisons (plank three). Finally, we *devote* ourselves to building up a relationship of mutual valuing (plank four).[18]

These steps are evident in the reconciliation that took place between Mama Aline and Jean-Baptiste as a result of their participation in the HROC workshop.

What HROC lacks is a capacity to promote sustained healing for the individual participants, who carry profound trauma that often results in chronic depression. Nor does HROC have a program of sustained relationship building among the Tutsi and Hutu participants, as suggested by Worthington's fourth plank. Given the depth of the traumas and the

17. Ibid., 93.
18. Ibid., 176–77.

history of the hostilities, a short seminar can only be the beginning of a long-term work that must be sustained. HROC's efforts are heroic given limited resources. Other initiatives must address the longer term need for healing and reconciliation.

The HROC strategies, then, align well with the findings of theorist/practitioners like Worthington who have looked at forgiveness and reconciliation in a variety of contexts. These solid principles upon which HROC is built are likely to transfer well to other social settings, as the Kenya anecdote above illustrates. One can also imagine employing HROC strategies in settings in the United States, such as reconciliation efforts involving gang members, and even in conflicts that do not involve violence, like those between people on opposite sides of political issues.

WHAT CAN PENTECOSTALS LEARN FROM AND CONTRIBUTE TO EDUCATION FOR RECONCILIATION?

Much about the HROC education for reconciliation efforts resonates with Pentecostal experience. Note again the mission statement of the Friends Peace Teams which links its "Spirit-led" character with its peace and reconciliation efforts. This linkage was prominent both in the first century church born on the day of Pentecost and in the Pentecostal movement launched at the start of the 20th century. Note the diversity and harmony among the diverse people gathered for the coming of the Holy Spirit in Jerusalem (Acts 2) mirrored by the diversity and reconciliation of the people gathered for the outpouring of the Holy Spirit at Azusa Street in Los Angeles and around the world in the first generation of the 20th century.[19] The Apostle Peter's sermon on the day of Pentecost resonates across the millennia: "In the last days, God says, I will pour out my Spirit on *all* people" (Acts 2:17, emphasis added).

Moreover, the strong emphasis on the expression of emotion in both the HROC workshops and in Worthington's REACH model resonates with Pentecostalism's historic embrace of the emotions as key to God's work of healing and empowerment in the life of the believer.[20]

For Pentecostals in Africa and elsewhere, the local church can provide a community in which people of different ethnic (and even political) groups can meet to experience forgiveness and reconciliation as

19. Robeck, *The Azusa Street Mission and Revival.*
20. See Wacker, *Heaven Below.*

each one acknowledges his or her own need for God's forgiveness and reconciliation.

Pentecostalism is a movement of more than half a billion people around the world.[21] One can imagine the power of such a movement as a force for forgiveness and reconciliation if models such as HROC are adopted by Pentecostal churches, especially in regions of the world, like Africa, where Pentecostalism is growing exponentially in the midst of social and political upheaval.[22]

CONCLUSION

Perhaps a new awareness of the need for reconciliation, as an alternative to escalating tensions, is arising. Government and media efforts are vital, but they are not enough. This study suggests that those interested in promoting forgiveness, reconciliation, and peace would also benefit from looking at the principles and strategies of grass-roots, person-to-person efforts like HROC, a process by which victims and perpetrators alike and learn forgiveness and reconciliation.

BIBLIOGRAPHY

African Great Lakes Initiative. "Healing and Rebuilding Our Communities." http://www.aglifpt.org/Program/hroc.htm (accessed November 20, 2008).

Bizimana, Theoneste, and Anna Sandidge. "After the Guns Have Stopped: Searching for Reconciliation in Burundi." Africa Great Lakes Initiative. http://www.aglifpt.org/publications/articles/hroc/pdf/aftergunsstopped.pdf (accessed November 20, 2008).

Chico, L. S., and T. Bizimana. *Healing and Rebuilding our Communities (HROC): Training Manual—A Guide for Leaders*. St. Louis: Africa Great Lakes Initiative, 2005.

Friends Peace Teams. "About FPT." http://friendspeaceteams.org/FPTJ/index.php?option=com_content&task=blogcategory&id=74&Itemid=100 (accessed April 29, 2010).

Hittenberger, J. "Globalization, Marketization, and the Mission of Pentecostal Higher Education in Africa." *Pneuma: The Journal of the Society for Pentecostal Studies* 26 (2004) 182–215.

21. See "Status of Global Mission, 2010."

22. Jenkins, *The Next Christendom*; and Hittenberger, "Globalization, Marketization, and the Mission."

Jenkins, Philip. *The Next Christendom: The Coming of Global Christianity.* New York: Oxford University Press, 2002.

Mureithi, P., producer and director. *Icyizere.* Josiah Films, 2009. http://www.josiahfilms.com.

Robeck, Cecil M. *The Azusa Street Mission and Revival.* Nashville: Thomas Nelson, 2006.

"Status of Global Mission, 2010, in Context of 20th and 21st Centuries." Center for the Study of Global Christianity at Gordon-Conwell Theological Seminary. http://www.gordonconwell.edu/sites/default/files/IBMR2010.pdf (accessed May 1, 2010).

Staub, E., L. A. Pearlman, and A. Gubin. "Healing, Reconciliation, Forgiving and the Prevention of Violence after Genocide or Mass Killing: An Intervention and Its Experimental Evaluation in Rwanda." *Journal of Social and Clinical Psychology* 24 (2005) 297–334.

Wacker, Grant. *Heaven Below: Early Pentecostals and American Culture.* Cambridge, MA: Harvard University Press, 2001.

Worthington, Everett L. Jr. *Forgiving and Reconciling: Bridges to Wholeness and Hope.* Downers Grove, IL: InterVarsity, 2003.

Zorbas, E. "Reconciliation in Post-Genocide Rwanda." *African Journal of Legal Studies* 1 (2004) 29–52.

Epilogue

Everett L. Worthington Jr.

A VIEW OF CONTEMPORARY PENTECOSTAL VISIONS OF FORGIVENESS, RECONCILIATION, PEACE, AND RESTORATION

When my mother was murdered on that 1995 New Year's Eve night, I had been studying and writing about forgiveness and reconciliation for over ten years. At that time, though, I confronted, more immediately and emotionally, my faith and the call of Jesus to forgive than for any other harm or offense I had ever experienced. That first night, I stood in my brother's back room and pointed to a baseball bat, saying, "I wish that whoever killed Mama were here. I'd take that bat and beat his brains out." In retrospect, it was the Holy Spirit's conviction of my sin of that judgmental and vengeful heart-attitude that softened me for receiving forgiveness from God and passing it on to the murderer.

The night I forgave, I realized that all day I had thought of virtually anything to distract myself from considering forgiveness. It was the f-word that I didn't want to hear, didn't want to think about. I thought of the crime, of my loss, of justice for the murderer, of my pain, of missing my wife (Kirby) and our four children (and projecting my eventual death into the effects on our kids), of the fact that I was at 48 an orphan, of drawing together with my brother and sister to comfort and strengthen each other, and of feeling the love of people back home in Richmond

215

praying for us weathering the emotion down in Knoxville. But I was not thinking of forgiveness. No, I couldn't. I knew after all that Jesus had commanded us to forgive as he prayed, "Forgive us our debts as we also have forgiven our debtors" (Matt 6:12). And I knew all too well that Jesus picked that verse of all the verses in the Lord's prayer to expand: "For if you forgive men when they sin against you, your heavenly Father will also forgive you. But if you do not forgive men their sins, your Father will not forgive your sins" (Matt 6:14–15). It was too early to confront the possibility of not forgiving. It was easier to distract myself from thinking that *forgiveness* word.

But in the late night and early morning hours, the irony of my distraction came to me in force. I had sent to the publisher a month earlier my first book on forgiveness, *To Forgive is Human: How to Put Your Past in the Past*.[1] There I was, writer of a book to help people forgive by using a program of psychological and Christian research, yet I was unwilling even to think the word. I could sense the movement of the Spirit, encouraging me to confront the crime against my mother and my own heart's response. But I wanted to dwell on the injustice, and hope for justice, not think about anything that might lead me to forgive.

Under the leading of the Holy Spirit, I began to think through the five-step method we have developed and researched with Christians from the Philippines to Richmond and with people in secular settings around the world. The method helps people grant decisional forgiveness to wrongdoers and then REACH emotional forgiveness for the injustice and harm they have experienced. Experiencing emotional forgiveness is often the harder of the two. REACH is an acrostic cuing the memory of each step.[2] R=Recall the hurt without accusation or self-pity. E=Empathize, which includes Sympathize, feel Compassion toward, or Love—feeling positive emotions toward the offender who, by harming us or our loved ones, has temporarily declared himself or herself to be our enemy. A=Give an Altruistic gift of forgiveness because we ourselves have been graced with having been often forgiven. C=Commit to the forgiveness we experience. H=Hold Onto Forgiveness once we have experienced it and might doubt its reality.

By thinking through the steps, I was able to forgive the murderer—decisionally and emotionally. The culmination came after imagining

---

1. McCullough, Sandage, and Worthington, *To Forgive is Human*.

2. Worthington, *Forgiving and Reconciling*.

graphically the young intruder in my mother's home, facing her with a crowbar in hand and perhaps thinking, *This old woman is ruining my perfect crime, and what's worse, she's seen my face; I'll go to prison.* He struck her in the head. Twice. Once on the back.

But the Holy Spirit brought immediately to mind that I had earlier stood in the back room of my brother's house and emotionally proclaimed that if the young man were there, I'd hit him in the head until he died. I thought, *Whose heart is darker? Is it the youth acting impulsively under the threat of going to prison? Or is it me, a 48-year-old Christian psychologist who is willing to beat someone to death after having a long period to come to some grips with the wrongdoing?* Under the leading of the Holy Spirit, I knew it was my own heart that was darker.

Yet, I also knew that God could and did forgive me and bring about repentance in my heart. And I could only ask, *If the darkness of my heart can be forgiven, then who am I to withhold forgiveness from this young man?* With that realization, I forgave. I made a decision, and emotional relief also washed over me.

I knew that if the young man were captured, justice was still necessary. Forgiveness did not make justice unnecessary. The young man had committed a crime against his victim and society, and the consequences had to be dealt with. But justice, I knew, was in the social and societal realm, whereas my forgiveness was in the realm of my inner being.

My forgiveness was real and lasting. It has persisted for over fourteen years since the night I forgave. But what has amazed me, perhaps even more than my shock that I could experience the miracle of decisional and emotional forgiveness, is how that experience has rerouted my life. Foremost, I believe that God gave me a new mission in life after that murder. For years, I had written down what I thought God's mission for my life was (i.e., "to try to promote faith, work and love in the family, church and society"). But some time in 1996 or 1997, I began to see my personal mission not as before, but as promoting forgiveness. My mission became this: to do all I can to promote forgiveness in every *willing* heart, home, and homeland.

The benefits of forgiveness flowed from God to me (from Heart to heart). Then, I was able to forgive the young man who killed my mother (from heart to home), though he has not ever been tried for his crime. Finally, the benefits will, I hope, spread far beyond my own personal experience to others in times and lands far away (from home to homeland).

A BIRD'S EYE VIEW OF THIS BOOK ABOUT
PENTECOSTALISM AND FORGIVENESS

Like you, I have read this interesting collection of essays about forgiveness and reconciliation as seen from within the Pentecostal tradition. I'm sure that you have drawn some lessons for your life from these essays. Geoff and Marty have honored and tasked me with providing some concluding thoughts for you to consider. I am coming at this task from a non-Pentecostal perspective, though my experience in the Charismatic renewal movement from 1970 in California through today make me highly sympathetic to much of the Pentecostal experience. Perhaps this slight bit of distance—from Pentecostal to Charismatic Presbyterian— can give me a slightly different perspective to evaluate these essays.

AN OUTSIDER'S VIEW OF THE DISTINCTIVES OF PENTECOSTALISM

My understanding of Pentecostalism (and the Charismatic Christian experience) suggests what makes Pentecostalism unique can be summarized under two general groupings. First, *God's supernatural breaks in on the natural world*. We observe that God acts boldly and visibly in the world today. The direct result is that we, as believing Christians, see and recognize God's hand in doing miracles—most frequently seen as immediate changes—communicating visions, answering prayers, doing miraculous healings and transformations, and delivering people from Satan, sin, and self. God speaks to us. God prompts us to pray and to act. These immediate in-workings of God's Holy Spirit accelerate in time the processes that C. S. Lewis (and indeed even Augustine) had recognized as miraculous in-workings of God through nature. Jesus changed water to wine immediately at the Canaan wedding (an immediate miracle) while God changes water to wine over time through natural processes of rain, soil, and plant, growing grapes (with and without the help of humans), and fermenting the grape juice (with and without the help of humans). The first distinctive of Pentecostal and Charismatic experience that I see is immediate miraculous intervention of God in both the natural world and the supernatural realm (e.g., demons), and thus the reality of the supernatural.

The second distinctive of Pentecostalism is, I believe, the divinely inspired *human response to God*. We respond to God's initiation in faith. Personal experience is important. This divinely inspired human response shows up particularly in emotional experience and personal story or testimony. It also shows up as a reverence for the authority of Scripture. It shows up in an emphasis on Arminian-conceptualized choice and free will, which empowers the sense of mission to the world that Pentecostals and Charismatics hold to so strongly. It also shows up as a response to grace by manifesting behavioral evidence (e.g., tongues, other manifestations of the Holy Spirit) of inner spiritual transformation. Finally, the human response shows up as a sense of interpersonal inclusion, peace, and reconciliation that flows directly from Pentecost. At Pentecost, we have a prototype of Christian experience. People spoke in other people's tongues, demonstrated unity in the Spirit of different tongues, ethnicities, sexes, religions, worldviews, beliefs, and values.

When the authors in this present book write about their Pentecostal perspective on forgiveness and reconciliation, then, they have many choices from the treasure trove of Pentecostalism about what they will bring to bear in understanding forgiveness and reconciliation, giving a distinctive Pentecostal perspective. They could focus on the grace of God in giving Jesus and leaving the Holy Spirit after his ascension—that is, on divine forgiveness of humans. They could focus on God's initiation of forgiveness and reconciliation. They could focus on ways that the immediacy of people's reception of God's grace and mercy could create individual transformative experiences that make us sinners seek forgiveness and us sinners grant forgiveness instead of holding onto self-justifying right to revenge. They could focus on the social aspects of forgiving— how one individual talks to another about an unjust transgression. Or they could focus on the societal fallout of transgressions and about how societal transgressions are healed. The choices are rich and varied and we could expect a blended choir of voices singing in harmony.

SUMMARY OF THE CHAPTERS

I anticipated a collection of essays that favored the individual experience of experiencing forgiveness from God, granting forgiveness to wrongdoers, and seeking forgiveness as a result of our own wrongdoing. Now that you have read the essays, you can see that there really wasn't much of that within the book. Mittelstadt (chapter 1) sets the stage by focusing on reconciliation and peace in the Luke-Acts historical narrative by Luke. Reconciliation and peace are both social (which use as interpersonal

relationships among two or three participants) or societal (which I use
to refer to groups and individuals acting according to or within group
identification and influence).

Berg (chapter 2) discussed *The Shack*, but rather than zero in on
the experience of forgiving a murderer of one's child, Berg encouraged
us to think more about the relationship of a postmodern worldview to
one of modernity. Modernity is based on propositional truths or what
cognitive psychologists today call system one (logical, rational) thinking.
Postmodernity is more about system two thinking (i.e., intuitive, non-
rational, relational and experiential truth), contexts of truth, and relationships. Berg's essay is stimulating and helpful, but it focuses our attention
to a less immediate and more societally contextualized level than I would
have anticipated prior to reading the book. In Quigley and Awbrey's essay
(chapter 3), forgiveness is largely personally experienced.

In the section of the book on historical perspectives, Brathwaite
(chapter 4), Olena (chapter 5), and Richie (chapter 6) describe the history of Pentecostalism. They draw from the different historical episodes,
but they each recount a sense of historical remorse and repentance for
Pentecostals' failures in race and ethnic reconciliation and relationships
with other faiths.

Even the two chapters on psychological perspectives on forgiveness spend their efforts less on the individual experience of forgiving
and more on social (Sutton, chapter 7) and societal (Mostert and Van
der Spuy, chapter 8) aspects associated with forgiving. Sutton considers
restoration of morally fallen pastors to community and leadership—a
distinctively societal aspect associated with forgiving. Mostert and van
der Spuy consider the case of South Africa's experiment with the South
African Truth and Reconciliation Commission, again describing the
bold societal experiment by Mandela and Tutu to bring about societal
healing through truth-telling, public communication of forgiveness, and
reconciliation.

Wilkinson (chapter 9) examines a variety of public apologies by
churches and governments for transgressions. Wilkinson is most immediately concerned with churches and the Canadian government apologizing
to the Native People of Canada. Hittenberger and Mureithi (chapter 10)
write about educating for peace in Rwanda, which must occur if the country is to heal from the genocide and mass killing of over three-quarters of
a million countrymen.

ANALYSIS OF THE PROPHETIC VISION OF THESE CONTEMPORARY PENTECOSTAL WRITERS

Throughout the book, these contemporary Pentecostal perspectives draw on individual experiential and expressive Pentecostal doctrine and experience. But for the most part, they are prophets calling the church to a place that isn't as often identified as Pentecostal—social and societal justice. Of course, this social and societal justice is a large part of Pentecostal or any Christian church's doctrine. The fact is, though, that different churches emphasize it less often than other churches.

Worthington and Berry identified eighteen classic virtues possessed by individuals. They had participants rate themselves on the degree to which they valued each virtue, and they subjected the results to a statistical analysis called exploratory factor analysis (EFA).[3] EFA essentially asks the data, to which virtues do people respond similarly? The researchers found that some people simply endorsed most of the virtues more and others rarely said they valued any virtues. Some people are more virtue-valuing than are others. No surprise there. But in a second order factor analysis, which followed up the first EFA, Worthington and Berry found that half of the virtues tended to be valued by some people and the other half by other people. Mostly people gravitated toward one set more than the other rather than arraying themselves mostly in some bell curve that split the difference.

We called one set of these virtues warmth-based virtues and the other set conscientiousness-based virtues. *Warmth-based virtues* are more empowered by redemptive emotions, and they encourage emotional and behavioral expression of those redemptive emotions. They emphasize qualities like love, compassion, forgiveness, empathy, and sympathy. *Conscientiousness-based virtues* are more powered by restraint of negative emotional and behavioral expression. They emphasize qualities like self-control, justice, conscientiousness, respect, responsibility, and accountability. Note that both sets are indeed virtues, and both sets are preached from almost every Christian pulpit. The key is how much is each set preached?

Religions tend to major on one set of virtues and minor on the other. You can probably correctly classify whether Islam, Judaism, Christianity, Buddhism, and Hinduism each lean mostly toward warmth- or

3. Worthington and Berry, "Virtues, Vices, and Character Education."

conscientiousness-based virtues. Importantly, though, units within each religion also might lean different ways. For example, there are compassionate Buddhists (for instance think of the Dali Lama) and more disengaged-and-detached-from-life Buddhists (like Zen). Both types advocate both warmth- and conscientiousness-based virtues, but the difference is in the emphasis.

Pentecostalism is a tradition that will differ from other Christian traditions. To take just a few examples, Pentecostals (in general) might differ from Anglicans, Roman Catholics, Orthodox believers, Methodists, Presbyterians, and Baptists. But *within* the Pentecostal tradition, the holiness tradition might be more closely aligned with conscientiousness-based virtues, but the Assemblies of God denomination (with its historic emphasis on worshipful praise and music) might shift more toward the emotionally expressive warmth-based virtues. Even within each tradition or denomination, individual congregations will differ from the overall body, and within each congregation, believers will differ in the degree to which they value each type of virtue.

I am not trying to pigeon-hole or fit Pentecostalism into some Procrustean bed. I am merely observing that Pentecostalism has had an emphasis of individual emotional expression, corporate emotionally expressive worship, personal holiness, and evangelism—not to the exclusion of other aspects of Christianity, but to their de-emphasis. But almost all of the current volume's writers have taken a prophetic perspective, calling the church into needed repentance and commitment to "let justice roll on like a river, righteousness like a never-failing stream!" (Amos 5:24) and to balance the things that God requires of people—"to act justly and to love mercy and to walk humbly with your God" (Micah 6:8).

MY UNDERSTANDING OF JUSTICE, FORGIVENESS, PEACE, AND RECONCILIATION

Let me try to put into context the emphasis on societal aspects of forgiveness by surveying forgiveness and its contexts. I believe that most people similarly understand the phenomena surrounding transgressions, their repair, and the repair of relationships (social and societal) that are damaged by transgressions. However, they indeed often use different language to label the processes surrounding transgressions. By noting the dissimilarities of language, we often give an impression of a chaos of understanding that in fact does not exist. Language is important. I have done my share of fighting over the turf of the right definitions of forgiveness, reconciliation, and related terms. Partly this is because I am a psychological scientist, and science requires that scientists make precise definitions if they are going to hope to test those definitions and the conclusions that arise from them. Partly, of course, my argumentative side is brought out because I am a sinful, self-justifying person who is beset by pride, the human condition, and want to be influential and to "make a name for myself." (We recall that the rich young ruler wanted to make a name for himself [see Luke 18:18–25], but today he is the nameless rich young ruler.)

So, it is with some trepidation that I present my understanding of forgiveness and reconciliation. After you have read it, I hope you'll say— even if you disagree about the meaning of terms—that we understand (for the most part) what is going on in the same ways. I have written more detailed explanations in *Forgiving and Reconciling: Bridges to Wholeness and Hope*, and (for professionals) *Forgiveness and Reconciliation: Theory and Application*, and I will draw from them and direct the reader to the latter source for detailed references.

TRANSGRESSIONS AND WAYS TO DEAL WITH THEM

Transgressions violate boundaries—psychological, moral, or physical (or all three). They are perceived as unjust, and they trigger people's God-given justice motive. People keep a rough mental tally of the amount of injustice, which I call the injustice gap. People generally consider transgressions against themselves as stressful, and they attempt to cope with the stress of unforgiveness in many ways that do not involve forgiving, and also by forgiving. These non-forgiveness methods of coping include (1) getting justice through the courts, natural consequences, or revenge; (2) forbearing (through self-control, people try not to respond negatively to the injustice and try to suppress emotions and emotional expression); (3) accepting and moving on with life (which accepts that bad things happen, but does not forgive); (4) relinquishing the matter to God (for God's presumed judgment of the offender or simply because it is not our place to judge). Note that, with the exception of seeking revenge, each of these ways of coping is consistent with Scripture.

WHAT IS FORGIVENESS? DO WE REALLY DISAGREE?

We also might forgive. Forgiveness is of two distinct types, which I do not believe are necessarily linked, but which in fact do often occur in sequence. These are decisional forgiveness and emotional forgiveness. I say that these are not always linked because, as we all know, we can make a decision to forgive and still be emotionally unforgiving. (Yes, God desires that we emotionally forgive, but it is the decision to forgive that is the subject of Matt 6:14-15, which I quoted earlier). We also could in fact emotionally forgive without deciding to do so. Note that both decisional and emotional forgiveness occur within a person.

Reconciliation is restoring trust in a relationship. Forgiveness does not have to lead to reconciliation. For example, sometimes it is impossible to restore a relationship. One cannot restore trust with one's dead parent, one's moved-away ex-partner, one's child who has emotionally cut one off, one's former business partner who refuses to have anything to do with one, the criminal who robbed and injured one and is incarcerated, the member of a terrorist group who refuses to reconcile and in fact wants only to kill you. Yes, we can love these people. Yes, we can make a decision to forgive them and perhaps even emotionally forgive them, but we cannot reconcile with them. Sometimes it is not wise to reconcile. A con man who bilks me out of my retirement-savings would love nothing more than to reconcile; after all, I still have my savings for health. If a woman has been repeatedly beaten and threatened by a nonrepentant husband, it would be unwise to return to that almost certainly abusive relationship. To the ex-spouse who is so embittered he or she wants to destroy one, or the parent who is so full of bitterness that he or she seeks to destroy the adult child, it would be unwise to put oneself in the vulnerable position of seeking reconciliation. Decisional forgiveness is *required* by God (Matt 6:12, 14–15). Emotional forgiveness is *desired* by God, but it is often much slower to come than is decisional forgiveness. But reconciliation is not required by God. Even God will not reconcile with those who turn their backs on Jesus.

In a valued and ongoing relationship, however, we might use forgiveness to motivate our reconciliation (i.e., restoration of trust). That is, we might forgive but attempt to set limits on the relationship until the offender can prove himself or herself sufficiently trustworthy to merit some growth of trust. We are dealing with fallible people here—people about whom we cannot know the motives, intentions, and hearts. So, God makes it imperative that we forgive, but does not make it imperative that we reconcile. If our forgiveness from God depended on reconciling with our enemy, the enemy could deny us forgiveness from God by simply failing to reconcile with us.

There have been studies asking psychologists, pastors who preach, pastors who primarily counsel, and lay people whether they believe forgiveness—to be complete—requires that we reconcile. Some say it does. A minority of people believe that complete forgiveness requires reconciliation. But how people answer that question usually depends on how the question is asked. For example, how many people would actually say that complete forgiveness requires reconciliation if an offender is (a) dead, (b) dedicated to kill one and intractable in that intent, (c) or is a stranger who killed one's child? Yes, we should forgive all of those people. But reconcile? Paul recognizes the problem. He says, "If it is possible, as far as it depends on you, live at peace with everyone" (Rom 12:18). It isn't always possible to reconcile—or even to live at peace with everyone. Peace, after all, can be capitulation out of fear that simply ends conflict, can be relationship with no vitality yet no conflict, or can be shalom. Not all peace is peaceful. "'Peace, peace,' they say, when there is not peace," wrote Jeremiah.

WHAT IS RECONCILIATION?

I have defined reconciliation as restoring trust. Reconciliation requires mutually trustworthy behavior. If one refuses to act in a trustworthy fashion, then trust is not possible. It isn't that a person might not desire trust to develop. It is that one or both parties cannot act in ways that promote trust. They cannot act in ways that the other person perceives as trustworthy.

Can people reconcile and yet the two parties go their separate ways? Think of Jacob and Esau. They reconciled, yet they did not live together. Abraham and Lot reconciled after their families and employees fought. Yet, they too went their separate ways.

Reconciliation can repair damage to a relationship, and can even restore a sense of trust, yet people might decide that there are benefits of living separately, or that the risk of a relapsed conflict is too great.

SOCIAL AND SOCIETAL RECONCILIATION

In the present book, the authors almost without exception make a strong plea for societal reconciliation. Let me discuss some of the processes that surround the pursuit of societal reconciliation. Perhaps the best way to do this is to consider social reconciliation between two people who have transgressed against each other, and then imagine the complexity that must be accounted for in scaling that up to a society in which different societal members have different experiences, values, agendas, and worldviews. Furthermore, there will inevitably be provocations to return to conflict within society. There are those we might call the hotheads, who take extreme positions. They become suicide bombers, murderers of doctors who perform abortions, or others who take extreme acts that are certainly provocative and tend to pull people who might be living at peace back into conflict.

Social Reconciliation

The processes of social reconciliation are relatively uncomplicated in comparison to societal dynamics. Nevertheless, there are a myriad ways that reconciliation can be derailed by two well-meaning people who are intent on reconciling.

We must first distinguish between forgiving per se and saying that one forgives. One might say one forgives merely to avoid conflict or to disarm an opponent so one can stab the opponent in the back. One might also find it convenient actually to forgive, but not tell the other person he or she forgives. For example, a woman might use guilt to manipulate a husband into cleaning the toilets to atone for misdeeds that have, in truth, long been forgiven. Saying that one forgives (which is interpersonal) is not the same as forgiving (which is a decision or emotional process occurring inside the skin). Even a person who sincerely forgives internally, might not be able to tell the other person (e.g., the person is dead, unavailable, etc.).

Therefore, let's consider a first step in reconciling to be *deciding whether to try to reconcile*. This must be considered in light of knowing that it is sometimes unwise to reconcile or pursue reconciliation or one might be unable to do so. Other decisions involve deciding when is the proper timing to explicitly attempt to reconcile or whether to reconcile implicitly (without explicitly talking about it) or explicitly.

The second step is *talking about the transgressions*. Typically, people who discuss transgressions follow a predictable sequence. One person makes a *reproach*, which says to the other person, "I believe you have hurt me. Can you explain to me why you did so?" Of course, reproaches can be made with more or less tact. At one end of the spectrum is the accusation, "You idiot! How could you do such an insensitive evil act? You are a beast." At the other end, which simply keeps the parties in conversation, is something like, "Usually you are sensitive. I don't understand what happened. I feel that I was hurt. Can you tell me what was going on that led you to hurt me?"

When reproached, people often respond with *accounts*. These might (1) deny wrongdoing, (2) refuse to accept that wrongdoing occurred, (3) justify one's acts, (4) blame the other person, (5) make excuses to avoid taking full responsibility, or (6) make a concession or confession of wrongdoing. Confessions are complex. To be believable, they usually must confess without excuse. They offer a sincere apology and express empathy for the pain the other person experienced. They might offer restitution or reparations, if those are possible and appropriate. Usually, the wrongdoer promises to try to avoid such misbehavior in the future, and seeks forgiveness. All of this must happen in an environment of valuing the other person. Making this confession involves what we call *repentance*.

Just because an offender has confessed, repented, and asked for forgiveness does not mean that forgiveness may be experienced (as a decision or emotional change) or publicly granted (i.e., saying that one forgives). Basically, the offender has made a concession, has publicly suffered, and has accepted some public shame along with admitting guilt. That is costly to the offender. Often, the contrite offender (having paid a cost) feels entitled to having the other person say, "I forgive you." (Remember, saying this is not equivalent of actually forgiving.) If the victim does not say that he or she fully forgives the offender, then usually—in what, to the victim can seem to be a bizarre twist—the offender feels offended or aggrieved. This might be due to (1) the offender's self-justification of one's own offenses (e.g., "I groveled, and she wouldn't even forgive me, like the Scripture says to do; so *she* is evil, and I was justified in hurting her."), or simply to (2) awareness of how difficult it was to lower himself or herself and make a good confession and ask for forgiveness (e.g., "I really suffered—probably more than she did as a result of my insult"). Whether the victim answers the offender's plea for forgiveness with "absolutely not," "maybe someday, but I need more time," or "I forgive you but I'm still emotionally hurt," the offender is likely going to get hurt and offended by anything less than full forgiveness.

Even if the victim grants forgiveness to the offender, the offender might be dealing with his or her guilt and shame and thus might be unable to *accept the forgiveness*. The person might have to struggle for a long while with self-condemnation, and might repeatedly seek forgiveness from God or seek to experience self-forgiveness before being able to accept the victim's forgiveness.

Reconciliation, then, involves decisions about reconciliation, followed by discussion of the transgression. Two additional processes are necessary: *detoxification of the damage done to the relationship* and *devotion to building a positive relationship*.

Societal Reconciliation

As the authors have observed, repair of damaged societal relationships is difficult or (some would say) impossible. Namely, a pastor who is involved in a public indiscretion—say a male pastor's affair with a parishioner, as Sutton wrote about—might be able to reconcile with many members of the congregation. But the chances are high he or she will not be able to reconcile with all the members. Some might be oriented to justice or other conscientiousness-based virtues; other congregants might be more forgiving. Some might have been personally affronted by the affair (say they are the parishioner's friend). Others might simply be locked in a power struggle with other members in the congregation and be using the issue to gain influence within the congregation.

I have discussed societal forgiveness in *A Just Forgiveness: Responsible Healing without Excusing Injustice*, which focuses mainly on societal issues. My main point in that book is that societal issues—including the societal levels of family, justice system, workplace, community, church, or society in general—can only be dealt with by doing those things that Micah (6:8) wrote about: loving justice, doing mercy, and walking humbly with our God.

PROPHETIC ENCOURAGEMENT TO FORGIVENESS AND RECONCILIATION

I began this chapter by an anecdote about forgiving my mother's murderer and reflection on the effect on my life of that murder and its forgiveness.

It changed my life mission to focusing not just on private forgiveness, but on doing all I can to promote forgiveness in every willing heart, home, and homeland. In this excellent collection of chapters edited by Mittelstadt and Sutton, we see the same progression. The Pentecostal writers begin with the heart. They attribute good things to God's working in people's hearts. They also assume that forgiveness should make its way into the home (see especially Quigley and Awbrey, Chapter 3). But this collection of contemporary Pentecostals call the church to social and societal justice and to the practice of forgiveness and reconciliation, when appropriate, to bring about a lasting shalom.

BIBLIOGRAPHY

McCullough, M.E., Steven J. Sandage, and Everett L. Worthington Jr. *To Forgive Is Human: How to Put Your Past in the Past.* Downers Grove, IL: InterVarsity, 1997.

Worthington, Everett L. *Forgiving and Reconciling: Bridges to Wholeness and Hope.* Downers Grove, IL: InterVarsity, 2003.

———. *Forgiveness and Reconciliation: Theory and Application.* New York: Routledge, 2006.

———. *A Just Forgiveness: Responsible Healing Without Excusing Injustice.* Downers Grove, IL: InterVarsity, 2009.

Worthington, Everett L., and J. W. Berry. "Virtues, Vices, and Character Education," *Judeo-Christian Perspectives on Psychology: Human Nature, Motivation, and Change,* edited by William R. Miller and Harold D. Delaney, 145–64. Washington, DC: American Psychological Association, 2005.

Young, William P. *The Shack: A Novel.* Newbury Park, CA: Windblown Media, 2007.

Modern Authors Index

Adams, J. Wesley, 112n14, 120, 140nn46–47, 143
Akallo, Grace, 155, 155n35, 172
Aker, Benny C., 110n8, 120
Aldred, Ray, 191, 191n50, 192, 194
Alexander, Paul, ix–x, 20, 20n24, 21
Alexander, Estrelda Y., 79n40, 84
Ali, M. Amir, 143
Allan, Alfred, 159, 159n57, 170
Allan, Maria, 159n57, 170
Allen, Jonathan, 156n38, 170, 170n100
Allman, Jaimée, 128n14, 130, 131nn20–21, 133n33, 134n36, 143
Anderson, Allan, 70n9, 84
Ankomak, Baffour, 155nn31–33, 170
Arrington, French L., 113n17, 120, 121
Asmal, Kader, 148, 148n5, 151, 151n18, 152, 163, 163n74
Asmal, Louise, 148n5, 151n18, 163n74, 170
Awbrey, Diane, xix, 43–62, 44n2, 220, 229

Balch, David L., 22
Bartleman, Frank, 69, 69n6, 70, 70n9, 70n11, 73, 74, 75n26, 80n47, 81n48, 85
Bassett, Rodney, 132, 132n27, 133n32, 142

Battle, Michael, 163n72, 170
Beacham, Doug, 74n24, 85
Beck, Guy L., 143
Beckford, Robert, 20, 20n23, 22
Bekoff, Mark, 126n1, 142
Bellamy, Guy, 97, 97n34
Benda, Brent B., 131, 131n25, 142
Bentley, William H., 95n20, 104
Berry, J. W., 221, 221n3, 229
Berg, Robert, xix, 25–42, 220
Bergstrom, R. J., 91, 104
Beyer, Peter, 179, 182, 182nn15–16, 194
Bizimana, Theoneste, 204n10, 207, 207n11, 209n13, 212
Blumhofer, Edith Waldvogel, 28n8, 41
Boesak, Willa, 151, 151n13, 170
Borgman, Paul, 7n7, 12, 12n10, 22
Botman, Russell, 162, 162nn66–67, 167, 167n84
Bovon, François, 7n5, 22
Brathwaite, Renea, xix, xx, 65–87, 220
Brandt, R. L., 95, 95nn22–23, 96, 97, 104
Breytenbach, Cilliers, 162, 162n68
Brooks, John H., 28n8
Brown, Robert, 91nn7–8
Burgess, Stanley M., 85, 86
Burkinshaw, Robert K., 192, 192n52, 194

231

Subject Index

guilt, 30, 31, 60–61, 132–33, 146, 147,
    151, 162, 165, 177, 179, 182, 210,
    226, 227–28. *See also* Shame

Harrison, Robert ("Bob"), xx, 89–104
"Healing and Rebuilding our Commu-
    nities" (HROC), 200–213
healing, 33, 69, 129, 134n35, 138, 139,
    158, 159n59, 161, 163, 167,
    167n88, 180, 189, 190–92, 194,
    204
  community, societal, 129, 203, 220
  divine, supernatural, 11, 109–11,
    137, 218
  facilitation of, 202, 207, 210
  impediments, 191
  natural, 138
  psychological, 157, 161
  reconciliation, 160, 179
Hebrews, 58, 112
holiness theology, sanctification, 53,
    70, 71, 73, 80, 80n46, 138, 222
Holy Ghost, the. *See* Holy Spirit, the
Holy Spirit, the
  anointing, 15
  baptism of, 68, 69, 71, 73, 74, 78, 79,
    80, 109, 137
  communication, language, 72
  conviction of sin, 215
  empowerment, 141
  engagement, 59
  faith in, 58
  forgiveness, 58, 108, 117–18
  fruit of, 137
  gifts of, 40
  guidance, 60, 165, 170, 211, 216,
    217
  indwelling, 3, 6n4, 11, 61, 137
  inner working, 43–44, 56, 59
  inspiration, 5, 6, 43
  joy, 25
  leading of, 7, 49
  manifestations, 219
  move of, 84
  outpouring, 164, 211

peace, 7
power and authority of, 10, 15,
    19n21, 44, 69, 114
racial unity, 66
reception, 18
sanctification as requirement for, 71
truth, 169
universal authority, 15
Hutus (Rwanda), xx, 199–202, 209

Icyizere, 208
injustice, 102, 127, 146, 147, 168, 216,
    223, 228,
injustice gap, 127, 223
International Church of the Foursquare
    Gospel, 66
International Criminal Court of Justice
    (ICC), 154–55
intervention, divine, 9, 218
Ireland, northern, 134, 134n35
Isaiah, 11, 132
Islam, 177, 221
Israel, Israeli, 8, 9, 10, 14, 119, 120,
    148, 164

Jerusalem, 3, 5, 12, 13, 14, 15, 16, 17,
    19, 70, 76, 120, 211
Jesus Christ, xviii, xxi, 3–21, 25, 26, 32,
    33, 35, 36, 37, 39, 40, 46, 48, 49,
    50, 54, 55, 61, 69, 71, 76, 78, 108,
    109, 110, 114, 115, 117, 119, 129,
    130, 133, 134, 136, 137, 138, 139,
    162, 215, 216, 218, 219, 224.
"Jilting of Granny Weatherall, The," xix,
    43–62
Jim Crow Laws, 68, 77, 77n33, 82, 100
John, 7, 14n13, 26, 35, 76, 108, 109,
    110, 119
Judaism, 177, 221
justice, 19n22, 31, 33, 109, 110, 113,
    115, 116 117, 127, 129, 130, 136,
    139, 151, 152, 154, 155, 156, 161,
    162, 163, 170, 180, 181, 183, 189,
    206, 216, 217, 221, 222, 223, 228
Social and societal, 166, 221, 229

Pentecostalism
agents of forgiveness, 108
Arminianism, 37
Canadian, 178, 192–93
divine communication, 40
divine healing, 109
early missionary endeavors, 37, 69
ecumenism, xx, 107–22
education for reconciliation, 211
emotion, 139, 211
Evangelicals, 26, 39
experience, 3, 26, 43, 109, 110, 111,
137, 138, 211, 218, 219, 221
Full Gospel, 111
globalism, xviii, 70, 212
heritage, xviii
hermeneutics, xix, xx, 3–22, 28,
48, 49
holiness codes, 53
Holy Spirit, 53, 137
immediacy, 138, 139, 141
integration with psychology, 125
loss of identity, 39
miracles, deliverance, 138, 140, 218
mission, xviii, 4, 219
modernism, 28
patronization of, 26
pneumatological heritage, 4
pneumatological intimacy, 108, 117
political and social involvement,
110, 169–70
postmodernism, 25–42
race issues, xix
Shack, The, xix, 25–42
social sins and taboos, 53
soteriology, 111
South Africa, 145–73
Supernaturalism, 218
testimony, xix, 25, 26, 37, 43, 61
theology, xix, 108, 111, 139, 140,
141
Wesleyan perspective, 107–22
Pentecostal Assemblies of Canada
(PAOC), xxi, 192
Pentecostals and Charismatics for Peace
and Justice (www.pcpj.org), 19

Pentecostal Evangel, The, 90n5, 100,
101n48
Pentecostal Fellowship of North
America (PFNA), 66, 83
Pentecostal and Charismatic Churches
of America (PCCNA), 67, 83
Peter, the disciple, 15, 16, 18, 21, 53
Peterson, Bartlett, 93n14, 105
Pharisees, 55
pneumatology, 6, 6n4, 7, 109, 117
poor, the, 11, 53, 101, 146, 152. *See also*
marginalized, marginalization
Porter, Katherine Ann, xix, 44, 44n4,
44n6, 45nn7–12, 46nn13–15, 47,
47nn17–18, 48, 49, 49n21, 50, 62
postcolonial discourse, 76, 76n32
postmodern, postmodernism,
postmodernity, 25–42, 220
Poverty and Inequality Report
(Carnegie Foundation), 145
Presbyterian Church in Canada, 190,
190n44
proclamation, Spirit-led, 4, 15, 19, 21
prodigal son, parable of, 35, 129
prophecy, literary (and programmatic),
as literary convention, 5
Psalms, 120

Quakers, 203, 204

racism, racial issues
Canada, 187
Evangelical response as opposed to
mainline, 98
Pentecostal history, 67, 70–84, 90,
91, 102
South Africa, 148, 163
terminology, 66n1
reason, advance of, 26, 27
reconciliation, xvii–xxi, 3–7, 10, 11, 15,
19–21, 33, 36, 65, 66, 66n1, 68,
75, 82, 83, 84, 102, 103, 108–22,
125, 126, 128–44, 147, 150, 151,
152, 153, 154, 156, 157, 158, 159,
160, 161, 162, 164, 166, 167,
168–70, 178, 179, 180, 181, 183,

www.ingramcontent.com/pod-product-compliance
Lightning Source LLC
Chambersburg PA
CBHW060331100426
42812CB00003B/956